THE SACKVILLE ILLUSTRATED DICTIONARY OF
GOLF

ALAN BOOTH AND MICHAEL HOBBS

SACKVILLE
BOOKS

First published in 1987
by Sackville Books Ltd
Sackville House
78 Margaret Street
London W1N 7HB

©Sackville Design Group Ltd

Designed and produced by Sackville Design Group Ltd
Art Director: Al Rockall
Project Co-ordinator: Melanie Faldo
Executive Editor: Valerie Mendes

British Library Cataloguing in Publication data

Booth, Alan
    The sackville illustrated dictionary of golf.
    1. Golf – Dictionaries
    I. Title   II. Hobbs, Michael, 1934-
    796.352'03'21   GV965

    ISBN   0-948615-01-X

Typeset in Times by Hourds Typographica, Stafford
Colour reproduction by Aero Offset Ltd, UK
Printed in Great Britain by
Purnell Book Production Limited
Member of the BPCC Group

The publishers acknowledge the following picture sources, with thanks:

Lawrence Levy: pages 3, 8 (top), 9, 10, 12, 15 (top), 16, 17, 18, 21, 22, 23, 25, 26, 27, 28, (below), 29, 30, 31, (top), 32, 33, 35, 36 (top), 37, 41, 42, 44, 45, 46 (below), 49 (top), 50, 51, 52, 54, 55, 56, 58, 59, 62 (top), 63 (top), 67 (top), 69 (top), 70, 71 (below), 72, 73, 75, 78, 79, 80, 82, 85, 87, 88, 89 (top), 92, 93, 94, 95, 99, 100, 101, 102 (right), 104, 105, (left), 107, 109 (below), 110, 112, 116 (top and below left), 117, 118, 119, 120, 123 (below), 125 (top), 126, 127, 131, 133, 135, 136, 137 (below), 138, 143 (top), 146, 147, 148, 149 (top right), 149 (below), 150, 151 (top), 152 (top), 154, 155, 156, 159, 161, 162, 165 (top), 166 (top), 167, 168 (top), 169, 172, 173 (top), 177, 179, 181 (below)
Brian Morgan: pages 8 (below), 13 (below), 14, 15 (below), 19, 20, 24, 31 (below), 34, 36 (below), 38, 40, 43, 47, 53, 57, 61, 66, 67 (below), 69 (below), 76, 77, 86, 89 (below), 90, 91, 97, 98, 105 (right), 108, 109 (top), 111, 121, 122, 123 (top), 124, 128, 130, 132, 139, 140, 141, 142, 149 (top left), 151 (below), 152 (below), 157, 158, 170, 171, 173 (below), 174, 176
Michael Hobbs: pages 11, 49 (below), 28 (top), 64, 81 (below), 137 (top right), 163 (below)
The Bert Neale Collection: pages 62 (below), 65, 68 (below), 84 (top), 163 (top), 181 (top)

Irish Tourist Board: pages 48, 129
J. Arthur Dixon: page 106
Peter Dazeley: page 180
World Allsport: pages 118 (inset), 125 (below)
BBC Hulton Picture Library: 13 (top), 39, 46 (top), 60, 71 (top), 74, 80 (below), 84 (below), 96, 102 (left), 113, 114, 115, 116 (below right), 134, 137 (top left), 143 (below), 164, 165 (below), 167 (below), 168 (below), 175
Hunstanton Golf Club: page 68
Royal Liverpool Golf Club: page 83
Little Aston Golf Club: page 81
The Burlington Gallery: pages 1, 4, 5, 183, 192
Woodhall Spa Golf Club: page 178

Foreword

As well as playing golf for a vocation, many of you know how fascinated I am with the many wonderful facets of golf. In fact, I love the game as much as life itself, and the more I study and observe I am continually humbled with its magnetic splendours. At the same time my opinion is reinforced with the notion that this is the game in which our very lives and beings come under close scrutiny from someone or something. This mystical and magical feeling is felt all over the world no matter what level of golf one plays. Simply, you and I experience the very same emotions at different and sometimes inconvenient times because we are golfers.

Clearly no other sport has been written about more than golf, and we should naturally protect these proper traditions with our beliefs through fine handsome volumes of future golfing literature. The authors' and photographers' devotion to golf shine through brilliantly in this book of golf and golfers past and present. I am extremely proud to have it in my library so that I may refer to it from time to time.

Ben Crenshaw
Austin, Texas

The Evolution of Golf

Europe

Golf has no sure birthplace. The game must really date back to the first man or boy who swung a stick at some rounded object with the idea of propelling it a satisfactory distance. But this is certainly not golf as we know it. Nor are other activities which resemble play on the putting green, perhaps with the aim of hitting an object such as a post.

In Europe, something of the sort [...]s far back as 1296 at [...]e Vecht. The game [...]n kolve or 'play with [...] easy enough to see [...]een the Dutch [...]ord 'golf'. [...]nged [...] [...]ome [...]cot- [...] the

ideas that make up the game of golf probably came across the North Sea. It is almost as likely that the Scots invented it themselves: certainly all the essential features of the modern game developed on the east coast of Scotland.

The first written mention of the game in Scotland came in 1457 when the Parliament of King James II of Scotland 'decreeted and ordained': 'that the Fute-ball and Golfe be utterly cryed downe, and not to be used'. Instead 'all men, that is within fiftie, and past twelve zeires, sall use schutting' — in other words, archery.

In 1471, James III returned to the subject. He decreed that 'Fute-ball and Golfe be abused in time cumming and schuting used'. So also James IV, 20 years later, who said: 'in na place of the Realme there be used Fute-ball, Golfe, or uther sik unproffitable sportes'.

The House of Stuart later gave up their attempts to ban the game

A photograph taken on Leith Links, 17th May 1867, of a Grand Golf Tournament by Professional Players. Tom Morris is at the centre.

and took it to themselves. By the middle of the 17th century, golf was certainly being played at Dornoch, Aberdeen, Montrose, Leven, Leith, Musselburgh and, of course, St Andrews. Here it is thought that golf arrived early in the 15th century, but the first written reference occurs when the Archbishop of St Andrews was given a licence to 'plant and planis cuniggis within the northe pairt of thair commond linkis nixt adjacent to the Wattir of Eddin'. Although the archbishop could set up his rabbit warrens and feed the animals, he was reminded that the townsfolk must not be prevented from enjoying their golf.

In all parts of Scotland, however, the game was for years, even centuries, a minority sport. Only the well-off could afford the expensive feathery balls (made from hide stuffed with boiled feathers), which cut quite easily and had to be changed quickly in wet weather. Others had to use wooden balls which, though much cheaper, split, damaged clubs and cannot have flown well.

This changed from the year 1848, when the first gutta percha balls were made. Rubber was both better and much cheaper. Modern golf was on its way, from Scotland into England and Europe and further afield.

Golf is claimed to have been played at Blackheath from 1608 but 150 years later there is the evidence of a silver club which was competed for. The first Continental club was at Pau in France. The club was founded by the Duke of Hamilton and others, as a result of earlier visits from officers of Wellington's army.

Blackheath apart, the first still active English golf club is Royal North Devon, founded in 1864 at Westward Ho! Close after it came Alnmouth in Northumberland, Royal Liverpool at Hoylake (both 1869), London Scottish at Wimbledon Common (1865), Crookham (1872) and Bath and Felixstowe (1880). Old Manchester, founded in 1818, used to play over the moors but does not currently have a course.

Few people, however, were playing the game, even in Scotland. The great expansion came as sports of all kinds grew in popularity. In the 10 years from 1887, the game quadrupled in popularity and that rate was more than maintained up to World War I. There were about 50 club and societies in Britain in the mid-1870s and well over 4000 by the war. Today there are more than 1900 courses in the British Isles, well over 2000 clubs and an unknown number of societies.

It is generally supposed that the Gentlemen Golfers of Edinburgh,

as they were known in their early days, existed before the Provost of Edinburgh presented a silver cup for competition among them in 1744. The Honourable Company of Edinburgh Golfers, who acquired their official name in 1795, take the minutes of 1 May 1744, recording the Provost's gift, as their real date of origin. The minutes kept from that date are the oldest continuous record of any golf club in the world.

The Company was responsible for forming the first set of rules of golf, and in 1754 for the foundation of the Royal and Ancient Golf Club of St Andrews, whose rules were virtually the same. The Company played over five holes of Leith Links.

In 1836 they moved from the Golf House in Leith to Musselburgh, where the Open Championship was staged for the first time in 1874. They shared the course with the Edinburgh Burgess and Bruntsfield Links Societies, and when it became overcrowded they moved to Muirfield in 1891; the first Open Championship there in 1892 was

won by the amateur Harold Hilton from Hoylake.

In 1897, the Rules of Golf Committee of the R and A was formed and the rules they produced have been followed ever since, though much modified, in consultation with the US Golf Association.

The game was becoming organized. The next group to band together were the professionals, spurred on by the intention of some clubs to let their shops to the highest bidder. The London and Counties Professional Golfers' Association was formed with J H Taylor, chairman, and James Braid, captain. As the organization became countrywide, the name was changed to the Professional Golfers' Association.

All this time, the character of the game had changed. Because it was cheap, the gutty ball allowed more people to play and it became a composition ball by the 1880s. Instead of several wooden clubs, irons were increasingly used. In 1902, the Haskell ball, with rubber core, thread winding and gutta percha cover arrived. It could travel a good deal further; courses had to be lengthened. Average players found it made the game more enjoyable; purists thought the great days of the game had gone for ever.

There was no such outburst of nostalgia when steel shafts replaced hickory at the end of the 1920s. The need to judge the twist of hickory disappeared overnight.

Professional tournament play developed more slowly in Europe than the USA. A player had a club job, went off during the week in the summer months for occasional tournaments and was on hand at weekends to tend to the needs of his members. Even the Open Championship ended on a Friday. The money available to tournament players in Europe has risen as dramatically as in the USA, though not in totals. In 1947, the Australian Norman von Nida smashed the money-winning record and won £3,263. In 1953, Bernard Hunt, who had a similar tournament performance to von Nida, still took home much the same amount. The real growth in the total prize fund only came in the early 1970s, but only one player, Severiano Ballesteros, had passed £1-million in European career money winnings by 1987.

The standard of European golf has so improved that now it rivals anything the USA can offer.

The Americas

In 1743, 96 golf clubs and 432 balls were despatched from the port of Leith to Charleston. Somebody must have been playing the game ... However, there is no actual hard evidence of this, even though two golf clubs were formed not much later, the South Carolina Golf Club in 1786 and the Savannah Golf Club in 1795. At this time there were references to the clubs in local papers but mainly notices of forthcoming social events. Clubs and balls were also advertised for sale in New York.

Such references peter out in the early part of the 19th century. No traces of a possible course or the remains of a single wood or iron have been found. The next wave came 50 or more years later when Royal Montreal, the first continuing club in North America, was formed. Fifteen years later John Reid, a Scot from Dunfermline, persuaded a few friends to try their hands at knocking a golf ball around three primitive holes on a cow pasture. That year, their St Andrews Golf Club was formally established. Others swiftly followed: Newport, Shinnecock Hills, Chicago and The Country Club. Golf was on its way. In 1894 the United States Golf Association was formed. Today, it has 5,600 member clubs.

In those early years, English and Scottish influence was very important. The first good amateurs were either immigrants or had learned about golf while on trips overseas. As the popularity of the game grew, the men of Dornoch, Carnoustie and Fife heard there was a living to be made. Instead of becoming professionals at the new English clubs, they crossed the Atlantic.

Soon, good American-bred amateurs appeared but Scottish-born professionals dominated the tournament scene into the 1920s. The need for an organization for the professionals was obvious enough but it took longer than the very quick foundation of the USGA. Although there had been an earlier friendly grouping, the PGA was not formed until 1916. Tom McNamara, one of those candidates for the title of the best player who did not quite win the US Open (he was second in 1909, 1912 and 1915), organized a lunch early in 1916 on behalf of the Wanamaker company, who were interested in stealing a march on Spaldings in obtaining the support of US golf professionals. From that lunch, the PGA was born, and also the PGA Championship.

It was mainly intended to guard the interests of club professionals, but the glamorous side was the future PGA Tour. As in the British Isles, this took many years to develop before it became today's multimillion dollar enterprise. For a long time there was no Tour — just a few scattered events. These mainly took place in the winter months in warmer parts of the USA when the professionals could take time off from their livelihoods — dealing with the various needs of their club members.

The real start of the PGA Tour was 1934, when Paul Runyan was leading money winner with $9,543. In this period, however, a player had to finish in the top 10 most weeks to make a living. Much later, it was possible for Tom Kite to be leading money winner in 1981 with some £375,000 by such consistency yet with just one win to his name.

In 1940, not much more than £100,000 was on offer. Byron Nelson's phenomenal play in the years 1944 to 1946, and the dominance of Ben Hogan afterwards,

Jack Nicklaus

made little difference. The growth of Tour purses was largely a reflection of inflation. By 1955, the Tour was still worth only $782,000.

Arnold Palmer and Jack Nicklaus changed all that. By the mid-1960s more than $2¾-million was at stake, then $8¾-million in 1973. By 1986, the total prize money during the season was $25,442,242. First to reach $1–million in prize money was Arnold Palmer in 1968; first to win $2–million (1973), then $3–million (1977) and $4–million (1983) was Jack Nicklaus. Early in 1987, he was only a few thousand dollars short of $5–million.

Women's Golf

The first woman to have expressed an interest in the game was Catherine of Aragon, Henry VIII's first wife. In a letter dated 13 August 1513 she remarked: 'All his subjects be very glad, I thank God, to be busy with the Golfe for they take it for pastime; my heart is very good to it.' A little more than 50 years later Mary, Queen of Scots caused enquiring eyebrows to be raised by playing the game 'on the playing fields outside Seton' just two days after her husband's murder.

After that, all is silence until, on 14 December 1810, the Musselburgh Golf Club resolved to 'present by subscription a new Creel and Skull to the best female golfer who plays on the annual occasion on 18 January to be intimated to the Fish Ladies by the Office of the Club.' Apart from the desirable creel and skull, women's golf made no known progress for quite a few more years. But it did prosper increasingly from the 1890s onwards on both sides of the Atlantic.

The first ladies' club was formed at St Andrews in 1867 but England was not far behind: a club started at Westward Ho! the very next year. By 1890 there were clubs to the total of 25 all over the British

Isles. In the early days, however, these were often merely putting courses. It was still thought unladylike to raise a club above shoulder height — even if cumbrous clothing made this a possibility.

Clothing remained a hindrance for another 30 years, but the demands of championship and other competitive play were soon to change it. The first British Ladies' champion, Lady Margaret Scott, who won in the years 1893–1895, had the fullest swing imaginable. So did the first American champion, Mrs Charles S Brown, when she played the Meadow Brook nine hole course with rounds of 69 and 63 to win by two strokes. As in this case, courses were often specially designed for ladies. Although they might not be restricted to the use of a putter only, few of the holes were much more than 100 yards. It was felt that 70 to 80 yards was about the limit of a drive.

In time, women made their way on to the full men's courses — though not in every club either side of the Atlantic. Restrictions on time of play relaxed over the years, but they still remain. Club professionals were a very important factor in the development of women's golf. The menfolk were often on hand either for lessons or as weekend customers at the professional shops. Their

daughters and wives kept the business going for the rest of time.

High standards of women's play were reached from about 1910. The occasional woman turned professional, even attempted to enter male competitions. In the 1930s Joyce Wethered and Babe Zaharias were paid for exhibition tours, playing with male partners, but professional golf did not arrive until 1944, when three Americans founded the Women's Professional Golf Association.

It got nowhere. Matters improved from 1950 when the Ladies' Professional Golf Association was founded. They had a star whom people would pay to see — the Babe — and several other very good players. There were 21 events by 1952 when the total Tour purse was some $50,000. However, even by the end of the 1960s, only $600,000 was shared out. Babe Zaharias was long dead; the excellent players who followed lacked spectator appeal. Even so, the LPGA Tour grew all the time.

Then the feats of Nancy Lopez in the late 1970s caused dramatic progress, so that from $1½–million in 1973 the purse rose to $4–million in 1979. In the 1980s, this growth has continued less dramatically to $7–million in 1983 and well over $10–million in 1987. In 1950, Babe Zaharias won $2,875. In 1963, Mickey Wright had her best money year, worth $31,269. It was 1976 before the $100,000 was passed, by Judy Rankin. In 1986, Pat Bradley won $492,021.

Professional women's golf in Europe still has far to go before it can compare with the men's Tour. In the USA, the two are growing closer. Even so, the Women's Professional Golf Association has made strides that were hardly imaginable when it first had a limited tournament schedule in 1979. Then the leading money winner was Cathy Panton with £2,495. The 1986 leader, Laura Davies, earned £37,500.

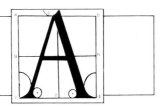

Aaron, Tommy

1937–. Born Gainesville, Georgia, USA

Aaron's successful career has one notable blemish in the 1968 Masters. His partner, Roberto de Vicenzo, was playing the round of his life and birdied the 17th. Aaron, marking his card, wrote down four instead of the three the Argentine had taken. That error cost de Vicenzo a tie and play-off with Bob Goalby because he failed to spot Aaron's mistake.

By one of life's ironies, Augusta was also the scene of Aaron's greatest achievement. In 1973 he won the US Masters. Going into the final round, he was four strokes adrift of Peter Oosterhuis, but shot

Tommy Aaron

a 68 to the Englishman's 74, and won by a stroke from J C Snead.

This was one of Aaron's two US Tour victories, the other coming in the 1970 Atlanta Classic, and he also won the 1969 Canadian Open

after a play-off with J C Snead. He also played in two Ryder Cup matches.

Aaron is an elegant swinger of the club. He will probably do well on the Seniors Tour, for which he qualified in 1987.

Aberdeen, Royal, Scotland

Ranked as the sixth oldest club in the world, the Royal Aberdeen was formed in 1815, though golf had been played on linksland in the 16th century. A Society of Golfers of Aberdeen was formed in 1780. The course became established on its site at Balgownie in 1888 and received its Royal accolade in 1903. A traditional links lay-out of hillocks and valleys, it stretches virtually straight out for the first nine holes. This makes it a longer test than the inward half, especially in the wind.

Royal Aberdeen, Scotland: a traditional links lay-out which has staged many Scottish events.

The club has staged many major Scottish events, amateur and professional, as well as the British Boys Championship, won in 1935 by John Langley. He became a Walker Cup player the following year, aged 18, and English Amateur champion in 1950.

Adelaide, Royal, Australia

Adelaide was the first club to be established in Australia in 1870. It went out of existence six years later, and was re-established in 1892. It settled on its present course at Seaton in 1904 and was given its Royal title in 1923.

In 1926 Alister Mackenzie, British-born architect responsible for Cypress Point in America, made changes to the course, one with links characteristics, improving it to championship standard. It staged the first of a number of Australian Open Championships in 1910, and has also been host to the country's Amateur and Ladies championships.

Gary Player won the second of his seven Australian Open titles here; an earlier champion was Jim Ferrier, runner-up in the British Amateur in 1939, who won both the country's Open and Amateur titles in 1938 and later left Australia to become a US professional. A testing course, with the wind a factor, one of its best holes comes early on. The third requires an accurate tee shot to a narrow fairway.

Alcott, Amy

1956–. Born Kansas City, Missouri, USA

Most women take a full backswing, needing as much time and space as possible to develop club-head speed. Not so Amy Alcott, who plays most of her shots with a backswing not much longer than Doug Sanders' telephone box method. Alcott is exceptionally strong and athletic, able to play

Amy Alcott

superbly with a short backswing.

As an amateur, Alcott won the US Junior Championship in 1973 and in 1974 she was second in the Canadian Amateur Championship. She became professional in 1975, winning her first tournament, the Orange Blossom Classic, on only her third start — an LPGA record.

Since then, Alcott has achieved the rare feat of winning at least one tournament on the US Tour every year, an achievement only rivalled by JoAnne Carner. Her two victories in 1986 brought her career total to 26. Her worst year financially was her first, when she finished in 15th place. From 1978 to 1986 she has been no lower than ninth place, and in the top four in 1979, 1980 and 1985–1986. She won well over $200,000 each year between 1984 and 1986.

Alcott has collected three of the women's major titles, the 1979

Peter Jackson Classic, the 1980 US Open and the 1983 Nabisco Dinah Shore Invitational. Her greatest performance came in the US Open, where her total of 280 was then a record for the championship. She finished nine strokes ahead of the second place finisher.

Aldeburgh, Suffolk, England

One of the oldest clubs in East Anglia, Aldeburgh dates from 1884, and vies with the courses of Hunstanton and Brancaster as the best in the area. Laid out on a gently rolling terrain, it is a heathland test, with linksland characteristics and a wealth of gorse, presenting masses of yellow colour in season. There is no record of the designer, but in his time J H Taylor put his experience to good effect in making a few necessary alterations.

The result is an excellent course with plenty of variety, especially over the second half. The 14th which calls for a drive between two trees and over a ridge, and a second shot to a plateau green, is outstanding. On sandy soil, although slightly inland from the sea, its fairways are fast drying, to provide fine golf most of the year. The English Ladies Championship has been held here on four occasions; the first winner was Enid Wilson, three times British champion.

Alison, Charles Hugh

1882–1952. Born Preston, Lancashire, England

Charles Alison began course designing in partnership with H`S Colt, whom he met when secretary of the newly formed Stoke Poges Golf Club. Colt was designing the new club's course and Alison then developed his interest in the subject.

Alison first worked with Colt in Britain; later he became the first architect to work internationally when he became responsible for the firm's many courses in the USA. He was particularly influential in the development of Japanese golf: two of his designs were among the best in Japan.

Alliss, Percy

1897–1975. Born Sheffield, Yorkshire, England

Like most professionals of his time, Percy Alliss was introduced to golf by working as a caddie at a local golf club. Equally talented as a cricketer as golfer, he turned down a trial for Yorkshire because the offer of an assistant's job at Royal Porthcawl came at much the same time, shortly after World War I.

In 1926 he took up the professional's job at the Wannsee club in Berlin, where he remained for several years, winning the German Open as a matter of routine. His son, Peter, was born there.

The Open Championship was his Achilles' heel. Percy Alliss was undoubtedly one of the best British players from the mid-1920s until World War II, but he failed this hurdle where such lesser players as Alf Perry, Reg Whitcombe and Dick Burton succeeded. In 1929, he

broke the course record at Muir-field to lead after the first round and eventually tied for fourth place, the same position as the previous year — in both cases behind the champion, Walter Hagen.

Two years later at Carnoustie, Alliss looked certain of a tie, if not of winning, with two holes to play, but drove out of bounds and finished third, two behind Tommy Armour. His last really clear-cut chance came in 1932 at Prince's, Sandwich. Although Alliss finished nine strokes behind the winner, Gene Sarazen, in fourth place, he reckoned that his game through the green was at a peak — if he could only have managed to average two putts per green.

Putting was always Percy Alliss's main problem. He was called a peerless long iron player, and all his striking was of high quality. People marvelled at how simple Alliss made golf seem — until he was on the greens.

He had 16 major victories which included an Italian Open, where his 262 total stood as a record for a national championship for many years. Even so, his outstanding

wins were in the British Professional Matchplay Championships of 1933 and 1937. Alliss was also outstanding in another matchplay event, the Ryder Cup, where he represented Great Britain three times. He would have been chosen more often but professionals working outside the British Isles were ineligible.

Alliss, Peter

1931–. Born Berlin, Germany

Peter Alliss's golf career is broadly similar to his father, Percy's. Blessed with great power, and recognized as the best striker in British golf during his long playing career, Alliss was also less convincing on the greens. Nevertheless, he won some 20 tournaments. He had many outstanding putting rounds and was also an excellent approach putter but, after a change in grip, was always unsure of his ability to get the short ones on line for the hole.

His most successful year was 1958 when he won the Italian, Spanish and Portuguese Opens. In all, he won five national championships in his career and was long regarded as the British player most likely to succeed in the Open Championship. However, as with his father, it was not to be; 8th place proved to be his best finish, the great rounds came too late.

Although not at his best as a matchplay golfer, Peter Alliss seemed to reserve his best performances for the Ryder Cup, in which he played eight times. After a bad start in 1953, when he was made to bear a great deal of the blame for a narrow Great Britain defeat at Wentworth, he became one of the most reliable performers, halving with, and beating, Arnold Palmer at the peak of the American's career.

Peter Alliss retired from tournament golf at the end of the 1969 season, during which he had won

Peter Alliss, now famous as a presenter of golf on television.

an event. He went on to become internationally recognized as a commentator on and presenter of golf on television. At first a little in the shadow of Henry Longhurst, he came to be accepted as the leading practitioner of the craft for the BBC, the ABC in the USA and also in Australia and other countries.

Author of many books on golf, his *Bedside* series was particularly successful, as was his autobiography. His other books deal mainly with the history of the game and are very well researched.

Alwoodley, Yorkshire, England

Close to the busy industrial city of Leeds, this moorland course, one of the finest in the area, offers great beauty as well as testing golf. With fairways set among heather, whins and gorse, it calls for great accuracy, notably at the 15th hole, an excellent dog-leg. Founded in 1907, it owes its lay-out to its first greenkeeper C W Brown, with help from notable designers, H S Colt and Alister Mackenzie. The latter was the club's first secretary who later achieved fame for his creative work in the design of Cypress Point and Augusta National in America, and Royal Melbourne in Australia.

Very much a private club, it was not until 1965 that Alwoodley welcomed outside events. The first was the county championship, followed in 1967 by the English Ladies and in 1971 the British Ladies Championships. This featured the then youngest winner this century, Michelle Walker, then only 18 years old. In 1986, Marnie McGuire of New Zealand took the title at the age of 17.

Amateur Championship

On 13 December 1884, Thomas Owen Potter, Honorary Secretary to the Royal Liverpool Golf Club, proposed that: 'A Tournament

Michael Bonallack, winner of the Amateur Championship.

open to all Amateur Golfers be held at Hoylake in the Spring Meeting Week of 1885'.

This was ample notice and drew a field from St Andrews, Carnoustie, Glasgow, London, Worcester, Westward Ho!, Dublin and other parts of the UK. Although the event was not recognized for a good many years as having been the first championship, the decision to do so was undoubtedly correct — there were no greater number of entries for some years, and the best players were there.

There was one great oddity in this first year. Halved matches were replayed. This meant that the champion, Allan Macfie, played the same man three times before struggling through. When he eventually reached the semi-final there was the compensation that he received a bye into the final!

For many years, none of the best

amateur golfers considered turning professional, so fields were of excellent standard. To win through the many rounds of matchplay was a feat equal to winning the Open Championship. Two amateurs, John Ball and Harold Hilton, did succeed in also winning the Open and others. Freddie Tait, Johnny Laidlay, Robert Maxwell and Horace Hutchinson — before World War I — came close. Even as late as 1921, Roger Wethered tied, only to lose the play-off over 36 holes. These feats were achieved in spite of the fact that amateurs often did not regard the Open as nearly as much a priority as the Amateur Championship. The best amateurs of the 1890s were no more than a notch below the professionals in playing ability, and three won the Open Championship that decade. Since then, only Bobby Jones has done so.

To those great players who have contested the Amateur Championship must be added Cyril Tolley, James Bruen, Joe Carr and Michael Bonallack.

The field in the Amateur has always been formidable. It reached 100 before the turn of the century and was 200 by 1907. Even today, there is not likely to be an entry of much more than 300, mainly because of increasing stringency in handicap qualifications.

The first overseas player to win the Amateur was Walter Travis. Australian born, he learned to play golf in the USA when in his mid-30s. The first American to win was Jess Sweetser, who won in 1926 although probably suffering from tuberculosis.

After 1926, Americans came to play a central role in the event: Bobby Jones, Lawson Little (twice), Robert Sweeny and Charlie Yates all won in the 1930s. After World War II they became even more dominant, providing five champions in the six years 1947–1952. Players from the UK rarely won in Walker Cup years, when the US team was entered. However, British amateur golf reached a very high standard in the 1950s and 1960s, when Joe Carr won the title three times and Michael Bonallack five. Bonallack's three victories in a row in 1960-1970 are a record.

Bonallack himself once said that he would have turned professional if he had reached his peak earlier. His British successors as champions have usually done so, with the notable exception of Peter McEvoy.

Although the championship was so often won by USA players, it did not fall to another overseas golfer until 1954, when Australian Doug Bachli won, followed in 1966 by Bobby Cole from South Africa. The first European champion was Philippe Ploujoux of France in 1981, followed by José-Maria Olazabal of Spain three years later.

Like the Open, the Amateur Championship is a bastion of links golf although there have been exceptions. Both Royal Porthcawl, seaside rather than links, and Ganton, about nine miles inland, have found favour with the R and A. The championship has once been staged in a country which is foreign in the political but not the golfing sense: in 1949 it went to Portmarnock, near Dublin.

Anderson, Willie

1878–1910. Born North Berwick, Scotland

Anderson emigrated to the USA while still in his teens at about the time he was beginning to show real promise. He first attracted national attention when he finished second in the 1897 US Open. His first title was delayed until 1901, when he won a play-off by 85 to 86 over Alex Smith.

This level of scoring later led people to think that Anderson established a brilliant record in the US Open only because the quality

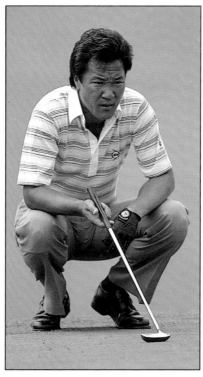

Isao Aoki

of the fields was low. In fact, it was much more the conditioning of the courses which led to high scores. People who had seen him play felt he was the equal of the great names who were to follow.

All a golfer can do is beat the people who turn up to play – which Anderson did. From 1903–1905, he set the record of three successive wins, while his career total of four US championships has never been bettered. With very little tournament golf available during his playing career, Anderson was equally dominant in the other major event, the Western Open, which he also won four times.

Aoki, Isao

1942–. Born Abiko, Chiba, Japan

With the possible exception of Tsuneyuki Nakajima, Aoki is the most internationally known Japanese golfer. Even so, his overseas appearances have been limited, although they include

some important victories. In 1978 he won the World Matchplay Championship at Wentworth, where his exceptionally wristy style, which makes him look a little like a man swinging a stick at the heads of daisies, caused some surprise. With such a narrow swing arc, it is hardly surprising that Aoki is not a long hitter. His real strengths lie in the touch shots. The nearer he gets to the hole, the more effective he becomes.

This is particularly noticeable with his putting. Using a centre-shafted putter, Aoki plants the heel of the club on the ground with the toe in the air, and is apt to knock the ball into the hole from all kinds of distances. Such putting enabled him in 1980 to equal Mark Hayes' Open Championship record with a round of 63 at Muirfield. His card showed all fours and threes, equally divided. Even so, at no time did he threaten to win the championship — he finished 13 strokes behind Tom Watson.

Aoki's best performance in a major championship had come a few weeks earlier in the US Open at Baltusrol, where he began with three 68s to beat the 54 hole scoring record for the championship. Alas for Aoki, Nicklaus's scoring was at exactly the same level. Out together in the fourth round (and by chance throughout) Aoki, with a final round of 70, beat the previous scoring record for the US Open. Nicklaus did even better, however, and although the result was in doubt to the end, he won by two strokes with his 68 to Aoki's 70.

In 1983, again in the USA, Aoki played one of the famous shots of modern golf, holing a full wedge shot on the last hole to win the Hawaiian Open. He left one onlooker, Jack Renner, disconsolate. Renner thought he had won the title until Aoki's shot from the rough ran into the hole from 128 yards. That same year, Aoki also won the European Open.

Tommy Armour

Aoki's main efforts, however, have been concentrated on the lucrative Japanese Tour, where he has won 41 tournaments, including a long-delayed Open in 1983 and five PGA Matchplay titles.

Arana, Javier

1904–. Born Bilbao, Spain

Spanish amateur champion in 1928, 1933 and 1934, Arana began designing golf courses in the 1930s. Although he has seldom worked outside Spain, his work there has been outstanding. Two of his best-known designs are El Prat and El Saler; the latter is considered to be one of the finest courses in Europe.

Armour, Tommy

1895–1968. Born Edinburgh, Scotland

Emigrating to the USA early in the 1920s, Armour had achieved little in amateur golf. However, he found a good teacher in J Douglas Edgar, and as a professional his standard of play was transformed.

Armour was a superbly accurate driver who very often left himself a good line to the flag for his second shots. This earned him a reputation as the greatest iron player of his time.

In 1927, Armour won the US Open after a tie with Harry Cooper, winning the play-off 76 to 79. That year, his best, he won a total of seven events. In 1930, he added the US PGA to his record but his greatest triumph lay ahead. It came in 1931 at Carnoustie when he took the British Open, the last Scottish-born player to do so.

As his golf game declined, Armour moved into other fields. He became the highest paid golf teacher in the USA ($50 a lesson) and seemed to be unbeatable in 'friendly' money matches, even though he had the putting yips, a term he himself invented (see Glossary). Armour produced two instruction books, *How to Play Your Best Golf* and *A Round of Golf with Tommy Armour*.

Auckland, North Island, New Zealand

Although it dates from 1894, the club moved to its present Middlemore course in 1910. After World War I it became really established as changes were made to its parkland-type lay-out. It is one of New Zealand's finest courses, appropriately chosen as the venue for the Commonwealth Tournament in 1971, the centenary year of New Zealand golf. It has been host to the New Zealand Open Championship many times, and New Zealand's famous Bob Charles has played and won there.

Augusta National, Georgia, USA

Home of the famous Masters Tournament, this course was built in 1931, the year after the legendary R T (Bobby) Jones achieved golf's Grand Slam by winning the Open and Amateur Championships of Britain and the USA. Retiring then from competitive play, Jones

Augusta National, Georgia, USA: the 12th hole, played from a central grove of trees across Rae's Creek.

Augusta National, Georgia, USA: the 16th hole, elegant and beautiful, has been the scene of many spectacular and legendary battles.

Augusta National Golf Club

OUT		3,510 yards		36
No1	White Pine	400 yards	par 4	
No2	Woodbine	555 yards	par 5	
No3	Flowering Peach	360 yards	par 4	
No4	Palm	220 yards	par 3	
No5	Magnolia	450 yards	par 4	
No6	Juniper	190 yards	par 3	
No7	Pampas	365 yards	par 4	
No8	Yellow Jasmine	530 yards	par 5	
No9	Carolina Cherry	440 yards	par 4	

IN		3,520 yards		36
No10	Camellia	485 yards	par 4	
No11	Dogwood	445 yards	par 4	
No12	Golden Bell	155 yards	par 3	
No13	Azalea	485 yards	par 5	
No14	Chinese Fir	420 yards	par 4	
No15	Fire Thorn	520 yards	par 5	
No16	Red Bud	190 yards	par 3	
No17	Nandina	400 yards	par 4	
No18	Holly	420 yards	par 4	

TOTAL	7,030 yards		par 72

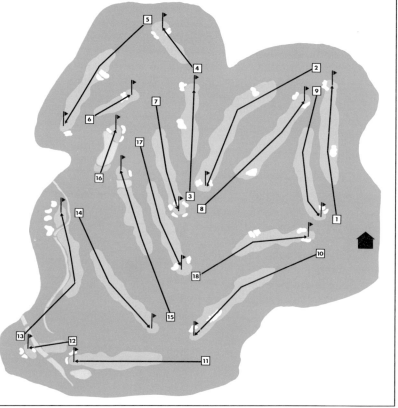

embarked on his long held ambition to build a dream course. He found the ideal site on a former nursery plantation, with a manor house to serve as clubhouse. With Alister Mackenzie, the Yorkshire-born architect who had designed Cypress Point, they constructed an outstanding course, as well as a beautiful one. Each hole is named after the flower, shrub or tree which make it a riot of colour for the tournament each April. Designed to encourage attacking play, the Augusta National has broad fairways, virtually no rough and fewer than 50 bunkers, but severely contoured, fast greens.

The Augusta National Invitation Tournament, later to become the Masters, was inaugurated in 1934. A sensational shot by Gene Sarazen in its second year created nationwide interest in the event, and, as its prestige grew, led to its acceptance as one of the world's major championships. Jack Nicklaus holds the record for the most victories, claiming his sixth title in 1986 at the age of 46.

The Australian, Sydney, Australia: the ninth hole of the oldest golf club in the continent.

Austin, Debbie

1948–. Born Oneida, New York, USA

A player on the US Tour since 1968, Debbie Austin had easily her best season in 1977, when she won five tournaments and finished sixth in the money list. Although she has won only two other titles, she was in the top 20 money winners seven times in the years 1973–1981. A chunky player, the long game has been her strength; her putting is sometimes hesitant. Her career now seems on the wane, with very little money won in 1985 and 1986.

Australian, The, Sydney, Australia

First established in 1882, The Australian lays claim to being the oldest club in Australia, for although Royal Adelaide was founded in 1870, it went out of existence until 1892. The Australian, which founded the New South Wales Golf Association together with Royal Sydney, itself suffered a break in continuity for five years from 1888 because of road building. It eventually came to its present site at Kensington in 1903.

Paul Azinger

In 1968, road building again disrupted the course: the construction of a new highway resulted in the rebuilding of a number of holes. In 1975, Jack Nicklaus, who had won one of his Australian Open titles here, was commissioned to make further alterations to the course, and over his new lay-out he won the Open in 1978 for the sixth time. On undulating sandy terrain, with few trees, it has almost links-like turf and is subject to winds from the sea.

Azinger, Paul

1960–. Born Holyoke, Maryland, USA

Azinger has had to qualify to play the US Tour three times, having twice forfeited his playing privileges in his early 20s. However, in the autumn of 1984 he was medallist in the qualifying event. He is now regarded as a future star. He won over $250,000 in 1986.

In his first appearance in the British Open in 1987, Azinger bogeyed both the 17th and 18th holes to finish runner-up, a stroke behind Nick Faldo.

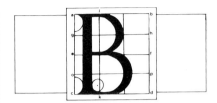

Baiocchi, Hugh

1946–. Born Johannesburg, South Africa

After a fine amateur career during which he won both the Brazilian and South African titles, Hugh Baiocchi has been a consistent rather than a brilliant performer in professional golf since 1973. In that year he took two South African tournaments and in Europe won the Swiss Open and finished third in the money list. Since then he has always made good money in Europe where his best year was 1977, when he was second in the money list.

Tournament titles have regularly come his way. In South Africa his best years were 1976 and 1980, with three wins in each. In 1978 he won the South African Open. In Europe,

Hugh Baiocchi

he has won six tournaments, including the 1977 Matchplay Championship, a second Swiss Open in 1979 and the 1983 State Express Classic.

Baker-Finch, Ian

1960–. Born Nambour, Australia

For the last few years, Baker-Finch has been regarded as one of the Australians most likely to succeed. He won his first title, the New Zealand Open, in 1983, but came to world attention in the 1984 Open Championship at St Andrews.

With opening rounds of 68 and 66 he led at the halfway stage by three strokes and gave little away with a 71 in the third round. At this point, he was tied for the lead with Tom Watson; Ballesteros and Langer were a couple of strokes behind. Beginning his final round, Baker-Finch's pitch to the first green cleared the burn but bit too well and twisted back in. With hindsight it seemed that he never recovered from this blow, and came home with a 79 in ninth place.

Baker-Finch has since won three titles in Australia and on the European Tour the 1985 Scandinavian Enterprise Open.

Ball, John

1861–1940. Born Hoylake, Cheshire, England

If major championship victories are the sole measure of a golfer, John Ball is the greatest British golfer ever. Harry Vardon won the British Open six times and the US Open once. Ball can go two better with a record eight wins in the Amateur Championship and one in the Open. In 1890 he became one of only three amateurs to win the Open Championship (Harold Hilton and Bobby Jones are the others). With Jones, he is the only man to win both titles the same year.

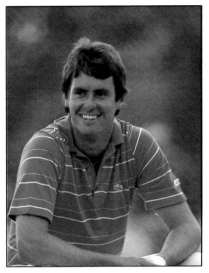

Ian Baker-Finch

Ball's eight victories in the Amateur Championship mean that he also holds the record for the most victories in any one event. Vardon and Nicklaus come closest with six victories in the British Open and US Masters respectively. Ball's titles came in 1888, 1890, 1892, 1894, 1899, 1907, 1910 and 1912, a span of close on a quarter of a century when none of the best amateurs turned professional.

Although J H Taylor is often given credit for being the first man to go for the flag rather than the centre of the green with his iron shots, it is likely that Young Tom Morris, a professional, and John Ball had already shown the way and were just as effective. Although Ball employed an ugly grip, with his right hand well under the shaft, many observers commented on the beauty of his style. Bernard Darwin even ranked him well above Vardon and Jones.

Playing with relatively few clubs, Ball was a superb manipulator of the ball and despised those who needed the club to do the job for them. He preferred to hood the face of an iron for low shots into wind and open the face and cut across the ball when he needed height.

often proved a good as well as long driver.

He appeared from nowhere as a 19-year-old at the 1976 Open Championship at Royal Birkdale, when he led for three rounds and finished joint runner-up to Johnny Miller. He led the European Order of Merit that year and held it for the next two years.

His first major, the 1979 Open at Royal Lytham, has gone down in golfing legend. Before the event began, Ballesteros' chances were discounted, as it was thought he would often be in the rough and it was severe at Lytham. But it was not severe enough. Ballesteros claims that he deliberately drove off the fairway to reach the best line in to the flag. As he once drove

One of the greatest all-round golfers, Severiano Ballesteros wins the Open Championship at St Andrews in 1984.

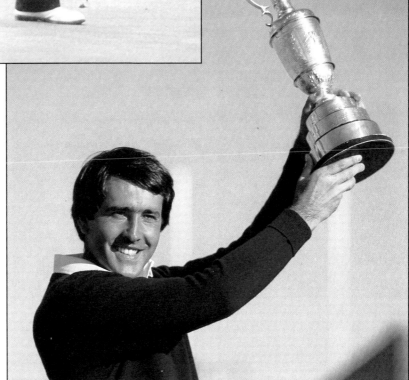

Ballesteros, Severiano

1957–. Born Pedrena, Santander, Spain

Although it is impossible to decide who is the greatest golfer, Ballesteros may have the greatest all-round talent. Of no other great golfer has it been claimed that he could play all the shots. Ballesteros is one of the game's long hitters with both woods and long irons; a master of the short irons; one of the best sand players; a deft chipper; and a very good putter although perhaps occasionally fallible on short putts. With his extreme length, he must be more likely than most to finish far from the fairway when he is off line, but the mature Ballesteros has among cars and vans, he became known in the USA for a while as 'the car park champion'.

Acceptance in the USA came with his performance in the 1980 Masters. His 66 in the first round gave him a share of the lead; his 69 to follow put him four ahead. It seemed all over when he had a 68 in the third round to lead by seven; then, on the final day, he was 10 in the lead after the first nine. Then came disaster: three putts on the 11th; into Rae's Creek on the par-three 12th for a five, and into it again with a deplorable iron shot on the 13th. Five shots gone at Amen Corner. Was this about to become the most abject collapse in Masters' history? Not so. His nerve held. Ballesteros played the remaining holes in one under par and won by four strokes.

Three years later he won again, in very different style. After rounds of 68, 70 and 73, he lay a stroke behind Floyd and Stadler. All was changed when he virtually won the

event on the first four holes which he played in birdie, eagle, par, birdie. Both Stadler and Floyd seemed to give up. Ballesteros again won by four.

Although Ballesteros regards the British Open as his favourite event, the Masters is not far behind in his affections, and his record in it is even better. In 1985 he tied for second, he was fourth in 1986 when he threw it away with one bad iron shot at the 15th, and he tied and lost the play-off in 1987.

Ballesteros' remaining major is the 1984 Open Championship at St Andrews. As at Lytham, he had a game plan and a very simple one — avoid the bunkers off the tee (he did not consider the rough nearly as severe a hazard). He kept in touch with leaders throughout, putting beautifully but with little luck. With two to play, he was level with Watson. On the dreaded 17th he hit his tee shot well left into the rough, but then, from a very difficult angle, hit the shot of the

championship, and holed out for his four. Just behind, Watson hit the ideal tee shot, but an equally poor second shot which finished almost against the wall beyond the road. For the first time, Ballesteros led the championship and made sure with a birdie on the last.

In tournament play, his record is even more impressive and it is a truly international one. He has won in Japan, Australia, South Africa, New Zealand, Kenya, almost every country in Europe as well as the USA. No one in golf history approaches his 36 European Tour victories and he has another 14 elsewhere, five of which are in the USA. His record is especially notable in the World Matchplay Championship, with four wins in the years 1981 to 1985. The first of these was a year when, because of European Tour politics, he was not selected for the Ryder Cup. In 1986, he again led the European Order of Merit after six victories during the season.

Ballybunion, County Kerry, Ireland

Towering sand dunes dominate the play of this superb links course, lying right by the sea — so close that erosion some years ago threatened its existence until golfers responded to a world-wide appeal to save it. Dating back to 1896, the Old course has seen changes, including a new clubhouse in the early 1970s which altered the order of play, the 14th becoming the first. Different from most links courses, the ridges of dunes run roughly at right angles to the shore. When the wind blows, finding the greens with approach shots can present a formidable challenge. The Old course has provided a fine test for many Irish championships, including the Men's and Ladies Amateur, and the Irish Professional was won here in 1957 by the popular Harry Bradshaw.

1984 World Matchplay Championship – Ballesteros driving and putting.

If the Old course is outstanding, it cannot overshadow the New. This was completed in 1982 by the famous American architect Robert Trent Jones, who created what has been described as 'a masterpiece', with splendid holes. Jones himself said of the 328-yard 10th, 'There is no more natural golf hole in the world, an outrageously beautiful stretch of God-given terrain.'

Baltusrol, New Jersey, USA

This club, established in 1895, is one of the oldest in the USA. Its professional for 36 years was Johnny Farrell, US Open champion and member of the first Ryder Cup team, who gave lessons to the Duke of Windsor on his frequent

Ballybunion, County Kerry, Ireland: the 15th hole on this magnificent links course lying right by the sea.

visits. It takes its name from Baltus Rol, a Dutch farmer who lived nearby and who was murdered by thieves in 1831.

Both courses, the Upper and the Lower, have been host to the US Open Championship; the former has been the venue for the earlier US Opens. In all, a dozen national championships have been played here. The Opens of 1903 and 1915 were played on the original course, which was replaced by the two layouts designed by A W Tillinghast in the 1920s. The Lower course has a demanding finish of two par fives; at the 17th of 630 yards in 1980

Jack Nicklaus birdied the hole to seal his second victory over the course (his first was in 1967) to win his fourth US Open title.

The most famous hole is the short fourth over a lake with alternate tees, to give a distance of either 162 or 194 yards to a two-level green sloping towards the water, with three bunkers at the back.

Banff Springs, Alberta, Canada

Set among the Canadian Rockies, this course of championship standard boasts the most spectacular scenery of peaks, lakes, glaciers and the wild life of a huge national park. Built in 1911 by Canadian

Card for the course

No1	469 yards	par 4	No10	449 yards	par 4
No2	390 yards	par 4	No11	410 yards	par 4
No3	438 yards	par 4	No12	193 yards	par 3
No4	194 yards	par 3	No13	383 yards	par 4
No5	388 yards	par 4	No14	399 yards	par 4
No6	470 yards	par 4	No15	419 yards	par 4
No 7	470 yards	par 4	No16	214 yards	par 3
No8	365 yards	par 4	No17	623 yards	par 5
No9	206 yards	par 3	No18	542 yards	par 5
OUT	**3390 yards**	**34**	**IN**	**3632 yards**	**36**

Baltusrol, New Jersey, USA: the 4th hole, 194 yards long and all of it over water, leads to a most difficult green. Below: the lay-out of the course reveals it to be an architectural oddity. The last two holes are both par fives.

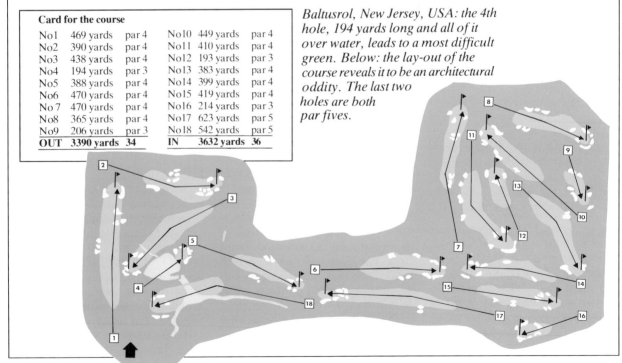

Pacific Railway as a nine-hole course, it was later extended to 18 holes. It was redesigned in 1927 by Canadian architect Stanley Thompson, who created one of the finest of short holes in his lay-out. The eighth hole, aptly named Devil's Cauldron, is 175 yards from tee to green over a lake, but swirling winds make it a far from easy shot from the elevated tee.

Barnes, Jim

1887–1966. Born Lelant, Cornwall, England

Jim Barnes, at 6ft 4ins may have been the first very tall man to play golf to championship level. Until quite recently it was thought that nobody much above 5ft 9ins could expect to play golf to a high standard.

Barnes was certainly an exception and a formidable performer in the major championships, where he had victories in the US PGA Championship in 1916 and 1919, in the US Open of 1921 and in the British Open of 1925. His most remarkable performance was in his US Open victory when he left his pursuers in disarray: Walter Hagen and Fred McLeod were nine strokes behind at the finish.

Barnes learned to play golf while an assistant in Cornwall, and he emigrated to California in the early 1900s. Like many others during this period of golf history, it was his experiences in America that made him a champion.

Barton, Pam

1917–1943. Born London, England

The greatness of Pam Barton can never be fully assessed for she was killed in an air crash at Manston in Kent during World War II when only 26. She had joined the Women's Auxiliary Air Force at the outbreak of war.

Before the war she had already won three women's major titles, two of them in 1936 when she won the US Amateur and the British Amateur — at the age of 19 only the second player to do so. In 1939 she won the British title again. She won the French championship at the age of 17 and the same year reached the final of the British Amateur, a feat she repeated in 1935. By the time of her death, she was considered to be one of the all-time greats of British women's golf. In the USA, she was elected to the Hall of Fame.

Barton, unusually for the 1930s, was a great believer in practice, and worked relentlessly to cure faults. Before her 1936 US championship she wrote, 'In America I practised five or six hours a day. First I played seven holes with 20 balls, and that took two hours; then I had an hour each of putting, driving and iron play.'

Baugh, Laura

1955–. Born Gainesville, Florida, USA

Laura Baugh was an early starter. She won the Southern Amateur in 1970 aged 15 and repeated her victory the following year, when she also won the US Amateur title, the youngest to do so at 16. Amid fanfares, she turned professional in 1973. In her first tournament, she caused fresh sensations by taking the lead at 36 holes before eventually finishing second.

Surprisingly, Baugh has never done substantially better: her best result was to reach a play-off in 1979, which she lost. This is one of 10 second-place finishes in her 13 years of professional golf. Her short game has always been outstanding, and her relative lack of success in professional golf stems from her lack of power, which means she may be hitting woods into greens when others are using mid-irons.

Once voted 'Most Beautiful Golfer', Baugh's indirect earnings have been even higher than her

Andy Bean

substantial tournament winnings – perhaps more than $250,000 a year from endorsements, modelling and other sources.

Bean, Andy

1953–. Born Lafayette, Georgia, USA

Bean, 6ft 4ins tall and broad to match, has long been one of the most powerful men in modern golf. After an excellent amateur career which brought him both the Western and Eastern titles, Bean joined the US Tour in 1976. By 1977 he was a success, taking his first tournament, the Doral-Eastern. The following year he won three times, an achievement which is becoming increasingly rare.

Bean has added a title most years since then and his consistency brings him many high finishes. In the years 1978–1986 he was four times in the top four money winners. He has won more than $200,000 six times and exceeded $400,000 in both 1984 and 1986 when he came close to the rare

$500,000.

Bean very much needs a major championship title, both to set a seal on his career and perhaps to lead on to a new plateau of success.

Belfry, The, West Midlands, England

One of Britain's newer courses, opened in 1977 and designed by former Ryder Cup player David Thomas, The Belfry has two layouts, the Brabazon and the Derby, named after Presidents of the Professional Golfers Association, whose headquarters are here. American in style, it features water hazards, notably the 18th on the championship Brabazon where both the tee shot and approach must carry a lake.

The 10th, a short par four, is generally played with a pitch second shot from the angle of a dog-leg across water to a long, narrow green; but in the Hennessy Cognac Cup of 1978, Severiano Ballesteros scorned the easy route. He smashed a towering drive which dropped all of 285 yards over trees on to the green, giving him an eagle chance from eight feet. He missed this but ensured a tap-in birdie.

The course has attracted many professional tournaments, but its most dramatic moment came in 1985. It was the venue for the Ryder Cup, when Europe gained its first victory for 28 years over the USA.

Beman, Deane

1938–. Born Washington DC, USA

If you judged a golfer solely by the prettiness or otherwise of his swing, Beman would rate no better than a 16 handicap. However, it is hard to think of even a handful of golfers who have made better use of their talents.

Four times a Walker Cup selection, Beman collected most of the amateur titles available during his career. In the USA he won the Eastern Amateur four times, and his first major championship came in 1959 when he won the British Amateur at Royal St George's. In 1960 he added the American title, and repeated his victory three years later.

Beman financed his amateur golf with a prosperous insurance business; his decision to turn

The Belfry, West Midlands, England: the 10th hole of a course transformed from 15 adjacent potato fields. It features many water hazards.

Deane Beman

professional in 1967 had little to do with money. He wanted to see how he managed against the best players in the world. He was a limited success. He did not win a major title but he came within sight of the 1969 US Open. Beginning with rounds of 68 and 69, he led, and his finishing rounds of 73 and 72 left him one stroke behind the champion, Orville Moody.

By the end of 1973, Beman had won four titles on the US Tour and faced a new challenge. In 1974 he became Commissioner for the US Tour. Rumour now has it that having left amateur golf to test himself against the professionals, Beman has been hitting a very large number of balls on the practice grounds. He may follow his spirited performance in the 1986 British Open by joining the US Senior Tour when he reaches 50.

Beman's successes have been largely due to his putting. He was once good enough to use only 19 putts in a US Tour round!

However, his determination and nerve have been just as important. He was once voted the best Tour player with fairway woods.

Bendelow, Tom

1872–1936. Born Aberdeen, Scotland

Emigrating to the USA as a journalist, Bendelow joined the US golf boom of the 1890s as a course designer, working for the Spalding sporting goods company. At that time, fees for laying out a course were not much more than $20 and designers did a rudimentary job. In, perhaps, an afternoon they marched around planting stakes to indicate tees, greens and the then standard cross bunkers to catch poor tee shots, and generally bar the route to the green.

In this rough-and-ready way Bendelow 'designed' hundreds of courses before World War I — and he certainly gave golfers somewhere to play. After the war he began to refine his work and to write and lecture on golf architecture. The finest example of his later work is the Number 3 course at Medinah, Illinois.

Berg, Patty

1918–. Born Minneapolis, Minnesota, USA

Berg began to play golf at the age of 12, and was soon on the way to her 29 amateur titles. In 1935, she competed in the US Amateur for the first time and reached the final, where she was beaten by the great Glenna Collett. She also reached the final in 1937 and 1938, facing the same opponent, Estelle Page, on each occasion. Page won comfortably in 1937 — and lost equally decisively in 1938.

In 1940, Berg signed one of the first women's professional contracts with the Wilson Sporting Goods Company. As a competitive golfer there was almost nothing to

play for although she did win the 1941 Western Open, with its first prize a handsome $100. In spite of a severe injury and later war service, Berg managed to fit in six wins by the time the WPGA was formed in 1946. She added another seven before 1948, when the LPGA was founded. Berg was a charter member.

In those early LPGA years, the Tour was really Berg and Babe Zaharias; although Betty Jameson also deserves mention. Babe was undoubtedly the greatest attraction but Berg was not far behind: she was leading money winner in 1954, 1956 and 1957.

From that first Western Open victory in 1941 to her last in 1962, Berg is credited with 55 victories by the LPGA. Eleven were rated as majors in their day. Her money winnings cannot be calculated accurately because early LPGA records have been lost. She continues to be active in promoting the game.

Berkshire, The, England

The two courses, the Red and the Blue, of the Berkshire club, set in glorious countryside, with heather, pines, open heath and a variety of splendid holes, are among the finest inland in the British Isles. Frank Pennink, noted player and course designer, applied that description in praising its 'golf of spectacular grandeur'. Although the Red is classed as the major layout, there is little to choose in their excellence and appeal. The Red is notable for its six testing par threes and six par fives. The courses were built in the late 1920s to Herbert Fowler's design and were made possible when large areas of forest on Crown land outside Ascot were cut down during World War I. The 1965 English Amateur Championship was played here on a composite course, giving Michael Bonallack the third of his five titles;

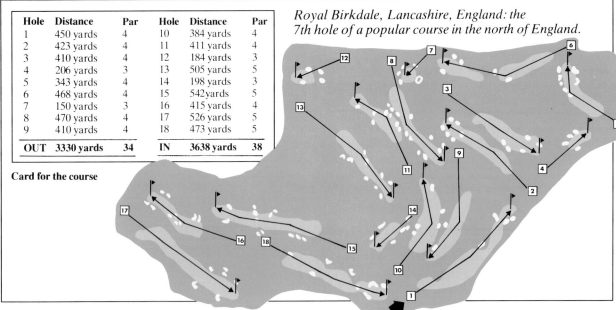

Hole	Distance	Par	Hole	Distance	Par
1	450 yards	4	10	384 yards	4
2	423 yards	4	11	411 yards	4
3	410 yards	4	12	184 yards	3
4	206 yards	3	13	505 yards	5
5	343 yards	4	14	198 yards	3
6	468 yards	4	15	542 yards	5
7	150 yards	3	16	415 yards	4
8	470 yards	4	17	526 yards	5
9	410 yards	4	18	473 yards	5
OUT	**3330 yards**	**34**	**IN**	**3638 yards**	**38**

Card for the course

*Royal Birkdale, Lancashire, England: the
7th hole of a popular course in the north of England.*

in the Berkshire Trophy, the club's major event, he claimed six victories. The ladies Avia Foursomes have also been held here since 1966.

Birkdale, Royal, Lancashire, England

Founded in 1899, Birkdale is one of the oldest clubs in the North of England, and received the Royal accolade in 1951. This great seaside course ranks high in Britain's linksland lore, and although the youngest of the Open Championship venues until 1977 when Turnberry came into the rota, many rate it as the most popular. It has certainly attracted more important events than many comparable courses — six Opens, including the 100th Open in 1971, the Ladies Open, the Ryder, Walker and Curtis Cups, the Amateur and English championships, and the PGA championship among major professional events.

It is distinctive among links courses: play is along valleys between sandhills, with unusually soft fairways, but fierce willow scrub provides hazards. It was from the cloying rough in 1961 that Arnold Palmer fashioned a near miracle shot to the 15th green (now the 16th) and went on to win his first Open. When Birkdale welcomed its first Open in 1954, Australian Peter Thomson won the first of his titles; 11 years later it was at Birkdale in 1983 that he claimed his fifth success. Tom Watson also captured his fifth Open here, making sure with a superb two-iron shot to the final green.

A teenage Ballesteros first commanded attention here when he led the Open of 1976 for three rounds before conceding the title to Johnny Miller. Three years after he first came to Birkdale — and to Britain — as US Open champion for the Alcan tournament of 1968, Lee Trevino was back to claim his first Open as he held off the challenge of the popular 'Mr Lu' (Lu Liang Huan) of Taiwan. The Ryder Cup of 1969 saw high drama in the first tied match of the series as Tony Jacklin and Jack Nicklaus halved the final singles encounter.

Blackheath, Royal, London, England

The Society of Blackheath Golfers was probably formed in 1608 by Scots who moved south when the thrones were united under James I, but the foundation of the club itself is difficult to establish. It is the premier club in England, although there must have been clubs in Scotland long before. In 1766 a silver club was presented to 'the Honourable Company of Golfers at Blackheath' while records start with a list of subscribers in 1787.

Originally there were five holes on the heath, followed in 1844 by a new lay-out of seven holes. A famous quartet of J H Taylor, James Braid and Harry and Tom Vardon played a medal competition over 21 holes in 1908, which Taylor won.

After World War I, when play became impossible on the heath, the club merged with Eltham and the course at Eltham Park was redesigned by James Braid. Its superb 17th century clubhouse, formerly Eltham Lodge, contains

Royal Blackheath, London, England: the superb 17th century clubhouse at Eltham Park.

fine trophies, including the silver club of 1766, and the Spring Medal, originally the gold medal of the Knuckle Club (the old winter club) which dates back to 1792.

Its most famous player, George Glennie from St Andrews, captain and then honorary secretary of the club, with Lieutenant J C Stewart, won the first golf championship played: 11 clubs competed in a foursomes knock-out tournament at St Andrews in 1857, and Royal Blackheath beat the Royal and Ancient in the final by seven holes.

Blairgowrie, Perthshire, Scotland

The heathland Rosemount course, with its wealth of pine and birch trees and heather-lined fairways, is considered to be Scotland's finest inland course — and with good reason. Its glorious setting is matched by its testing qualities, among them many dog-leg holes and the occasional pine encroaching into the fairway. Its tiny 15th hole of 128 yards, which lends comparisons to Troon's Postage Stamp, is followed by two fine holes: the 16th of 468 yards calls for an uphill drive with water to the left, and the attractive 17th of 170 yards leads across a valley to a two-tiered green.

Established in 1899 with nine holes on forest land owned by the Marquess of Lansdowne, it was extended to 18 in 1927 and James Braid later designed new holes. In recent years a second course of equal merit has been added, called Lansdowne, the name first given to the original nine-hole lay-out.

Blalock, Jane

1945–. Born Portsmouth, New Hampshire, USA

After a good but not outstanding amateur career, Jane Blalock was Rookie of the Year on the 1969 LPGA Tour. In 1970 she won her

Jane Blalock

first tournament and was 13th on the money list. Since then she has been one of the LPGA's most consistent players, only twice out of the top four between 1971 and 1978. This consistency is well illustrated by her record of not missing a cut between 1969 and 1980, a run of 299 events.

Most of Blalock's victories came in the years 1972–1979. She appeared to be past her peak in the early 1980s but revived in 1985 when she won twice, finished seventh on the money list and won her greatest money total, $192,426. Her best years in real terms were 1972 and 1974 when she accumulated nine victories.

In 1981, it looked as if she might be the first woman to earn more than $1–million in tournament winnings, although in fact she did not do so until 1983, when she was the seventh to reach that target. She has won 29 times on the LPGA Tour.

Bolt, Tommy

1918–. Born Haworth, Oklahoma, USA

Always a mercurial player, the most published press photographs of Tommy Bolt show him either breaking a club or throwing one — or other kinds of mayhem. This was partly due to the fact that he had an almost permanent corps of press photographers ready to record him doing his worst. Such a reputation has obscured the fact that Bolt has been one of the smoothest swingers of a golf club, and an equally superb shot-maker. As a putter, he was considered just about the worst on the US Tour — a judgement Bolt himself endorsed.

'Thunderbolt' did not begin playing tournament golf until he was 32, but proved himself by winning in his second season. In 1955 he won four times, but his greatest achievement came in the 1958 US Open, which he won decisively from Gary Player. If it had not been for a three putting spasm towards the close of the 1952 Masters, Bolt might well have taken that title too.

More remarkably, Bolt was still good enough at the age of 53 to come third in the 1971 US PGA. He would have made a fortune as a Senior golfer, but the development of that Tour from 1980 came too late for him. In 1969 he won the US PGA Seniors title, and then defeated Scotsman John Panton for the World Seniors.

Bombay Presidency, India

The club took its present name in 1931, after its formation near the docks in 1927 as the New club. It moved to its present site at Chembur in 1940. Previously there were two nine hole courses, no longer in existence, and a quite short course. Back in 1842 the Royal Bombay club had been founded, the second oldest in the world outside Britain; that, too, no longer exists.

Chembur became the home of the Western Indian Championship and, later, the All India Amateur Championship. Australian Peter Thomson, often a welcome visitor, won the Indian Open three times. He used his vast experience to good effect when he redesigned the course, bringing it to first-class condition, with some testing holes and fast greens.

Bonallack, OBE, Michael

1934–. Born Chigwell, Essex, England

On his record, Bonallack must be

Michael Bonallack on the Swilcan Burn, R & A Golf Club, St Andrews.

considered the best amateur golfer in the UK since Harold Hilton and John Ball. His greatest achievement was to win five Amateur Championships in 1961, 1965, 1968, 1969 and 1970. No one else has taken three titles in a row, and only John Ball, with eight, has taken more. Not even Ball won twice consecutively, something only four players have ever managed.

Bonallack went on to win five times in the 1960s, his most astounding win being over David Kelley in 1968. Kelley decided to follow the Jones philosophy of playing the course and trying to keep to par. For the first 13 holes he did just that and found himself seven down! Bonallack was out in 32 and then came home in 29. Bonallack won by 12 and 11, a record margin as are his five victories in this event.

The short game was Bonallack's strength, putting in particular. When his swing was off, he could miss green after green and still make his pars by getting down in two. In one championship final, he managed to do this 22 times.

Bonallack was an automatic Walker Cup choice from 1959 to 1973. A high point for him came when he was playing captain of the winning 1971 team. He represented Great Britain and Ireland seven times in the World Amateur Team Championship. With his best playing days behind him, Bonallack became increasingly involved in administration. In 1975 he became chairman of the R and A Selection Committee, and chairman of the PGA from 1976–1982 when he took up the presidency of the English Golf Union. His later appointment as Secretary to the R and A was unanimously welcomed.

Boros, Julius

1920–. Born Fairfield, Connecticut, USA

An apparently effortless swinger,

Julius Boros

Julius Boros's career emphasizes how well many of such players last. At the time of his second US Open victory in 1963, for example, he was, at 43, the second oldest winner. In spite of the recent victories in their 40s by Raymond Floyd and Jack Nicklaus, Boros, with his 1968 US PGA, is easily the oldest player to win a major championship. Seven years later, he came within a whisker of being the oldest winner of a US Tour event. At 55 he tied with Gene Littler (another smooth swinger who has the secret of eternal golfing life) but lost the sudden death play-off. (Sam Snead, at the age of 52, is actually the oldest winner.)

Boros was a late starter on the US Tour and was 32 at the time of his first win in 1952. He had added another 17 victories by 1968. Some of these achievements were due to his mastery of the wedge. He helped to combat nerves by walking up to the ball, taking up his stance and wristily flicking the ball away in one continuous movement. Boros is one of the great players who virtually did without practice. He reckoned he already had too

many aches and pains to want to risk any more. One of his rare appearances in Britain was in the 1965 Ryder Cup match at Royal Birkdale.

Bradley, Pat

1951–. Born Westford, Massachusetts, USA

After a good, but by no means outstanding, amateur career, Pat Bradley was quickly a success as a professional. Her first victory came in her second season, in 1975, when she won the Colgate Far East Open in Australia. In the USA she was already on the threshold of stardom, 14th on the money list. Since then, she has steadily improved and from 1976–1986 has only twice been out of the top six.

In 1981 Bradley won the US Women's Open. From being six strokes behind the leaders, she finished with scores of 68 and 66, the latter one of the lowest rounds ever played in the event.

Consistency, rather than tournament wins, was for long Bradley's hallmark. From 1977 to the end of 1986, she missed only three cuts

Pat Bradley

and at one time, 1980–1985, went 121 events before doing so. At the beginning of the 1983 season, she still had only nine wins but then came a change. She won four times that year, missed out in 1984 (she was still fourth on the money list) and added three more victories in 1985.

In 1986 Bradley was the dominant player on the Tour: she won five times and came within reach of the Grand Slam of all major titles. She won the Nabisco Dinah Shore, the LPGA Championship and the du Maurier Classic. She failed only at the US Open hurdle, where she was fifth. Her total of six majors in the 1980s is the highest. Not surprisingly, her $492,021 was comfortably a record. Only one other player, Nancy Lopez in 1985, has passed the $400,000 mark. Bradley became in 1986 the first woman to pass the $2–million mark in prize money.

Bradshaw, Harry

1913–. Born Delgany, County Wicklow, Ireland

Bradshaw has gone down in golfing folklore as the man who lost an

Harry Bradshaw

Open because his ball came to rest in a beer bottle. The incident occurred as early as the fifth hole in only the second round and the ball was not in a bottle but lying against a broken one.

He moved his ball only about 20 yards and was struck in the eye by the glass — though fortunately it did him no harm. His putting was the most affected. Having been at a lifetime peak, it became unsteady for a few holes. He finished in 77 on a difficult day for scoring, only one worse than the eventual champion in 1949, Bobby Locke, who won the 36-hole play-off. Bradshaw never came as close again.

Bradshaw won four events during the 1950s, including the Dunlop Masters twice, and with Christy O'Connor won the World Cup in 1958. He made an unlikely-looking figure on the golf course with his short, flat swing. A closer look revealed a very strange grip with three fingers of his right hand overlapping. By today's standards, he was under-powered but he did have two equalizers. He was a superb wedge player and putter, one of the few who have managed to hit his putts and listen to them falling into the cup. For many years, he was professional at the Portmarnock Club.

Brae Burn, Massachusetts, USA

Scotsman Donald Ross put his stamp on this course which dates back to the 1890s, and finally saw it completed to his satisfaction in 1947. Trees play a crucial part in it, and it offers a great challenge, typical of the many courses Ross designed.

Brae Burn was host to the first US Open after World War I, won in a play-off by Walter Hagen. It was also the scene of a unique meeting in the final of the 1928 US Amateur between American Amateur champion Bobby Jones and

James Braid

British champion Phil Perkins, of Birmingham. Victory went to Jones by 10 and nine.

Two Curtis Cup matches were played here in 1958 and 1970. On the first occasion Mrs Frances Smith (formerly Bunty Stephens) won the final singles for Britain to tie the match. Britain retained the trophy after winning at Prince's in 1954.

Braid, James

1870–1950. Born Earls Ferry, Fife, Scotland

A member of the Great Triumvirate, Braid ranks behind Vardon in golf history. Perhaps J H Taylor should also be placed ahead of him, mainly because Braid's five victories in the Open Championship were compressed into a short period, 1901–1912. Between 1903 and 1911, he also won the matchplay championship five times. Many years later, in 1927, Braid reached the final, one of the great feats of an older player.

Braid took longer to emerge than Vardon and Taylor, mainly because he did not find a putter that suited him until the turn of the century and was a fairly short hitter. Legend has it that Braid's hitting changed overnight and he became the longest of the three. Later, he became a prolific designer of golf courses and a very good one.

Brancaster

See West Norfolk, Royal, England

Brand, Gordon J

1958–. Born Cambridge, England

Although Brand has yet to win on the European Tour, he had won four times on the Safari Tour by the end of the 1986 season. 1987 saw his outstanding career achievement, second place behind Greg Norman in the Open Championship at Turnberry. In spite of the pressure, Brand had a 71 in the last round. The £50,000 he won was more than his total in any one year on the European Tour.

Brand, Gordon, Junior

1958–. Born Burnt Island, Fife, Scotland

After a brilliant amateur career, Brand easily adjusted to professional golf. He won the PGA

Gordon Brand, Junior

Tour qualifying event and quickly followed this with good performances on the South African Tour. In his first year on the European Tour he won twice: the Coral and the Bob Hope Classics. He finished seventh on the money list and was without a rival for the Rookie of the Year award.

1983 was not a good year for Brand, perhaps because he took too much conflicting advice on his swing. Since then, however, he has established himself securely in the top 12 in Europe.

Brown, Eric

1925–1986. Born Edinburgh, Scotland

Eric Brown had an unfortunate start to his tournament career. He turned professional shortly after winning the Scottish Amateur Championship in 1946, but the PGA rules of the day did not allow him to win money until he had served a five-year apprenticeship. He made up for lost time quickly, however, and won his first national championship, the Swiss Open, in 1951. He added three more such titles in the early 1950s and won seven tournaments in Britain in the years 1952–1962. Only a couple of loose drives at the end of the 1958 Open prevented his winning.

Perhaps Brown's most memorable performances came in Ryder Cup matches in the 1950s, when he won each of his four singles. He was subsequently non-playing captain of the 1969 Ryder Cup team which tied at Royal Birkdale.

Brown, Ken

1957–. Born Harpenden, Hertfordshire, England

Active on the European Tour since 1975, Ken Brown quickly gained recognition. This was partly because of his appearance. A lanky 6ft 2ins without a spare ounce of flesh, he was nicknamed 'the walk-

Ken Brown

ing one-iron'. With a hickory-shafted putter or any other, Brown is one of the best putters in world golf.

Brown played in the Ryder Cup in 1977 at the age of 20 and made three subsequent appearances. In spite of this status, he has won fewer titles than expected. He won the 1978 Irish Open but did not have another victory until 1983. Now he has a total of four in Europe and one in Africa.

In the years 1984–1986, Brown has given most of his attention to the US Tour, where he has one second place to his name in 1984, but has not made great impact. However, on brief visits to Europe he has won twice and in 1986 came second twice in successive weeks.

Bruen, James

1920–1972. Born Belfast, Northern Ireland

James Bruen only had a brief spell at the top of amateur golf: several years both before and after World War II. He led the qualifiers in the

1939 Open Championship before finishing 13th, and won the first Amateur Championship after the war in 1946. Bruen was three times a Walker Cup player, and an inspiration to his team in 1938 when he played golf of superb quality.

Bruen had one of the strangest swings of all time. On the backswing he raised the club almost directly away and then looped it around. He eventually delivered a fearsome blow, able to carve the ball from the most severe lies in the rough. A wrist injury cut short his career.

Burnham and Berrow,
Somerset, England

Built among the sand dunes by the Bristol Channel in 1890, this fine links course has attracted many major amateur events, including the English Men's and Women's championships, as well as the British Ladies. It also stages the

George Burns

annual West of England Open amateur event.

Its first professional was J H Taylor who found it ideal for developing his mashie play. As early blind holes were changed it became, in his words, one of the most sporting courses conceivable. With the wind a factor, the short fifth and 17th holes, with greens well-bunkered in front, provide a real test, especially the latter where even a driver may be needed for the uphill tee shot to a green high among the dunes.

Burns, George
1949–. Born Brooklyn, New York, USA

After a good amateur career in which he won the Canadian title, the Porter Cup and the North and South, Burns played in the 1975 Walker Cup and the World Team Championship. He then turned professional.

Although he has had his ups and downs, Burns instantly established himself by winning twice in Europe, followed by a 30th place in the 1976 US money list. His best year was 1980 when he won over $200,000, was seventh on the money list and won the Bing Crosby Pro-Am.

In 1981, he seemed to be on his way to the US Open title: his first three rounds of 69, 66 and 68 set a 54-hole scoring record for the event. In the final round, however, too many tee shots finished in the rough and his 73 was not good enough. He came second, behind, David Graham's 67.

Burton, Dick
1907–1974. Born Darwen, Lancashire, England

Needing a par four to win the 1939 Open Championship at St Andrews, Burton finished the job with great panache. First came a daring drive down the line of the fence, then followed a good pitch. He casually tossed his putter to his caddie when his ball was still well short of the hole. A three indeed it was.

Burton lost some of his best years to World War II but at least had the consolation of holding the title for a record seven years! His first shot in defence of his title at St Andrews in 1946 went out-of-bounds.

Burton's first tournament victory came in 1935 and his last in 1949, bringing his total of major wins to seven. In one of them, the 1949 *News Chronicle,* he set a low aggregate record with 266.

Butler, Peter
1932–. Born Birmingham, England

In a career as a leading player which lasted from the early 1960s to the late 1970s, Peter Butler's playing record was good enough for him to be invited to the US

Peter Butler

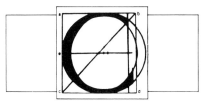

Calcavecchia, Mark

1960–. Born Laurel, Nebraska, USA

Mark Calcavecchia first played on the US Tour in 1981, but he had no success in his first four years, and was never better than 134th on the money list. He made great strides in 1986, shooting a record equalling 65 in the last round of the US Open to finish 14th and in all winning over $155,000. He won his first tournament, the South West Classic in Texas, towards the end of 1986, and in 1987 won the Honda Classic in Florida on a course where he had caddied the previous year.

Calcutta, Royal, India

Founded in 1829, this club came to its present site towards the end of the 19th century, and received its Royal title from King George V in 1911 during the Delhi Durbar. Calcutta was the first club outside Britain where golf was played. Two years after the club presented a cup to the Royal and Ancient, the first Calcutta Cup event was played at St Andrews. The first Amateur Championship of India was played in 1892 over the club's previous course, continuing when the change took place.

The new course was built on paddyfields, and trees were planted over the years. Its hazards include large tanks (or ponds), two of which feature on the fine 10th hole, the first calling for a long carry from the tee. The Indian Open, first played at Delhi in 1963, came to Calcutta two years later when the Indian amateur P G Sethi triumphed over Australian Peter Thomson, then British Open champion.

Campbell, Bill

1923–. Born West Virginia, USA

Bill Campbell had a swing good

Royal Calcutta, India: founded in 1829, it was the first club to play golf outside Britain.

Masters on several occasions. His 13th place in 1964 was the highest by a British player at that time. Two years later he led the field after 36 holes but followed with a 79.

Butler won his first big tournament in 1959 and by 1974 he brought his total in Europe to 14. In 1967 he had a tournament round of 61, but a 65 in the 1966 Open Championship was more significant. This second round put him one off the lead and broke the Muirfield record. The course was set up at its toughest that year, with tight fairways and exceptionally deep rough. Butler, with his faded wooded shots, was able to hold the fairways. This steadiness was always a feature of his play.

Bill Campbell

enough to keep him in the highest class of amateur golf for more than a quarter of a century — the late-1940s to the mid-1970s. In the Walker Cup, he has a remarkable record. In his eight singles he was never defeated, and only once allowed half a point to escape him.

Campbell was less successful in championship golf but reached the final of the 1954 British Amateur and won the US title in 1964. He won the North and South four times and his home state's championship 14 times. He won the USGA Seniors Championship in 1979 and 1980. In 1982 he became president of the USGA, his 'political' ambitions having perhaps changed course — he served in the West Virginia state legislature from 1949–1951.

Campbell, Dorothy

1883–1945. Born Edinburgh, Scotland

Dorothy Campbell was one of only three players to win the US and British Amateur Championships in the same year — 1909. Until Marlene Stewart Streit appeared,

Campbell was the only player to have won both these titles and the Canadian. She won another British title in 1910, before emigrating first to Canada, where she won their title three times, and then to the USA, where she won three US titles.

Campbell, Sir Guy

1885–1960. Born London, England

Although Sir Guy died in the USA, he was sufficiently attached to St Andrews to be buried there. A golfer good enough to reach the semi-finals of the Amateur Championship, he was a student of the history of golf and golf equipment.

He wrote for *The Times* and for golf magazines after World War I, and later became a golf architect. He is best known for his work at Killarney and Prince's, Sandwich.

Canizares, José-Maria

1947–. Born Madrid, Spain

José-Maria Canizares took a full 10 years to establish himself in European tournaments in the 1970s. He broke through in 1980, aged 33, when he won two tournaments and moved up to seventh place in the money list. His best earlier placing had been 21st. Although Canizares has won only twice since on the European Tour (and the 1984 Kenya Open) he is a steady money winner.

Steady, however, is hardly the word to describe his performance in the 1978 Swiss Open. He finished his second round with five consecutive birdies and the next day played the first nine in 27 strokes which equalled the world record. In the process, adding his finish and start together, he had 11 consecutive birdies and an eagle.

Canizares has twice been a member of the winning pair in the World Cup and also took the individual title in 1984. He has played in each Ryder Cup match in the 1980s and was the only unbeaten player in 1985 at the Belfry: some compensation for failing in his final match in America in 1983. He is a superb putter, although he seems not to believe it.

José-Maria Canizares

Canterbury, Ohio, USA

In his home state, Jack Nicklaus set one of his many records over this course, renowned for its formidable finish. In 1973 in the US PGA Championship, Nicklaus took the title by four strokes from Bruce Crampton for his 14th major championship victory, breaking Bobby Jones's record. The US Open was played here in 1940 and 1946, both resulting in play-offs. Lawson Little won from Gene Sarazen, and Lloyd Mangrum beat Byron Nelson and Vic Ghezzi. William C Campbell and Mark O'-Meara took the American Amateur title in 1964 and 1979 respectively.

An undulating but relatively short course, Canterbury calls for accurate placing of shots; here Jack Nicklaus was supreme in winning his title, dropping only five shots in the four rounds. The course was named in honour of Canterbury in England where Moses Cleaveland — who founded and gave his name to nearby Cleveland — was born. The course was built in 1922, many

JoAnne Carner

years after the American city was established, the 'a' in the name of the founder being omitted.

Caponi, Donna

1945–. Born Detroit, Michigan, USA

Donna Caponi's best years were 1968–1981, when she was only three times out of the top 10 and seven times in the top five. She still enters most of the events, but is drifting down the money list.

One of the quite frequent American women to take the US Open as her first title, she has 24 career wins, including four major championships, the LPGA twice and US Open twice. In 1981, she became the third woman golfer to earn $1 million. She has a very slow, deliberate swing and, because of a strong left-hand grip, a shut face at the top of the backswing, with the back troubles that tend to result.

Carner, JoAnne

1939–. Born Kirkland, Washington, USA

JoAnne Carner ranks among the top handful of women golfers. She first had a magnificent amateur career: she won five US Amateur titles in the years 1957–1968, reached two more finals and played in four Curtis Cup teams as JoAnne Gunderson before her marriage to Don Carner.

Carner would undoubtedly have beaten Glenna Collett's record of six had she not turned professional. Since then, she has won two US Opens and 42 tournaments in all. In the years 1970–1986, 26th has been her worst money list placing. She has been 10 times in the top six, three times as leading money winner. Carner is a big hitter and one of the best players ever of the long irons.

Carnoustie, Angus, Scotland

Although the first club was formed

Donna Caponi

at Carnoustie in 1842, golf was played there long before. The course, consisting at first of 10 holes, was extended to 18 by Old Tom Morris, and improved by James Braid in 1926. Its first Open was played five years later.

One of the great links courses, in some respects the greatest, Carnoustie offers natural golf of immense variety, and an exacting challenge, made even more so when the wind blows. The first hole introduces the famous, indeed notorious, Barry Burn, presenting a real hazard as it winds across fairways. There is also Jockie's Burn to contend with on the early holes, including the fifth, where the great Ben Hogan, in his one and only British Open appearance, holed a chip in the last round of the 1953 championship on his way to victory and a grand slam of major titles.

The Barry Burn is back at the 10th, 'South America' — so named, it is said, after one of the town's sons, set on emigrating, woke up there after a farewell party and decided to go no further! The last three holes provide a great finish, with the Barry Burn ready to swallow up the ball three or four times at the 17th, and again cause problems at the final hole.

Some of the greatest players have emerged here as Open champions — Tommy Armour, Henry Cotton, Ben Hogan, Gary Player and Tom Watson. Sadly, through lack of facilities it has fallen out of Open favour since 1975 although there are hopes of its future return. The Amateur Championship has also been held here, as well as Scottish events.

Hole	Distance	Par
1 Cup	395 yards	4
2 Gulley	432 yards	4
3 Jockie's Burn	345 yards	4
4 Hillocks	381 yards	4
5 Brae	376 yards	4
6 Long	529 yards	5
7 Plantation	384 yards	4
8 Short	169 yards	3
9 Railway	425 yards	4
OUT	**3,436yds**	**36**
10 South America	426 yards	4
11 Dyke	370 yards	4
12 Southward Ho!	476 yards	5
13 Whins	161 yards	3
14 Spectacles	482 yards	5
15 Luckyslap	460 yards	4
16 Barry Burn	248 yards	3
17 Island	432 yards	4
18 Home	440 yards	4
IN	**3,495yds**	**36**

Carnoustie Golf Club, Tayside
Championship course
Card for the course

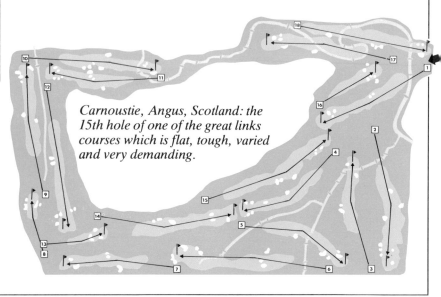

Carnoustie, Angus, Scotland: the 15th hole of one of the great links courses which is flat, tough, varied and very demanding.

Carr, Joe

1922–. Born Dublin, Ireland

In 30 years at the top of amateur golf, Joe Carr accumulated over 50 important titles. His peaks were three British Amateur titles in 1953, 1958 and 1960. In these finals he ended a US sequence in 1960 by beating the great Harvie Ward, and crushed another champion, Bob Cochran, eight and seven. He was still good enough to reach another final at the age of 46 when he faced Michael Bonallack, his only clear superior in British Isles amateur golf since World War II.

Carr was a 'typical' Irish golfer: by no means elegant, with a right-hand under-the-shaft grip and a sway into the ball. He changed his style without losing effectiveness. On the greens he had his days, but was renowned for using a long iron to putt with when all else failed. He made more Walker Cup appearances than anyone else — both sides of the Atlantic.

Casper, Billy

1931–. Born San Diego, California, USA

Undoubtedly one of the very best players at his peak, Billy Casper always lacked crowd appeal. At one stage, he was even thought of as a superb putter — and little else. In time, however, he did come to be recognized as a shot-maker although media attention concentrated more on his diet, which included buffalo meat, than his golf.

Casper won two US Opens, in 1959 and 1966. The second of these was the historic one in which Palmer lost seven shots over the last nine holes. In the play-off, Palmer again led after the first nine, this time by four but Casper won comfortably enough as a result of more errors from Palmer.

His other major title, the 1970 Masters, again came after a play-off, with Gene Littler.

Billy Casper

Casper was, in fact, much more formidable in US Tour play. He won 51 times, which ranks him behind only five others. He played every Ryder Cup match between 1961 and 1975, was captain in 1979 and won several events outside the USA.

Champions, Texas, USA

Two US Masters champions, Jimmy Demaret and Jackie Burke, built this Houston course on the grand scale, as befits the Texas image. With Ralph Plummer as architect, their design was to blend the characteristics of classic holes around the world into their dream course.

Champions opened in 1960 with many dog-leg holes and more than 70,000 trees which enclosed almost every fairway. Its fourth hole, a par three, is rated among the toughest in the world and one of the longest, with a tee shot that has to carry a deep gulch. It is impossible to play out of it, and both Ben Hogan and Lee Trevino have come to grief here.

The twelfth is another long par three: a pond all along the left bites into the fairway ahead of the green, so the tee shot has to clear the water. In 1967, the Ryder Cup was played over this championship course, named Cypress Creek, with an American victory by 21 matches to six, and two years later it hosted its first US Open, won by the former Army sergeant Orville Moody. A second course, the Jack-rabbit, was designed by George Fazio.

Charles, OBE, Bob

1936–. Born Carterton, New Zealand

Bob Charles has two unique distinctions to his name. In the first place, he is not merely the best New Zealand golfer ever, but the only one of really high class. He is just as distinctive as a left-hander. Nobody has attained anything remotely approaching his stature.

Ironically, Charles is not a true left-hander. He gives preference to the right hand for everything except the golf swing. He played with borrowed clubs to begin with and they were left-handed! His career could give backing to the argument that all left-handers should play right-handed and vice versa.

As left-handers are unusual, they are often thought to have ungainly swings. This has been said of Charles, but if you watch him in a mirror that impression disappears. Most people have concentrated on his putting. Although nowadays he complains of an occasional twitch in his putting action, Charles is an all-time great on the greens.

In the 1963 Open Championship, for instance, he played six rounds of golf. The most putts he used were 31 and the least 26. He tied with American Phil Rodgers and beat him in the 36 hole play-off. He is credited with having suggested at the end that 36 holes was too much golf — and his words were heeded.

Bob Charles

Coming from a small nation in the golfing sense, Charles has always been an international player. He has won well over 20 titles in his own country and has been successful all over the world, with multiple wins in Europe and the USA, and even a South African Open to his credit. Besides these, his most important wins were the Canadian Open, the World Match-play, the John Player Classic and his US Tour victories. Charles has been second twice in the Open Championship and once in the US PGA.

Chen Tze-Chung

1958–. Born Taipei, Taiwan

Chen Tze-Chung is one of the few Oriental players to make a concentrated attack on the US Tour, where he has played since 1983. In that year he tied for the Kemper Open, but lost the play-off. Even more dramatic was his performance in the 1985 US Open at Oakland Hills.

He began with a 65 and two 69s

kept him in the lead by two strokes going into the last round. Here Chen began to go further ahead until the fifth, where he had an eight on a par four, partly caused by a double hit from deep rough. After that he scattered strokes to the wind but then pulled himself together: his eventual 77 put him only a stroke behind the winner, Andy North. In 1987 he won his first US Tour event, the Los Angeles Open in a play-off with Ben Crenshaw.

Chen has won twice in Japan (and lost two play-offs) and once on the Asian and US Tours. He is a short hitter, but accurate.

Cherry Hills, Denver, Colorado, USA

More than a mile above sea-level, with the snow-capped Rockies in the distance, the ball flies long and far in the thin atmosphere of Cherry Hills, but the course is good enough to test the long hitters, especially the second nine. The 14th, a dog-leg with a creek on the left, is rated highly by the great Ben

Hogan, and a fine finishing hole, also a long par four with water on the left, has a long climb to the green. Designed by William S Flynn and opened in 1922, the course has twice been slightly altered.

Three US Opens have been played here: the first won by Ralph Guldahl in 1938, the second by Arnold Palmer in 1960 and the third by Andy North in 1978. Palmer, trailing by seven strokes, started his last round with six birdies in the first seven holes, completed his round in 65 and won by two strokes. That year Ben Hogan's hopes of a fifth Open victory ended with one hole to go when his ball found water in front of the green. Jack Nicklaus, aged 20, recorded the lowest score made by an amateur here in the Open in 1960, two under par 282, to finish second.

Christchurch, New Zealand

The second oldest club in New Zealand, Christchurch was founded in 1873, but it was not until 1900

Cherry Hills, Denver, Colorado, USA: the first hole.

that it settled on its present site at Shirley, a stretch of sand dunes which give links conditions, with a creek affecting several holes.

The course was altered after the New Zealand Open had been played there for the first time in 1910, but it returned 11 years later to become a frequent venue for the event. Australians Peter Thomson and Kel Nagle claimed the Open title here. Bob Charles failed to do so on his home course, although he succeeded at other venues.

Cinque Ports, Royal, Deal, Kent, England

One of the most testing of links courses, with its sandhills, humps and hollows, fierce rough, cavernous bunkers, and often subject to searching wind, Deal's qualities are summed up by that noted authority Bernard Darwin as 'truly great'. There are some fine holes calling for great skill — though luck, too, can play its part. The fourth, which replaced an old, blind hole, is a short hole played from a high tee to a plateau green,

Howard Clark

while another testing one-shot is the 14th to a green with a hollow on the left and bunkers on the right. Its last six holes provide a stern finish, especially against a prevailing south-westerly wind.

Founded in 1892, the club received its Royal title in 1908 when the Prince of Wales became president. It has been host to two Open Championships, as well as the British and English Amateur, the Brabazon Trophy and the Halford Hewitt Cup. J H Taylor's victory here in 1909 brought him his fourth Open title. In 1920 George Duncan, who had opened with two rounds of 80 (which today would have seen him miss the cut) fired a third round 71 to make up 13 strokes on Abe Mitchell to join him in the lead, and followed with 72 to win by two strokes from Sandy Herd.

Clark, Howard

1954–. Born Leeds, Yorkshire, England

Although Clark has long been recognized as a formidable talent from the days of his British Boys' Championship in 1971 and 1973 Walker Cup appearance, he took some years to establish himself on the European Tour. He seemed to have really arrived when he finished first, second and first in the Portuguese, Spanish and Madrid Opens at the beginning of the 1978 season. He continued with a sequence of high placings.

For several years thereafter, Clark achieved nothing as good, although he consistently made money. He moved up a gear from 1984 onwards, however, winning twice in each of the next three years and also being in the top six of the money list. His two most significant wins came in the 1984 PGA Championship and with the individual title in the 1985 World Cup. He also has a good Ryder Cup record.

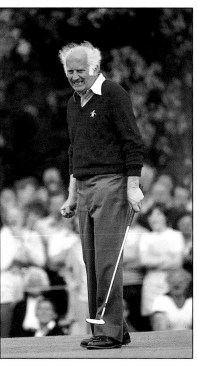

Neil Coles

Coles, MBE, Neil

1934–. Born London, England

A professional golfer since 1950, Coles began tournament golf more than 30 years ago in 1955. He had improved dramatically in those five years for at 16 he had a 14 handicap.

A top player since the beginning of the 1960s, Coles kept up his high standards to the end of the 1970s and as late as 1982 he won the Sanyo Open.

Coles was the first to total £200,000 in Europe, where he had 27 career victories from 1956 to 1982. He has always had a well-deserved reputation for consistency, achieved in spite of the doubtful method of a hooker's grip and shut face at the top of the backswing. He is by no means a top-class putter, but superb at the little shots around the greens, especially chipping. On reaching 50, Coles won the PGA Seniors title three consecutive years from 1985, and the first Seniors British Open in 1987.

Collett, Glenna

1903–. Born New Haven, Connecticut, USA

The winner of 49 championships in a long career, with a gloriously free swing and competitive nerve, Glenna Collett (Mrs H S Vare) is one of the greatest women golfers. Her reputation has suffered a little because, although she reached two finals of the British Ladies' Championship, she was defeated in the 1929 final by Joyce Wethered and by Diana Fishwick in 1930.

In the American Ladies', Collett reached eight finals in the years 1922–1935 and won six of them. Both achievements are records for the event. She is one of four women to win three in a row, which she did in 1928–1930. She also won the Canadian title twice, the French, the Eastern Amateur seven times and the North and South on six occasions.

Glenna Collett played in the first Curtis Cup match in 1932. Her last came in 1948.

Colonial, Texas, USA

This was the home club of the great Ben Hogan, and it was here he developed the game that was to make him a legend in his lifetime. Over a course calling for extreme accuracy Hogan was supreme, and when the Colonial National Invitation tournament was launched in 1946, he took the title in the first two years, and in all won it five times.

Built in 1936, the course was chosen for the US Open five years later, but on this occasion Hogan came third to Craig Wood, who took the title in spite of having to

Colonial, Texas, USA: the 13th hole. The course is a fierce challenge, as the great Ben Hogan knew.

wear a corset for a painful back. After flooding in 1969, the course was restored. It presents a fierce challenge, with small, tricky greens, narrow fairways winding through woods, and a river coming into play.

Colt, Harry S

1869–1951. Born St Albans, England

By profession a solicitor, Colt became the first full-time golf course architect who had not previously been a professional golfer. He began with work at Rye in the 1890s and later became the first secretary of the Sunningdale Golf Club, where he made changes to the course and later designed a second 18 holes, the New.

Colt was one of the first to develop heathland courses (perhaps the next best land for golf after links) and designed many in the belt to

the south of London. He was also the first to cut a course through forests, and designed one of the St Andrews courses, the Eden. Among his own favourite designs were Royal Portrush, Swinley Forest and Wentworth. He carried out improvements on such famous courses as Muirfield, Hoylake, Ganton and Royal Lytham. He also worked abroad and had a hand in Pine Valley. With James Braid, he was the most admired architect of his day.

Compston, Archie

1893–1962. Born Penn, Wolverhampton, England

The most well-remembered feat in Compston's golf career was his amazing 18 and 17 victory in a 1928 challenge match over Walter Hagen. This happened in the middle of his fairly brief career as a top British player which lasted from the mid-1920s to the 1930s.

Compston never won the Open Championship but he came close. In 1925 he came second, just one stroke behind Jim Barnes. In 1928, he came third, three behind Hagen. Perhaps Compston's best chance came in 1930 when, after a third round 68 (the only score under 70 in the championship) he led Bobby Jones by a stroke into the last round. Jones had a 75, Compston an 82 for sixth place and never recovered. However, he won the PGA Matchplay twice, the French Open and several more tournaments. He played against the USA four times.

Compston won a famous case against the Inland Revenue, who attempted to tax him on his winnings from betting on himself in private matches. He claimed they would not pay him if he lost.

Henry Cotton competing against Densmore Shute in a £500-a-side golf challenge match. Cotton was the first middle-class Englishman to turn professional golfer.

Connachan, Jane

1964–. Born Haddington, East Lothian, Scotland

Jane Connachan won her first tournament in 1978 at the age of 14 when she became Scottish Girls' champion and repeated this victory in 1979 and 1980. She also won the British Girls' twice and the Australian title. In women's golf she went on to win both the Scottish Championship and the British Strokeplay titles in 1982. She was in both Curtis Cup and World Cup teams in 1980 and 1982, and was the youngest ever Curtis Cup player at 16.

Playing professional golf since 1984, Connachan was eighth in the Order of Merit that year, winning once. In 1985 she won twice and moved to second money position. Poor putting dropped her to 18th in 1986.

Cotton, Henry

1907–. Born Holmes Chapel, Cheshire, England

Henry Cotton was the son of a successful iron-foundry owner. After an education at a public school, he planned to go to university. Instead, he became perhaps the first man of middle-class background to turn professional in the UK when a career in amateur golf would have been the norm.

Cotton had his sights raised well above the life of a club professional, however. He wanted to be the best British player and there is no doubt that he achieved his ambition. An assistant professional at 16, he was a full club professional at 19 and even then a man to watch. He was first noticed for his tournament performances in 1928, and he went to the USA to compete and to see how the Americans succeeded.

Although Cotton learned a great deal there, the Open Championship eluded him for several years. Then he began the 1934 Open with

rounds of 67 and 65, still the record for 36 holes. After three rounds he had a lead of 10 strokes, but began to play badly in the final round. All was well in the end, however: Cotton became the first British champion after a gap of 11 years.

Perhaps his finest Open performance came at Carnoustie in 1937, with the whole US Ryder Cup team in the field. In foul weather, Cotton routed them. Six championship years were lost to World War II when Cotton was at his peak. His next and final win came in 1948 at Muirfield, and included a round of 66 with King George VI in his gallery. After this third win, Cotton did not play in the Open for some years although he continued to compete occasionally in other tournaments. In Britain and Europe combined he won 30 major tournaments.

Cotton enjoyed an affluent and an elegant life style. He entertained and was entertained grandly, and was at home on the Continent. He had a suite at one of the best hotels in Paris and worked in Monte Carlo in the winter before he eventually settled at Penina in Portugal.

Here Cotton designed a splendid golf course, then several in Britain and others on the Continent; he made substantial changes to others. As a writer, he has worked for newspapers and golf magazines since the early 1930s, and has published nearly a dozen books. Perhaps the best of these is *This Game of Golf* (1948), which contains many reminiscences and illuminating thoughts on playing the game. He was also a widely respected teacher, especially good with the better players.

Country Club, The, Massachusetts, USA

Founded in 1882, the Country Club was the first to be formed. Golf was introduced 11 years later, but with only six holes. In 1894, however, it was one of four clubs to form the US Golf Association, and the scene in 1913 of one of the most significant championships, the US Open. Francis Ouimet, a 20-year-old local amateur, tied the great British pair, Harry Vardon and Ted Ray, and beat them comprehensively in the play-off, 72 to 77 and 78 respectively. Ouimet's victory saw an upsurge of interest in golf in the USA, marking the start of its popularity and later dominance.

Fifty years later, the 1963 US Open, held to celebrate the anniversary of Ouimet's victory, also ended in a tie, with Julius Boros winning the play-off against Arnold Palmer and Jacky Cupit.

Located at Brookline, outside Boston, this secluded course with its wealth of trees has small greens;

Royal County Down, Northern Ireland: the spectacular view of the 9th green and 10th tee on this most severe of championship tests.

although there are some short par fours and only three short holes, the many longer holes compensate. The 17th, where Ouimet holed a difficult, long downhill putt for a birdie as he forced a tie, is now a dog-leg left, with a plateau green beyond bunkers — changed somewhat from those far-off days. With 27 holes in existence by 1963, the lay-out for that championship was taken from the three nines.

The 1932 and 1973 Walker Cup matches, held here, made it the first American club to host the event twice. It has also been host to the US Amateur; on the last occasion, in 1982, Jay Sigel was the winner.

County Down, Royal, Northern Ireland

Under the shadow of Slieve Donard, the highest of the Mourne mountains, this great course offers breathtaking views as well as superb golf. It is rated as one of the most severe of championship tests, yet because of its remoteness and lack of facilities it has been denied an Open Championship. It has, however, staged the Amateur Championship, and has been popular with the ladies, hosting the British on seven occasions and the Curtis Cup in 1968. Irish championships and home internationals have also been held here.

Founded in 1889, the task of laying out the course was given to Tom Morris, with a budget 'not to exceed £4'. From rough ground and sandhills, two separate circuits of nine holes have emerged, with narrow fairways, severe rough and the emphasis on accurate driving. There is nothing more spectacular than the ninth hole, with a drive uphill, and from the top a fairway below with two protecting bunkers to a plateau green. From there, the landward nine gives flatter lies, but rough of gorse and heather. The club received its Royal title in 1908 from King Edward VII.

Fred Couples

Couples, Fred

1959–. Born Seattle, Washington, USA

One of the longest drivers on the US Tour, Fred Couples has been tipped for stardom since joining the Tour in 1981. He won the Kemper Open in 1983 and the Tournament Players Championship in 1984 — his best year when he won over $334,000. His third victory came in the Byron Nelson Classic in 1987 in a play-off with Mark Calcavecchia to pass the $1–million mark in prize money.

Couples holds the record for the lowest nine holes in the 1982 US PGA, 29 strokes, when he came third after a closing 66.

Crampton, Bruce

1935–. Born Sydney, Australia

Now extremely successful on the US Seniors Tour, Bruce Crampton first came to attention by winning the 1956 Australian Open. He soon had his sights set on the US Tour, but he found the going tough: his first victory was not until 1961. His problem was inconsistent driving,

Bruce Crampton

for which his excellent putting could not compensate.

From 1968 to 1975, Crampton was a model of consistency. He earned more than $100,000 each year although he was not a frequent winner until 1973. He won four events that year, taking the Vardon Trophy — and well over a quarter of a million dollars. He again took the Vardon Trophy for low stroke average in 1975.

When Crampton retired from the US Tour in 1977 he was the first non-American to top $1 million and the fifth to do so. He had 15 wins on his record.

Crans, Valais, Switzerland

Set 5,000 feet above the Rhone valley and ringed by the snow-capped peaks of the Alps, this course provides a spectacular setting for the Swiss Open, or, as it is now known, the European Masters. The original course, built in 1905 and closed during World War I, was rebuilt a few years later. Jack Nicklaus has since designed a new nine.

With the advantage of the rarefied

atmosphere, open fairways and little rough, low scores predominate, with Peter Townsend returning 61 when he won the Swiss Open in 1971 and Baldovino Dassu capping that with 60. Severiano Ballesteros has twice won the event; his countryman, José-Maria Canizares, created a world record with 11 consecutive birdies and an eagle in 1978, but finished third behind Ballesteros.

Crenshaw, Ben

1952–. Born Austin, Texas, USA

Possibly the best putter in the modern game, Ben Crenshaw also has a high rating for his recovery play. The results of his driving are often erratic. He came to the US Tour in 1973 with the best amateur credentials since Jack Nicklaus. He had won three NCAA championships in a row, the Western Amateur at both match and strokeplay, and had represented the USA in the World Team event. He was immediately a big success. He had already taken a third place as an amateur in a Tour event in 1972, and began his first paid event, the San Antonio-Texas Open, with a 65 and went on to win. A few days later, he was second in the eight-round World Open. Perhaps no one could have lived up to that start. Crenshaw certainly failed to — if only because he has never afterwards threatened to rival Jack Nicklaus.

Crenshaw's next victory was not until 1976, when he won three US Tour events and the Irish Open. He also had his best placing of second on the money list. He continued to win the occasional tournament so that by the end of 1986 he had 12 US Tour wins to his credit.

Crenshaw's sights were set a good deal higher than that: he wanted passionately to win major championships. He had very good sequences in the British Open, and was in contention in each of the years 1977–1981. He also came

close to the US Open in 1975: only a shot into water on the last-but-one hole ruined his chances. Then, in the 1979 US PGA, he played superbly, only to be defeated by David Graham on the third hole of the sudden-death play-off.

Finally, in the 1984 Masters, Crenshaw putted beautifully, in almost perfect control of his long game, and at last achieved his ambition of winning a major title. His game then collapsed until 1986 when he came back to form after illness, winning two tournaments and more than $380,000.

Crump, George

Died 1918. Born Philadelphia, Pennsylvania, USA

A one-off golf architect, George Crump had a dream of building a course in the sandy low-lying hills of New Jersey. In 1912, he sold his hotel property and bought his land. He died before the completion of his great course, which opened a few years after his death.

Ben Crenshaw

Pine Valley is a monument to the school of thought that believes a golf course should scare you at least half to death — but it is still one of the world's greatest courses.

Curtis Cup

Although the Curtis Cup was the last of the cup matches between teams from Great Britain and Ireland and the USA to take place, international matches between American and British women were the first to be staged. Possibly the first thought came from Issette Pearson who, as far back as 1898, expressed relish at the prospect. In 1905, to coincide with the Ladies' Championship at Cromer, a match was played in which 'England' won by six to one. Afterwards, two Americans, Harriot and Margaret Curtis, offered to present a cup, but travel and team selection problems prevented any real progress.

Even so, 'American and Colonial' played Great Britain in 1911, and in 1923 'Overseas' faced 'The Rest of England' — a very odd title indeed. In both cases the results were similar to the 1905 match. In 1930, however, when the last of such matches was played, the result was closer. The Curtis Cup was then presented for future competition with 'hope that other countries would join in later'. France and Canada were then the obvious candidates.

The first match was played at Wentworth in 1932. Three foursomes were played on the first day, six singles on the second; all matches were over 36 holes. The Americans practised; the British did not turn up until tea time on the day before play. (After all, the greatest American, Glenna Collett, had lost recent finals to Joyce Wethered and Diana Fishwick in the British Ladies.) The USA won with points to spare and repeated their victory comfortably in the first match in the USA. In 1936 at

Cypress Point, California, USA: the 16th hole of a magnificent course.

Gleneagles, the match was tied.

In the 1950s, Great Britain and Ireland had their best run in the Curtis Cup, winning in 1952 and 1956 and tying in the USA in 1958 — the first time a British Ryder, Walker or Curtis Cup team had not been defeated in the USA.

Thereafter, all was more or less disaster. It can be summarized by saying that the Americans won very easily on US soil but sometimes had minor problems in Britain. The results of 1980 and 1982 are more or less typical: the USA won 13-5 in Britain and $14\frac{1}{2}$-$3\frac{1}{2}$ in the USA. In 1984 the USA won its 13th consecutive match.

Even so, there was a change in 1984. Before, all had been controversy, with no Scots in the team when many thought three worth their place. There were no expectations of even a reasonable performance. However, the match was close all the way and, in the end, half a turn on a putt could have meant a tied match. The USA won nine and a half to eight and a half.

The 1986 team was a mix of the four nationalities with two English, two Welsh, one Scot and three Irish. Possibly inspired by the European Ryder Cup victory the previous September, all of the three foursomes went to Britain the first morning. After the singles the score stood six and a half to two and a half. There was no fight back in the second day foursomes from the USA where they lost two and halved one. With eight singles remaining, the match was virtually over. The first was halved and the American went down five and three in the second, which settled the match. The final result was 13 to five. It has been to date the only victory in the USA for any of the Cup teams, a historic achievement by captain Diane Bailey's team.

Cypress Point, California, USA

This was the second course built on the Monterey Peninsula to follow Pebble Beach, and was laid out early in the 1920s by the Scottish architect Alister Mackenzie. His work here was so admired by Bobby Jones that he engaged Mackenzie for Augusta National. A magnificent course, with a great variety in its design, Cypress Point even has a patch of linksland, as well as pines and perfect greens. Above all, there is the blue Pacific smashing into the rocky shore to complete a superb setting.

After the opening hole the course moves inland among the pines, then to links country at the eighth and ninth. The three holes starting at the 15th provide outstanding, spectacular golf, with the crashing waves isolating the greens. The par three 16th, one of the world's most photographed holes, calls for a carry of more than 200 yards over the sea to a green on a narrow neck of land — a really daunting prospect — followed by a par four back over the ocean.

Bing Crosby, who gave his name to the National Pro-Am played over this and adjoining courses for many years, achieved the very rare feat of holing in one at the 16th. Jack Nicklaus was a three-times winner of the tournament, now sponsored by AT & T.

Daly, Fred

1911–. Born Portrush, County Antrim, Ireland

Daly caught the headlines in the years immediately after World War II and became an Open Championship and matchplay specialist. He had won nothing on mainland Britain before he took the 1947 Open. Here he was fortunate because he had posted his score at Hoylake when the wind got up. If there were any doubts about his performance, Fred put them to rest by winning the matchplay championship the same year, and going on to give a series of splendid Open performances. In 1948 he came second and in 1950 third after closing rounds of 69 and 66. In 1951 he was fourth on his home course, Portrush, and third in 1952.

Daly played in four Ryder Cup teams, won two other matchplay titles and several other tournaments. Ill health seemed to make him less effective after the early 1950s, when he was over 40.

Daniel, Beth

1956–. Born Charleston, South Carolina, USA

Twice a winner of the US Amateur, in 1975 and 1976, and in the Curtis Cup teams of 1976 and 1978, Beth Daniel shot straight to the top when she joined the LPGA Tour in 1979. By the following year she was the leading money winner, and repeated the achievement in 1981. She had been the first woman to top $200,000 in a season and by the end of 1982 had done this three times.

Since then, Daniel has been taking something like a stroke a round more, and her results have fallen away in proportion. She certainly no longer seems to be the leading woman player. She has a total of 14 wins, 11 of which came in the 1980–1982 seasons.

Dar Es Salam, Royal, Rabat, Morocco

A magnificent Robert Trent Jones course, which the famous architect carved out of a 1000-acre cork-oak forest at the invitation of the country's king, himself a keen golfer, the Royal Dar Es Salam has wide, lush fairways lined by trees, finely designed greens, vast bunkers and ornamental lakes. A monster course, which can be stretched to 7500 yards, everything is on the grand scale, with three of the four par fives out of reach in two shots, and the short holes all with long carries.

Typical of the exotic surroundings is the setting for the ninth, a par

Beth Daniel

three with a long carry over a lake to an island green where flamingoes, wild fowl and colourful foliage provide a spectacular setting. Since 1971 it has been the venue for the Hassan II Trophy, inaugurated by the king, which has attracted many of the world's top players. Its winners include Billy Casper, Lee Trevino, and the only British winner, Peter Townsend. In 1987, in the first PGA European Tour event staged here, Howard Clark won the Moroccan Open.

Darwin, Bernard

1876–1961. Born Downe, Kent, England

Grandson of Charles Darwin, Bernard Darwin is generally accepted as the best writer to have given most of his attention to golf.

During his short career at the bar, the *Evening Standard* asked him to write on golf in 1907. *Country Life* and *The Times* followed. He left the bar and it was not until 1953 that he eventually retired from *The Times*.

In America in 1922 to report the Walker Cup for *The Times*, Darwin was asked to play and to captain the team when Robert Harris fell ill. He did both with great success, winning his singles.

Darwin was not quite of Walker Cup standard, but nevertheless twice reached the semi-finals of the Amateur Championship. His best wins were the *Golf Illustrated* Gold Vase, the President's Putter and the Worplesdon Foursomes with Joyce Wethered.

Darwin was the most prolific of golf writers. Besides his many articles and reports on golf, he wrote more than 30 books. He also wrote on boxing, cricket, Charles Dickens and for children.

Davies, Laura

1963–. Born Coventry, England

After a short amateur career which

Laura Davies, who made golf history in July 1987 when she became the first British woman to win the United States Women's Open at the age of 24.

brought her a place on the 1984 Curtis Cup Team, Laura Davies was an immediate success when she turned professional in 1985. In that year and in 1986 she was the leading money winner on the European circuit, winning five titles during the two seasons. The most important of these was the Ladies' British Open.

Davies holds the record for the lowest round of 63 on the WPGA tour, the most birdies in a round and a record low total of 268. She seems to have established herself as the star personality the young Tour needed. Her phenomenal hitting is particularly impressive. She has played on the US Tour, finishing a creditable 11th in the 1986 US Open. In July 1987, Davies made golf history when she became the first British woman to win the United States Women's Open.

Davis, Rodger

1951–. Born Sydney, Australia

A noticeable figure on the golf course in plus twos with his name embroidered into his socks, Rodger Davis became known for his second-place finishes — 30 by the end of 1986. After a slump, he virtually retired from tournament golf to go into business in the early 1980s, but returned to achieve his best season in 1986.

Davis's first win came in 1977 but he played in Europe for five years before winning a tournament. This came at The Belfry, a course where he had twice collapsed when in a strong position. The win was the 1981 State Express Classic. By this time he had also won five times in Australia. Nothing very much went right for Davis in the years that followed until he won the 1985 Victoria Open. In 1986, he won four titles, two of them high-quality ones: the PGA Championship at Wentworth and the Australian Open. He also took the New Zealand Open and the Air New Zealand Open. That same year he was on the winning Australian team in the Dunhill Cup and achieved an unexpected win in the World Matchplay by seven and six

over the favourite, Ballesteros, eventually finishing fourth. In 1987 Davis was joint runner-up to Nick Faldo in the British Open.

Deal *See* Cinque Ports, Royal, England

Demaret, Jimmy

1910–1984. Born Houston, Texas, USA

Jimmy Demaret was the first man to win the Masters three times, in 1940, 1947 and 1950. These were his peak years, for in 1940 he won six other titles. He repeated this achievement in 1947, when he was also leading money winner and took the Vardon Trophy.

Demaret never managed to win the US Open, but he had the galling experience in 1948 of being in the clubhouse after he had broken the US Open scoring record with his total of 278, only to have Hogan beat it by two strokes. In 1957, aged 47, Demaret came in only one stroke behind the first place play-off between Dick Mayer and Cary Middlecoff.

Rodger Davis

Demaret was not the first man to dress colourfully for golf, but he injected more variety into the effort than anyone before — or since. His sense of humour was legendary and he even brought a smile to the lips of the dour Ben Hogan, whom he often partnered in fourball events.

Devlin, Bruce

1937–. Born Armidale, Australia

Devlin's career goes back to the late 1950s when he was a gifted amateur. He was in the 1958 winning Australian team in the Eisenhower Trophy at St Andrews, and had the equal best individual score. In 1959 he won the Australian Amateur and followed with the Australian Open in 1960, while still an amateur. This encouraged him to turn professional. He quickly won the French and New Zealand Opens, but soon settled for the US Tour as a regular from 1964 when he won his first event.

Devlin went on to have a successful USA career for about 10 years; he was the most successful non-American after Bruce Crampton and Gary Player. He totalled eight

Bruce Devlin

Leo Diegel playing a golf challenge match at Moor Park, Rickmansworth.

US victories, with others on home soil, together with the 1966 Carling and the 1970 Alcan, both rich events.

Dibnah, Corinne

1962–. Born Brisbane, Australia

After winning her country's Amateur Championship in 1961 and the New Zealand title two years later, Dibnah joined the WPGA Tour in 1984. She worked her way to 13th place in the Order of Merit, but her jump to third in 1986, with two wins, established her among the top players.

Diegel, Leo

1899–1951. Born Detroit, Michigan, USA

Diegel has gone down in golfing history as the man who threw away national championships. What he might have achieved had he won the 1920 US Open, in which he finished second ... Much later, he missed a short putt to tie the 1933 British Open. In between, however, he had notable achievements. They included four Canadian Opens in the years 1924-1925 and 1928-1929 and also two majors: the US PGAs of 1928, when he stopped Hagen's run, and 1929.

Diegel played brilliantly in the

1929 Ryder Cup at Moortown and his revolutionary putting method was quickly copied. Basically, this involved his pointing both elbows out, one towards the hole, one away. His action was wholly an arm stroke and seemed to enable him for a while to hole all the short ones. Diegel was recognized as the greatest shot-maker of his day. Although he lost many championships, he still won over 30 tournaments.

Donck, Flory van

1912–. Born Tervueren, Belguim

In a phenomenally long career which began in the early 1930s, van Donck was still representing his country in the World Cup at the end of the 1970s. He amassed 26 national Opens, mostly on the Continent. In the 1950s he usually finished in the top group of the British Open, coming second in 1956 and 1959. He had five victories in Britain and in 1950 his 65 in the Open at Troon set the course record, and equalled the lowest round ever in the championship.

Dornoch, Royal, Sutherland, Scotland

A pilgrimage to this most northerly of top-class courses is one that never disappoints: it is a wonderful

links, praised by many famous players including Tom Watson and Ben Crenshaw, as well as British stars who have spread its fame such as Roger and Joyce Wethered.

The course is split in two levels, the top on a ridge of sandhills, then down to play between them, with the sea always within sight. Its outstanding holes include the eighth — a drive over a sheer drop towards the sea, then down to a green in a hollow — and the 14th, named 'Foxy', a double dog-leg long par four to the left and then the right, to a plateau green, and without a single bunker.

Golf is said to have been played at Dornoch as early as 1616, but it was not until 1877 that the club was formed. Tom Morris laid out nine holes a few years later, with a second nine following. The club was brought up to championship standard by one of its respected servants John Sutherland, for 50 years its secretary. It was then improved after World War II.

The great trio of Braid, Vardon and Herd played here, and the club has been host to the Scottish Professional and Ladies Championships. It was also host to its first major event when the Home Internationals were played here in 1980 — so successfully that the R and A took the Amateur Championship to Dornoch in 1985.

Douglas, Kitrina

1960–. Born Bristol, England

After an excellent amateur career which included three national titles — one the 1982 British Ladies' — Kitrina Douglas was immediately successful on the WPGA Tour. She won twice in her first season and came second in the Order of Merit. Douglas has been less effective since then, but she won again in 1986.

Royal Dornoch, Sutherland, Scotland: the sea is always within sight on this most northerly of top-class courses. It is split into two levels, the top on a ridge of sandhills.

Dowling, Debbie

1962–. Born Wimbledon, Surrey, England

After earning international selection but with only a county championship to her credit, Debbie Dowling turned professional to compete on the WPGA Tour. She has won five events since then and her play has improved all the time. She finished fifth in the Order of Merit in both 1985 and 1986.

Dublin, Royal, Irish Republic

A fine links course, the Royal Dublin lies on Bull Island, connected to the mainland by a causeway. The club, which cele-

brated its centenary in 1985, moved here in 1899 after first being at Phoenix Park and then at Sutton.

The second oldest club in Ireland, and the oldest in the republic, it was founded by a Scots Army captain, John Lumsden. After World War I it was redesigned by H S Colt, as the course had been ruined by military operations. With virtually a straight out and home lay-out, the inward nine can be a tough test against a prevailing west wind.

The great Christy O'Connor, whose home club it has been since 1959, picks out the fifth hole — a marvellous driving examination into a narrow tunnelled fairway and a big second shot with out-of-bounds on the right — and the 18th — a great finish with the notorious 'garden' out-of-bounds beckoning round a sharp right-hand dog-leg — as two outstanding holes. In

Royal Dublin, Irish Republic: this links course on Bull Island is connected to the mainland by a causeway.

the 1966 Carrolls International, O'Connor finished eagle, birdie, eagle for a sensational victory. The home of many Irish championships, it has also been the venue for the Carrolls Irish Open, won twice here by Ballesteros.

Duncan, George

1883–1964. Born Methlick, Aberdeenshire, Scotland

Golf at the Gallop was the title of one of Duncan's books. It was appropriate, for he was one of the quickest golfers ever. He and Abe Mitchell were the best players between the days of Vardon, Taylor and Braid and the arrival of Henry Cotton. Duncan had a long

career from early this century to the 1930s.

Duncan became the first Open Champion after World War I. At Deal in 1920 he began with two rounds of 80, but swept up the field on the last day with rounds of 71 and 72. He was just as mercurial two years later at Royal St George's. While Walter Hagen accepted congratulations for having won the Open, Duncan was still out on the course, and came to the last needing a four for a 68 and a tie. With a speed that almost deceived the eye he played a run-up not too well, then glanced at the line of his putt — missed, and finished runner-up.

Among Duncan's other successes were victories in the PGA Match-play, the Belgian and French Opens and numerous tournaments. He saved some of his best performances for matches against the USA, winning his singles in 1921, 1926, and in 1927 and 1929 when the Ryder Cup started, and in the process winning over Hagen by six and five and ten and eight — the latter a record margin.

Durban Country Club, South Africa

This club was formed in 1920 after the course of nearby Royal Durban, the country's oldest club, had been flooded and it was feared the city might lose its chance of staging national championships. Opened two years later to the design of Laurie Waters, former South African Open champion, and George Waterman, it has remained basically unchanged in spite of a few alterations over the years.

It staged its first South African Open in 1922. In 1956 Gary Player won his first title here, and in 1976 he beat Bobby Locke's record of nine Open wins, going on to complete 13 victories in all. When Royal Durban staged the 1970 Open, Tommy Horton became the first British winner.

Built on sand dunes along the Natal coast, the third hole, a par five, is played from an elevated tee at the highest point of the course. At the next, the dunes give way to flatland, later varying between the two. Towards the close, there is a climb to a green high among the dunes at the 16th, followed by an elevated tee at the next, with a good

George Duncan (right) accepts the 1929 Ryder Cup from Sam Ryder after beating Walter Hagen.

Pete Dye

drive needed for a clear shot to the green from a fairway of violent undulations. It is said that the Duke of Windsor (the Prince of Wales) took 17 shots at the short 12th.

Dye, Pete

1925–. Born Urbana, Ohio, USA

After reaching state championship level in amateur golf and making a modest fortune in life insurance, Pete Dye went into golf architecture in the late 1950s. He began to tour Scottish courses, returning home with many ideas.

Railway sleepers became one of Dye's trademarks, used to support tees, bunkers and even greens. He also uses pot bunkers and undulations in both his small greens and fairways. Among his most famous courses are the Harbour Town Links on Hilton Head Island, Casa de Campo in Dominica, The Golf Club, Ohio, Oak Tree in Oklahoma and the controversial Players' Club at Ponte Vedra, Florida, which has been both lavishly praised and reviled. Overall, Dye has been the most innovative architect since Robert Trent Jones.

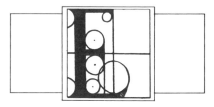

Edgar, J Douglas

1884–1921. Born
Newcastle-upon-Tyne, England

Although known locally, Douglas Edgar attracted little attention until he won the French Open of 1914, leaving the great players of the day far behind. After World War II, he emigrated to the USA, and in 1919 produced a miraculous performance in the Canadian Open. With rounds of 72, 71, 69 and 66 he won by 16 strokes against a top-class field. He seemed to have the ball on a string.

In 1920 Edgar was harder pressed, winning only after a play-off. He also reached the final of the US PGA but three-putted the last green to lose.

In 1921 he was found dead. The cause was loss of blood from a deep cut in the inside of .the thigh. The Atlanta police never solved the case. Harry Vardon said of him: 'This is the man who will one day be the greatest of us all.' And Tommy Armour: 'He was the best golfer I ever saw.'

In 1920 Edgar published *The Gate to Golf*. It was a revolutionary instruction book, the first to argue for hitting from in to out. Illustrations show that his swing was modern in its full shoulder turn, but far more restricted hip movement.

Elder, Lee

1934–. Born Dallas, Texas, USA

In his first year on the US Tour in 1968, Lee Elder tied for the American Golf Classic and took Jack Nicklaus to five extra holes before losing. His best year was 1978 when he won two tournaments. Elder

Lee Elder

became the first black golfer to play both in the Masters in 1975 and in the Ryder Cup in 1979. He won four tournaments and over $1-million before joining the Seniors Tour in 1984 and since then he has won seven Seniors events and a further $720,000.

Evans, Chick

1890–1979. Born Indianapolis, Indiana, USA

Only one man has obscured the fame of Evans' great feats in golf — Robert Tyre Jones Junior, whose achievements as an amateur were far greater. However, Jones retired in 1930 while Evans kept on playing. He qualified to play in the US Open as late as 1953 and for considerably longer in the US Amateur. He was over 70 when he last qualified.

Evans first came to the fore when he won the 1909 Western Amateur, the first of eight wins. National championships escaped him for a while but he made up for this in 1916 when he won both the US Amateur and the US Open — the first man to do so.

Evans won the US Amateur again in 1920 and twice more reached the final in 1922 and 1927. He lost to Jones in 1927 by eight and seven. He also took the Western Open in 1910, the only amateur ever to win.

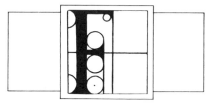

Faldo, Nick

1957–. Born Welwyn Garden City, Hertfordshire, England

Nick Faldo was a brief comet in amateur golf. In 1974, he was a boy international. The following year he won a host of titles, which included the Berkshire Trophy, the Scrutton Jug and the County Champion of Champions. More important, he also won the British Youths' and, aged 18, became the youngest winner of the English Amateur.

In April 1976 Faldo turned professional, winning £130 in his first event and learning his trade while another new arrival, Balles-teros, produced the high drama. In 1977 Faldo won his first event and played in the first of his five Ryder Cups, beating Tom Watson. He was to remain unbeaten in Ryder Cup singles until 1985.

In 1978, Faldo easily won the first of his three PGA champion-ships at Royal Birkdale. This was the performance that established him as a player who had 'arrived'. The spotlight has been on him ever since, relentlessly at times.

In Europe, the PGA seemed to be his speciality, although he did also win the Tournament Player's Championship in 1982. By this time he had begun testing himself on the US Tour, mostly playing out of the European season. In 1983 he flew to France at the last minute to play in the French Open, won it, and followed up by winning the next two tournaments. Instead of playing the US Tour for most of the year he aimed instead to be the leading money winner in Europe. Later in the season, he fought for the Open Championship and won

Nick Faldo, who achieved a boyhood dream in 1987 when he became the second Briton in three years to capture the Open Championship.

two more tournaments. He was leading money winner, improving on four other years when he had finished in the top four.

In 1984, Faldo had his best year on the US Tour, becoming the first British player since Tony Jacklin in 1972 to win when he took the Sea Pines Heritage Classic with four rounds in the 60s. Soon after, he won on the European Tour. Since then, he has been constructing an improved golf swing, which brought him victory in the Spanish Open in 1987.

Nick Faldo achieved a boyhood dream in 1987 when he became the second Briton in three years — the other is Sandy Lyle — to capture the Open Championship.

In the tense finish at Muirfield, Faldo completed all 18 holes of the final round in level par figures for 71 and a 279 total, five under par,

to win by a stroke from American Paul Azinger, making his first appearance in the championship. As a 14-year-old in Hertfordshire, Faldo took up the game after watching Jack Nicklaus on TV and set his goal on becoming a champion. A day after his 30th birthday, his dream came true.

Faulkner, Max

1916–. Born Bexhill, Sussex, England

The most multi-talented player of his time, Max Faulkner wasted a great deal of it on endless experimentation with both his methods and his clubs. His outstanding achievement was to win the 1951 Open Championship at Royal Portrush when it seemed as if he had overcome the problem of putting for ever. 'I'll never miss another of

those', he said, extending his arms to indicate putts in the four to six feet region.

Nor did he during the championship. Afterwards, normal problems returned and the pencil-slim putter that had served him so well lost its magic. He made many other putters, the most famous of which had a head made from driftwood, and part of a billiard cue for a shaft.

Faulkner was in the Ryder Cup team during the period 1947–1957 and had 16 tournament wins in a much longer period. He won the Portuguese Open in 1968 at the age of 52. With three Spanish Open titles, perhaps he flourished in the sun which complemented his colourful clothing.

Fernandez, Vicente

1946–. Born Corrientes, Argentina

Vicente Fernandez was three times winner of the Argentine Open and twice of the Brazil Open. He could claim to be the best player to emerge from his country, perhaps even from South America as a whole, since Roberto de Vicenzo. Although no one is likely to rival that great player's longevity,

Fernandez has done better than most. His career began in the late 1960s, when he had his first championship win, and continues to the present day.

Fernandez first won in Europe in 1970, but the finest achievement of his career was undoubtedly taking the 1979 PGA championship at St Andrews. He won largely because he played the dreaded 17th in four while his closest rival, Baldovino Dassu, took seven.

Ferrier, Jim

1915–. Born Manly, New South Wales, Australia

The first Australian golfer of genuine world class, Jim Ferrier began by dominating amateur and professional golf in his own country in the late 1930s much as Bobby Locke did in South Africa at the same time. Ferrier won the Australian amateur title four times and the Australian Opens of 1938 and 1939. He then turned professional and sought fame and fortune in the USA.

There, Ferrier became a major

Marta Figueras-Dotti

force, reaching his peak from 1945–1951. In 1947, he won the US PGA Championship, and three years later experienced one of the most famous of the many collapses seen in the US Masters. Over the final six holes, Jimmy Demaret picked up seven strokes on him to win. Ferrier found the creek on the 13th and then bogeyed the next four holes as well.

Although his swing was inelegant, dipping into the ball as a result of a knee problem, Ferrier was one of the great putters.

Figueras-Dotti, Marta

1957–. Born Madrid, Spain

Daughter of a president of the Spanish Golf Association, Figueras-Dotti won the amateur championships of Spain, France and Italy in 1979 before going on to win the 1982 British Ladies' Open against a professional field. This achievement gave her the rank of the best amateur in Europe. That same year she was also an All-American as a result of her performances at the University of Southern California.

A professional who has played the LPGA Tour since 1984, Figueras-Dotti was also the first Spanish golfer to turn professional. Her career in the USA has been steady rather than brilliant, with her rookie year, 1984, being her best. She finished 15th in the money list.

Finsterwald, Dow

1929–. Born Athens, Ohio, USA

Finsterwald was professional for over 20 years at Broadmoor, Colorado Springs, one of the USA's most attractive courses. He also competes on the US Seniors Tour where he has yet to win. On the full US Tour, he won 12 events between 1955 and 1963, and was four times a Ryder Cup team member during that time.

Finsterwald was highly thought of for his consistency, which came

Dow Finsterwald

from straight hitting and excellent putting. He also had great shot-making skills, and enjoyed the challenge of having to draw or fade shots into the flag.

He won one major, the 1958 US PGA Championship, the year the event became strokeplay. He was twice second in the money list, winner of the Vardon Trophy in 1957 and PGA Player of the Year in 1958.

Firestone, Ohio, USA

Built by Harvey Firestone, founder of the rubber and tyre company for employees, the course at Akron, Ohio, opened in 1928. It was redesigned by Robert Trent Jones for the 1960 US PGA Championship, when it was lengthened, its greens changed, and water hazards and extra bunkers introduced. Most of the holes run parallel to each other, separated by trees.

The South course is renowned for its superb condition; the North course was added in 1968. The PGA Championship returned here in 1966 and 1975, and the World

Series of Golf, originally a 36-hole exhibition of four players, has been played here since 1962. Winners of main events world-wide have contested the event over four rounds since 1976. The first winner of this format was Jack Nicklaus, who also won the 1975 PGA title.

Fleck, Jack

1921–. Born Bettendorf, Iowa, USA

If Francis Ouimet's defeat of Vardon and Ray in the 18-hole play-off for the 1913 US Open was the greatest upset in golf history, Fleck's achievement is close behind. In 1955, he birdied the last hole at Olympic to tie Ben Hogan, whom everyone thought had won a record fifth US Open. Gene Sarazen, commenting on television, had to apologize for announcing the result too soon. However, he recovered his poise and raised a laugh by saying he had merely announced the result a little too early.

Hogan completed the 18-hole play-off the following day by holing a long putt. The trouble was that he had begun the hole one stroke behind Fleck, hooked his drive into rough almost the height of wheat and taken three more shots to get out to the fairway. The putt was for a six and a round of 72. Fleck, playing in a two-day trance, was champion by three strokes.

Fleck won two later Tour events and now competes quite steadily as a Senior.

Floyd, Raymond

1942–. Born Fort Bragg, North Carolina, USA

Floyd's start as a tournament professional was disastrous: he missed nine out of his first 10 cuts. But the next time out he won, and at the age of 20 was the fourth youngest to win on the US Tour.

Then Floyd disappeared from view, emerging only briefly into the limelight with another win two years later. During this period, he earned more of a reputation as a playboy than a golfer. This seemed to change in 1969 when he won three times, including the US PGA Championship, and made the Ryder Cup team. Floyd then promptly disappeared once again. By the spring of 1976 he had added only one more victory and had occupied such lowly positions as 70th and 77th in the 1972 and 1973 money lists.

Firestone, Ohio, USA: the 10th tee of the longest championship course in America, one of Robert Trent Jones's finest pieces of work.

Then in the Masters in 1976 Floyd gave one of the most dominant performances ever. Starting with rounds of 65 and 66 he was miles ahead, and had set the 36-hole scoring record. Some have faltered when in this good a position. Not Raymond Floyd, one of the great front runners. He finished the tournament with two rounds of 70. The first of these enabled him to set the 54-hole scoring record for the Masters and the second tied Jack Nicklaus's record aggregate set of 271 in 1965.

Floyd's eight-stroke victory caused an upsurge in the sales of two clubs: the Zebra putter with which he seemed to hole everything in sight, and the five-wood. Floyd had decided that what he needed to play the par fives with was the high flight of this club, rather than the

Raymond Floyd

one-iron. It worked well. He was 13 under par on these holes.

Floyd now became far more consistent, winning almost every year. His next major championship was in 1982. Again it was a front-running performance, which began with a round of 63 and ended with his needing a bogey five to beat the US PGA scoring record. He took six but still won with three strokes to spare, the lead he had established after the first round.

Floyd's next major came in 1986. In the US Open at Shinnecock Hills in bad weather he began with a 75, five strokes behind. His next two rounds of 68 and 70 brought him to within three strokes of the leader, Greg Norman, who finished with a 75 to Floyd's 66. Floyd won by two strokes, the oldest winner at the age of 44.

With this victory, Floyd needs the British Open to complete his Grand Slam of the majors. He has won 21 times on the US Tour and made six Ryder Cup appearances. At the end of 1986, Floyd was one of only four players to earn more than $3 million in career money winnings. The others are Nicklaus, Watson and Trevino.

Ford, Doug

1922–. Born West Haven, Connecticut, USA

Always in the top 10 of the US money lists in the years 1951 to 1960, Doug Ford won 19 Tour events between his first in 1952 and 1963. Two of these were major championships: one the 1955 PGA, where he beat Cary Middlecoff by four and three in the final, and two years later the Masters. His finish was dramatic: finding sand beside the 18th green, he holed out for a birdie three and a round of 66. Ford now competes quite successfully on the Seniors Tour, even though he is over 60.

Formby, Lancashire, England

A course of unspoiled linksland, the flat nature of Formby's opening holes contrasts with the sandhills and forest of firs which follow, but throughout the holes are of infinite variety. The fifth, a formidable par three to a plateau green, is the first of three fine short holes. Erosion around the turn necessitated the rebuilding of a few holes but this has not affected the quality of play.

The course provides a flat finishing stretch, with a large green at the 18th where in the 1967 Amateur Championship, the American Walker Cup player, Marty Fleckman, holed his second shot for an eagle two. Founded in 1884, its clubhouse was opened in 1901 by the then Lord Derby; the present Lord Derby is its president. It first

staged the Amateur in 1957 and for the third time in 1984. Formby has also been the venue for the English Amateur, the British and English Ladies championships and the Home Internationals.

Fowler, Herbert

1856–1941. Born Edmonton, London, England

Fowler took to golf in his mid-30s after his first love, cricket, and quickly became a golfer of good class. Early this century a group decided to put up the money to build a course at Walton Heath and asked Fowler to undertake the design. He did so with great enthusiasm and took his time — about two years — in contrast to the brief single visit to a site which was usual at the time. Fowler rode the land on horseback, looking for good sites for greens. In 1904, Walton Heath opened.

The course was a great success, visited by such political leaders as Lloyd George and Winston Churchill. Fowler was subsequently asked to undertake many other projects. Among these was a re-design of Westward Ho!, work at Saunton and The Berkshire. Fowler also worked in the USA.

Furgol, Ed

1917–. Born New York Mills, New York, USA

Ed Furgol came into tournament golf in 1945 with the most severe physical handicaps. His left arm was withered, stiff at the elbow and shorter than his right. However important the left side is said to be, Furgol had to hit with his right: the left hand was merely attached to the club.

Furgol never became a major figure on the Tour but he did take the 1954 US Open, six other events and was individual winner in the 1955 World (Canada) Cup. He played in the 1957 Ryder Cup.

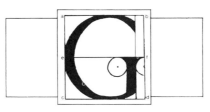

Gallacher, Bernard

1949–. Born Bathgate, Scotland

After a brief career in amateur golf which brought him the Scottish Strokeplay title, Gallacher's rise in professional golf was meteoric. In his first year, 1968, he was Rookie of the Year; he was leading money winner the following season, when he won two events. From then until the end of 1984, he was never worse than 30th in the money list and seven times ninth or better.

Never a very gifted striker or particularly powerful, Gallacher's sheer determination was the equalizer, and he had an excellent putting stroke. He won 13 European Tour events and three in Zambia. Perhaps his best performance was to take the Dunlop Masters in the successive years 1974–1975.

As a Ryder Cup player, Gallacher was the youngest ever to

Bernard Gallacher

play in the matches in 1969 — though he later lost that record to Paul Way — and appeared each year from 1969 to 1983. His record in singles was very good but his best performance came in 1979, when he won four of a possible five points.

Ganton, Yorkshire, England

Although nine miles from the sea, this testing course has all the qualities of links play. It has provided a worthy venue for virtually every important event except the Open Championship. Banks of gorse, which give a blaze of yellow in the spring, and its trees make the contrast with seaside links, but the challenge it presents is much the same.

Founded in 1891, it had two great champions as its first professionals, Harry Vardon and then Ted Ray. Vardon won three Opens and the US Open while at Ganton. Seven architects have shaped the course, the first Vardon himself and the last C K Cotton, ahead of the Ryder Cup of 1949. Notable holes include the fourth, with the approach over a gully to a plateau green, the seventh, a long dog-leg, and particularly the finishing stretch, with the 18th hole calling for a long diagonal carry to get a clear shot into the well-bunkered green.

Ganton has twice hosted the Amateur Championship — the only inland course to do so — the English Amateur, the British and English Ladies championships, the Brabazon Trophy, Dunlop Masters and PGA Championship. Gordon Clark won the longest Amateur final in 1964 at the 39th hole, and when he won his fifth English title here in 1968, Michael Bonallack completed the first round in 61 to go 10 up. He said if he struck his putts correctly, he knew they would run true on the greens. He eventually won by 12 and 11 against David Kelley.

Antonio Garrido

Garrido, Antonio

1944–. Born Madrid, Spain

One of the many Spanish professionals who originally came into golf as a boy caddie, Garrido has had a long career as a journeyman professional who just keeps going. He won both the Spanish and Madrid Opens, and also the Benson and Hedges International, and in 1986 the Four Stars Pro-Celebrity. Perhaps this victory was a reaction to his disqualification a few weeks before, after carelessly replacing his ball nearer the hole than his marker in the Madrid Open.

In 1979, with Ballesteros, Garrido became one of the first two Continental Europeans to play in the Ryder Cup. He and Ballesteros won the World Cup for Spain in 1977. Garrido is an excellent striker and straight hitter, but his putting looks unconvincing.

Geddes, Jane

1960–. Born Huntington, New York, USA

A feature of the US Women's Open is the number of players who have claimed this title as their first victory. Eleven have done so, including Jane Geddes, one of the rising stars of the LPGA Tour. She won after an 18-hole play-off with Sally Little and then went on to win again the following week.

After playing only a few events in 1983, Jane Geddes made good money in her first two full seasons and was ranked 17th in 1985. But 1986 was her first big year when she moved up to fifth in the listings.

Geiberger, Al

1937–. Born Red Bluff, California, USA

Blessed with a relaxed swing, Geiberger has also been plagued by an unruly stomach. Earlier in his career the stress of competitive play was thought to be the problem. Geiberger combatted it for a while by eating the occasional peanut butter sandwich during a round.

But there was more to the problem than nerves. He needed intestinal operations in 1978 and then a series of them in 1980. Since then, although he appears in about half the Tour events, Geiberger has not been a force in US golf. He may well prove effective on the Seniors Tour, for which he qualifies in 1987.

Geiberger's main career lasted from 1960 to 1980, in two phases.

Al Geiberger

He was quite successful early on and first won in 1962. He slumped at the end of the 1960s, returning to form from 1973. He has had 11 Tour wins, including the 1966 PGA Championship.

Geiberger is remembered for his record round of 59 in the 1977 Memphis Classic, played over a very long course of 7,249 yards. He used 23 putts, the last of which was from eight feet, to break 60.

Glen Abbey, Ontario, Canada

Designed by Jack Nicklaus and opened in 1976, the Glen Abbey course is now the home of the Canadian Open Championship — one event Nicklaus himself has never been able to capture, although he has been runner-up several times. The event was held here for the first time in 1977, giving Lee Trevino his second title, and it provided Peter Oosterhuis, the 1981 winner, with his only US Tour victory.

Gleneagles, Perthshire, Scotland: the 16th hole of the outstanding King's course set in wonderful moorland.

Mounds were built around the course, with the spectator in mind, and five holes wind through a ravine, in which a creek is a feature. At the final hole there is a lake fronting the green and to the right, with bunkers on the left. It is a course to rival Nicklaus' own well-loved creation, Muirfield Village in Ohio.

Gleneagles, Perthshire, Scotland

The glories of this wonderful moorland setting, with its hills and valleys, gorse and heather, makes Gleneagles one of the most beautiful golfing centres in the world. The views are superb, with the Ochil mountains to the south and the

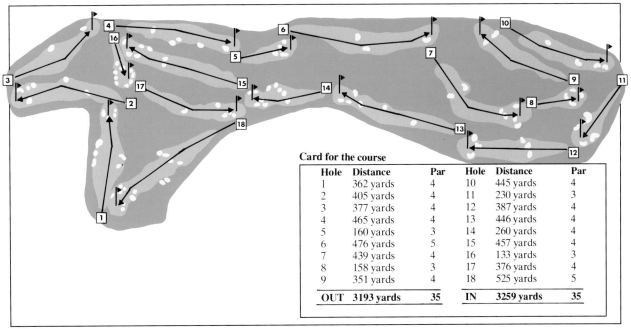

Card for the course

Hole	Distance	Par	Hole	Distance	Par
1	362 yards	4	10	445 yards	4
2	405 yards	4	11	230 yards	3
3	377 yards	4	12	387 yards	4
4	465 yards	4	13	446 yards	4
5	160 yards	3	14	260 yards	4
6	476 yards	5	15	457 yards	4
7	439 yards	4	16	133 yards	3
8	158 yards	3	17	376 yards	4
9	351 yards	4	18	525 yards	5
OUT	**3193 yards**	**35**	**IN**	**3259 yards**	**35**

Grampians to the north — and always the green, inviting fairways, wide enough not to be intimidating.

Gleneagles has four courses: the King's is rated the most challenging, but is closely followed by the Queen's, with two other shorter lay-outs. James Braid designed the King's and Queen's, which were opened in 1919. In 1921 the King's was the venue for the first professionals match between Britain and America, later to become the Ryder Cup. On the outward half, the short fifth, followed by two long par fours, are a fine test. Braid's Brawest is the outstanding 13th hole, with a long, high drive needed to carry a bunkered ridge, and a long approach to a well-bunkered plateau green.

Enid Wilson won the third of her British Ladies titles here; and Jessie Valentine won her British title on the course where 21 years earlier, in 1936, she holed a putt across the final green to halve the Curtis Cup. Gleneagles also staged the Double Diamond World Classic on three occasions, and in 1987 its first Bells Scottish Open won by Ian Woosnam.

Bob Goalby

David Graham

Goalby, Bob

1929–. Born Belleville, Illinois, USA

Many people remember that Roberto de Vicenzo lost a US Masters because of an error in marking his card. Fewer recall that it was Bob Goalby who benefited, becoming outright winner instead of contesting a play-off over 18 holes. The de Vicenzo tragedy made Goalby a forgotten champion in spite of his brilliant final round of 66.

Overall, Goalby won 11 Tour events. The peak of his career came at the end of the 1950s and lasted until the end of the 1960s. More recently he has been successful on the Seniors Tour, coming third on that money list in 1981 and 1982. Goalby also works on NBC's golf telecasts.

Graham, David

1946–. Born Windsor, New South Wales, Australia

David Graham is one of several Australians who have based themselves in the USA for their main playing career. In winning his two major championships, he played two of the greatest rounds of golf. In 1979, he became the first Australian since Peter Thomson in 1965 to take a major championship, the US PGA — and he did it in remarkable style. Playing the last, he needed a par four for a round of 63. Then there were a few minutes of farce. Too strong with his approach, he next chipped short of the putting surface, then past the hole and then missed the putt to take six. All was not lost, however. He had tied and won the play-off against Ben Crenshaw.

In 1981, Graham became the only Australian ever to win the US Open, and he is the only non-American champion in the years 1971–1986. His final round of 67 at Merion in 1981 was almost flawless, his drives and shots to the green remorselessly finding their targets.

Graham is also the all-time leading Australian money winner on the US Tour, which he has played since 1971, winning eight events. Like most Australians, however, Graham is an international player with nearly 20 other wins to his credit, including the 1977 Australian Open. In Britain, he won the World Match Play in 1976, and was in the winning Australian team in the Dunhill Cup in 1985 and 1986. His style is stiff and graceless but he proves there is more than one way to play the game.

Green, Hubert

1946–. Born Birmingham, Alabama, USA

In 1978, Hubert Green missed one of the most famous putts of golf history. It happened on the last green of the Masters, from about two and a half feet, and would have tied him with Gary Player. Putting has been a strong feature of Green's game, however. He uses a 50-year-old club and a split-hands grip. His chipping is possibly even better.

Green's best year was 1974 when he won four times — including the rare feat of three in a row — and was third in the US money list. As he had only joined the Tour in 1970, and improved every year, he seemed to be heading for super-stardom.

It never happened, but he remains capable of producing superb performances. Two of these have come in major championships. In 1977 he won the US Open, leading throughout. Towards the end he was offered a suspension of

play because of a telephone threat to kill him, but he decided to play on.

With his best years apparently behind him, Green resurfaced at Cherry Hills in the 1985 PGA Championship, beating Lee Trevino by two strokes. It was his ninth and last win to date. He has also won in Japan and he took the Irish Open in 1977.

Like his putting grip, Green's swing is unusual. He takes his club away well on the outside and then loops it round.

Guldahl, Ralph

1912–1987. Born Dallas, Texas, USA

Guldahl was one of the players who foiled Sam Snead's ambition to win the US Open. Having finished second in the 1937 Masters, Guldahl needed to par in to tie Snead's total in that year's Open. He did better: he won by two strokes and beat the scoring record

Hubert Green

for the US Open. In 1938 he won the US Open again, after being four behind the leaders as he went into the final round.

Guldahl's third major championship came in 1939, when his 33 for the last nine in the Masters at Augusta pushed Snead into second place.

Suddenly Guldahl disappeared as a force in golf. Some said he wrote a book on how to swing the club and that it set him thinking about his own method, not an orthodox one. Guldahl himself claimed he lost interest and just wanted a club job and time with his family.

Gullane, East Lothian, Scotland

Set in the heart of Scotland's finest golfing country, Gullane has three courses, with its No. 1 course of championship standard and highly rated, even if it has not attracted the renown of nearby Muirfield. It has been the venue for many outstanding tournaments, and is a qualifying course for the Open Championship when it is held at Muirfield.

Established in 1882, its most notable feature is the big hill which has to be climbed early on, but from which there is a glorious view over the Firth of Forth to the mountains beyond. The seventh hole marks the highest point, and the pleasure of a long hit downhill. A similarly inviting prospect comes at the 17th, often helped by a following wind, but a heavily bunkered green awaits.

The great American woman golfer Babe Zaharias created history here in 1947 when she won the British Ladies Championship, the first American to do so. It was again played here in 1970. The Gullane No. 1 course has also staged many Scottish events, among them the Amateur and Professional championships, as well as the Ladies championship.

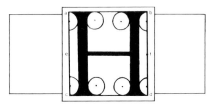

Hagen, Walter

1892–1969. Born Rochester, New York, USA

Walter Hagen hit so many bad shots in the course of almost every event he played it is remarkable that he made a living. However, he may well have had the best temperament for the game in the history of golf. Hagen could whirl them away off line, but it never upset him. He expected to bend a few long shots and calmly got on with the job of recovering — and he never played two bad shots in a row.

Some of this erratic play was probably because as a mature golfer Hagen never practised. He thought he might either leave his best shots on the practice ground or, just as bad, find out he was off form. However, he never lost events because of bad shots late on in a round.

Hagen's greatest strengths were from 150 yards and in: pitching, chipping, bunker play and putting. On the greens, he was reckoned the best of his generation. From bunkers, he produced many delicate flicks, nipping the ball from the surface — and all his best years were before the invention of the modern sand iron.

Hagen quickly rose to the top. The first important tournament he played in was the 1912 Canadian Open and he finished 11th. The next year he finished fourth in the US Open.

In 1914, opening with a 68 for the lead, he held on all the way to win the US Open. And in 1919 he did it again, surprisingly his last victory in that championship.

Hagen's greatest achievements were in the US PGA and the British Open. He became the first native American to win the PGA in 1921, then a matchplay event. In 1923, he lost the final to Gene Sarazen. Then he produced the greatest run in a major championship since Young Tom Morris 50 years before. Hagen won four PGA titles in a row. In 1926 he beat Bobby Jones in a challenge match by 12 and 11 over 72 holes in 1926. All in all, Hagen is considered the greatest matchplay golfer ever.

Hagen first played in the British Open at Deal in 1920 and aroused much interest — but not because of his golf. He wore a dozen different colour-harmonized golfing outfits when such smart attire was rare. He was irritated not to be allowed to use the clubhouse (no

Walter Hagen in 1928 at a £750 golf challenge match over 72 holes against Archie Compston.

professionals were in Britain at that time and not often in the USA either). Instead, he had his hired limousine parked in front of the clubhouse and a footman to serve him lunch.

Hagen went round Deal in 84, 82, 78 and 85. Although scores were much higher those days, his 329 put him 53rd, 26 strokes behind the champion, George Duncan. In spite of this disaster, the resilient Hagen went off to win the French Open. In 1922 he became the first American to win the British Open at neighbouring Royal St George's, and in 1923 he finished second in the Open. At Hoylake in 1924, he regained the Open title but he did not defend it in 1925. In 1926, Jones had revenge for his matchplay thrashing by Hagen earlier in the year. Hagen was third as Jones won the Open.

On his next appearance in 1928 at Sandwich, Hagen won the Open

again, only a matter of days after losing a 72-hole challenge match by 18 and 17. The man who beat him, Archie Compston, was third.

There was a similar pattern in the 1929 Open. In the Ryder Cup, George Duncan beat him over 36 holes by a record 10 and eight. At Muirfield, Duncan finished 19 strokes behind Hagen's winning total of 292. Some think this his finest career performance. When the weather was good, he set the Open record with a 67 and, in foul weather on the last day, had two 75s, better than any other competitor. He won by six strokes.

Harbour Town, South Carolina, USA

Jack Nicklaus worked with Pete Dye to create this natural course in 1968. It had been opened only three weeks when it staged a US Tour

Harbour Town, South Carolina, USA: the 17th and 18th holes of a famous course, created by Jack Nicklaus and Peter Dye in 1968.

event late in 1969, the Heritage Classic, won by Arnold Palmer.

The final holes of the course on Hilton Head Island are close to a bay, and Nicklaus said their designs were influenced by Pebble Beach, although he added there was also 'some Scioto, some Merion and Pine Valley'. Deep greenside bunkers lined with railway sleepers are reminiscent of Scottish courses. Narrow fairways wind through oak trees draped with Spanish moss, pines and magnolias, with greens in natural contours, giving a course which Nicklaus described as 'the kind that makes you play good golf shots'.

The 18th provides a spendid finishing hole, a long par four; the

drive and approach have to be played across the Calibogue Sound. Nick Faldo became the first European to win the Heritage Classic here in 1984, followed in 1985 by Bernhard Langer.

Harlech, *See* St David's, Royal, Wales

Harper, Chandler

1914–. Born Portsmouth, Virginia, USA

In the 1953 Tam o' Shanter, which then carried the biggest golf prize, Chandler Harper watched Lew Worsham, 100 yards or so out from the flag, attempt to get down in two to tie his total. Lo and behold, Worsham holed his wedge shot. However, Harper won as many as 20 titles, not all now credited as full US Tour events.

Harper was at his best from the

late-1940s to the mid-1950s. He won the Canadian Open, the 1950 US PGA and in 1954 took only 259 strokes to win the Texas Open. His last three rounds of 63, 63 and 63 are the record for 54 holes in a Tour event. Harper's best year was 1953 when he was fourth in the money list.

Harris, John

1912–1977. Born Chobham, Surrey, England

After qualifying in civil engineering, John Harris joined his father's golf course construction firm. He gradually took to design, perhaps as a result of so often being in the company of golf architects. Although he undertook a considerable amount of design work in England, most of the courses he designed were overseas: in many European countries, Tunisia, Australasia, the Far East and in the West Indies. Some of his best work was done in Tobago and Jamaica, and at Royal Canberra in Australia, and Waireki in New Zealand.

Harrison, Dutch

1910–1982. Born Conway, Arkansas, USA

Although the 21 years between Harrison's first and last victories —

Fred W Hawtree

1937 and 1958 — are not a record, they help to show how well he lasted. Even two years after his last success at the age of 50, Harrison was still good enough to come third in the US Open. If the Seniors Tour had come earlier he would certainly have made a killing for he won the national over-50s title five times when there was little else to play for.

Harrison is still remembered at Ganton Golf Club for his performance in the 1949 Ryder Cup. With the USA in difficulties, Harrison fired five successive threes at Max Faulkner in their singles, a crucial factor in the eventual US success.

Havers, Arthur

1898–1981. Born Norwich, Norfolk, England

Havers first qualified to play in the Open Championship in 1914 at the age of 16. Nine years later he was champion, winning at Troon in 1923, the last British player to win until Henry Cotton's victory in 1934.

Although he represented Great Britain and Ireland against the USA five times in the years 1921–1933 Havers never achieved what might have been expected of a man who had been Open champion. This may have been because his left-hand grip was far too strong. He also lunged into the ball, and was sometimes addicted to shanking.

Hawtree, Fred G

1883–1955. Born Ealing, Middlesex, England

Setting out as a greenkeeper, Hawtree began to move into course design in his early 30s. After World War I, he formed a partnership with J H Taylor, in which Hawtree did most of the detailed work. His most famous legacy was his re-modelling, with many new holes, of Royal Birkdale. Most of his

Dale Hayes

designs were for English courses but he also worked in Europe.

Hawtree, Fred W

1916–. Born Bromley, Kent, England

After completing his education, Fred Hawtree joined his father's firm shortly before World War II. Later he became one of the most prolific English architects of his time. He has often had to work with rather unsuitable land but he is opposed to massive earth-moving operations. He believes the designer should attempt to fit the course into the landscape. Hawtree's son, Martin, has followed him into golf course architecture.

Hayes, Dale

1952–. Born Pretoria, South Africa

Although he is still only in his mid-30s, Dale Hayes has settled for a club professional job in South Africa. Yet in the early 1970s, he was a prodigious talent after winning the English and Scottish Amateur Stroke Play titles. He won the Spanish Open at the age of 18 and went on to win 10 South African events by 1976 including

Sandra Haynie

the South African Open and six in Europe in the 1970s as a whole. He tried his luck in the USA for two years in the mid-1970s with little success. He then returned to Europe, where he had come first in the money list in 1975. He won the Italian and French Opens in 1978 and then returned to South Africa, where he continues to play on their sunshine circuit.

Haynie, Sandra

1943–. Born Fort Worth, Texas, USA

From the time of her first LPGA victory in 1962, Sandra Haynie was a leading figure on the Tour and usually well up in the money list. Between 1963 and 1975, ninth was her worst placing and she was six times third or better. Haynie had one or more victories in each of the years 1962–1975, and her best years, 1966, 1971, 1974 and 1975 gave her multiple wins — six in 1974, including both the US Open and LPGA Championship.

Haynie played little in the four years 1977–1980 as a result of injuries and other interests, but she added more titles in 1982, taking her career total to 42.

Hazeltine National, Chaska, Minnesota, USA

Tony Jacklin made history here in 1970 when he followed his Open victory at Royal Lytham in 1969 by becoming the first Briton to win the US Open for 50 years. The previous winner was Ted Ray in 1920. Jacklin became the first British player since Harry Vardon in 1900 to hold both titles at the same time. Jacklin was the only player to finish under par. He won by seven strokes from Dave Hill, who criticized the course as a 'cow pasture', a description it did not merit and for which he was censured.

Winds of 40 miles an hour blew on the first day when Jacklin returned a one under par 71

Sandy Herd

followed by three rounds of 70. On the last day, after he sank a 30-foot birdie putt at the ninth hole, he was never threatened. It was the second longest course for a US Open, with many dog-leg holes, far from easy, but in spite of stumbling early on during the final round, Jacklin, then at the peak of his form, was masterly. Over this Chaska course Hollis Stacy won the US Women's Open here in 1977.

Herd, Sandy

1868–1944. Born St Andrews, Fife, Scotland

Sandy Herd was already one of the leading players by the early 1890s. He proved that Victorian golfers were not merely the best among the relatively few playing. He won the 1926 Match Play Championship at

the age of 58, one of the great feats by an 'old golfer'.

Herd is chiefly remembered, however, for being the first winner of the Open Championship to use the rubber-wound Haskell ball, which had only just arrived from the USA. He is said to have been the only player in the field to do so and played the six rounds — including the qualifying — with just the one ball. At the end, it was cut, with its inside protruding, but it had done the job. This was Herd's only championship but he was also second in 1892, 1895, 1910 and again in 1920, by then aged 52.

Herd played in the Open for the last time in 1939, aged 71. Although he ranked below Braid, Taylor and Vardon, he was regarded as the fourth best of his era and was famous for his fast and furious waggle before swinging.

Higuchi, Chako

1945–. Born Tokyo, Japan

Probably the best Japanese woman player ever, Chako Higuchi was still a force in Japanese golf into the mid-1980s. Her best years were the late-1960s to the late-1970s. Although Ayako Okamoto has improved on her achievements in the USA, Higuchi never played in the USA full-time but took the LPGA Championship in 1977. In Japan, she was repeatedly leading money winner, winning both the LPGA title and the Open three times. Her first major victory outside Japan came in the 1976 Colgate European Open at Sunningdale.

Hill, Dave

1937–. Born Jackson, Michigan, USA

Dave Hill justly earned the reputation for speaking his mind — and was sometimes fined for doing so. One occasion came after he lost the 1970 US Open to Tony Jacklin.

Hill was a perfectionist and delighted in practice as much as Ben Hogan. He was seldom satisfied with the standard of his stroke-making. After winning a tournament, he often announced that he had played very badly.

Hill joined the US Tour in 1959 and was soon a consistent, if moderate, money winner. His first win came in 1961 and his last in 1976, a total of 13 in all. His best year was 1969, when he won three times and was second in the money list. The following year he finished second behind Tony Jacklin in the US Open. Characteristically, he was rude about the course, saying the architect — Robert Trent Jones — was an idiot and that it was 'robbing sheep of good grazing'. He liked golf in Britain no better. In 1987 he qualified for the Seniors Tour.

Hilton, Harold

1869–1942. Born West Kirby, Merseyside, England

Harold Hilton was the second amateur after Bobby Jones to win the Open Championship and the last British one to do so. His wins came in 1892, the first time the Open was played over 72 holes, and again in 1897. In other good performances he was third in 1898 and again in 1911, one stroke behind the first-place play-off. Then aged 42, he won the British and the US Amateur titles, also in 1911.

The British Amateur Championship gave him more trouble than the Open. He had lost finals in 1891, 1892 and 1896 but then won in both 1900 and 1901. Two more Amateur wins are to his credit, giving Hilton the remarkable total of seven major championships. Among British amateurs, only his fellow member at Royal Liverpool, John Ball, has a better record.

Hilton played at a fast and furious pace and had a lashing swing. His grip was loose at the top and he was up on his toes at impact, yet he was renowned for his accuracy which was outstanding for wood shots to the pin.

Harold Hilton, the second amateur after Bobby Jones to win the Open Championship, in 1892 and 1897.

Hirono, Kobe, Japan

Built in 1932 by the English architect Charles H Alison, much of whose work was done outside Britain, this course is one of the finest in Japan, although with the Japanese golf boom, many courses have followed to rival it. It has been the venue for the Japan Open and Amateur championships. A flat course, it has streams which wind across fairways, ponds to create hazards, and a profusion of pine groves. Water comes into play at three short holes, the fifth, 13th and 17th and at the long 12th.

The fifth hole is outstanding, with a tee shot over a large lake to a fiercely bunkered green. The par five 12th rates as one of the best in the country, with a daunting drive over water and then a ditch. Few golfers are able to reach the green in two shots.

Hogan, Ben

1912–. Born Dublin, Texas, USA

Hogan is unique in the ranks of the great golfers. It took him longer than anyone to reach the top. He was 28 when he won his first US Tour event and 34 before he won a major championship.

Like most professionals of his generation, Hogan came to golf through caddying. In 1931, he turned professional and tried tournament golf, without success. In 1937 he won $380 when in despair because he had no money left and a thief had stolen the wheels of his car. In 1938 he won for the first time, but in a fourball event.

Two years later Hogan arrived. First he won the North and South tournament, following with four more victories and was leading money winner with some $10,000. He repeated this achievement in 1941 before joining the US armed forces. Although he had been the top star on the US Tour he had failed to win a major event.

When Hogan returned, Byron

The unique Ben Hogan at Wentworth in 1956.

Nelson was the outstanding player. Hogan set off in hot pursuit. In his short 1945 season he won five times. The following year he almost came within sight of Nelson's unprecedented run of wins with 13 of his own, one of which was the US PGA. In 1947–1948, he added 18 more victories and was again the leading money winner, winning the first of four US Opens with a new scoring record of 276, and the PGA. He also took the Vardon Trophy for the third time.

By this time, Hogan had changed his shape of shot. He had come on the tournament scene as a hooker. He began winning when he learned to control his hook. Later he learned the fade but was still prone

to hit a destructive hook. In 1948, he returned to the Tour with a slice rather than a fade, but it was one which infallibly found the fairways and the greens. In time, he came to hit a low, straight ball, which faded at the end of its flight.

Hogan began 1949 in fine style, winning two of the first four tournaments and losing a play-off in another. Returning from a tournament, he was gravely injured when his car was hit by a bus and this almost cost him his life. It was many months before he could play golf again and he never fully recovered from his injuries. He could no longer take the week-in, week-out grind of tournament play so he concentrated on the major championships. He had to abandon the US PGA championship because he did not think his legs would take 36 holes a day.

But they had to in the 1950 US Open, 15 months after his accident. Hogan got through the 36 holes on the final day at Merion and then won the 18-hole play-off the following day, showing immense courage as he was in constant pain.

In 1951, Hogan won the Masters with a perfect final round of 68. Every shot seemed to happen as planned. Next came the US Open at Oakland Hills, a course remodelled to be as severe as possible. Hogan hated it. He began with a 76 but improved in each round; many people think his final 67 is the greatest round of golf ever played. Afterwards Hogan said he was glad he had 'brought this course, this monster to its knees.'

He had a poor 1952, winning only the Colonial in his home town, but 1953 could be called the best year any professional golfer ever had — arguably the equal of Jones' 1930 Grand Slam. Hogan began by winning the Masters by five strokes in a record 274, five below the previous best. He

thought it his best four rounds ever. At Oakmont, he made winning the US Open seem easy. He led throughout, beginning with a 67, and won by five strokes. The British Open at Carnoustie, the only one in which he competed, was another triumph, as he lowered his score each round — 73, 71, 70, 68 — to win by four strokes from fellow American, amateur Frank Stranahan, and from Dai Rees and Peter Thomson.

Hogan believed a golfer could go on winning major championships until the age of 50. He did but this was to be his ninth and last major.

How unlikely this seemed at the time. In 1954, he lost a play-off for the Masters and then another to Jack Fleck in the 1955 US Open. The following year, he three-putted the last green, to cost him the chance of a play-off in the Open with Cary Middlecoff. By this time, his play through the green was still magnificent but his nerve with the putter had gone.

Hong Kong, Royal, Fanling, Hong Kong

Golf in the Crown Colony was

established in 1899 with the formation of the club and its first course, Happy Valley, followed by a nine-hole lay-out at Deep Water Bay on the island. In 1911 a third site was established at Fanling, not far from the border with China. War brought a halt to golf, and considerable restoration was needed after 1945 to bring the courses back to first-class condition after the Japanese occupation. Now Fanling has three 18-hole courses — the Old, the New and the Eden, named after St Andrews — and nine holes at Deep Water Bay.

It was granted its Royal title in 1897 by Queen Victoria. The Hong Kong Open is played on a composite course of nine holes each of the New and Eden courses. Its winners include Australians Peter Thomson, Kel Nagle and Greg Norman. In 1987 Ian Woosnam became the first British player to take the title. In 1984 the World Amateur Team Championships were staged, with Japan winning the men's Eisenhower Trophy and the United States the ladies Espirito Santo Trophy. In the early days at Fanling, members would arrive by rickshaw, and at Deep Water Bay by launch, or take a longer route on a pony.

Honourable Company of Edinburgh Golfers, *See* Muirfield and Introduction

Horton, Tommy

1941–. Born St Helens, Lancashire, England

Although second in the 1967 Order of Merit, Tommy Horton was not chosen for the Ryder Cup that year, although his record suggested he was worthy of selection, but earned his place in later years.

Horton began as a tournament professional in 1964 and was soon successful. He was at his best in the years 1967 to the early 1980s. He

Royal Hong Kong, Fanling, Hong Kong: 18th hole of the Eden course.

Tommy Horton

Beverly Huke

won six European Tour events — the 1978 Dunlop Masters was his best victory — and six others, including the 1970 South African Open, which disturbed Gary Player's near monopoly of the event. He also won his Ryder Cup place in 1975 and 1977, and was joint leading British player in the Open Championship in 1976, finishing in sixth place, and in 1977 when he finished ninth.

Hoylake, *See* Liverpool, Royal, England

Huggett, MBE, Brian

1936–. Born Porthcawl, South Glamorgan, Wales

Brian Huggett has been an outstanding Welsh player. His consistency on the European Tour from 1961 to his retirement at the end of 1980 was remarkable. He never finished worse than 52nd and he was five times in the top three. He was leading money winner in 1968.

Huggett won 18 titles, 17 of them in Europe, and came close to winning the Open Championship. In 1954 he finished a stroke behind winner Peter Thomson and was third in 1962. He captained the

1977 Ryder Cup team and made six appearances as a player. During the 1969 match, he holed a putt of about five feet to halve his match with Billy Casper at Royal Birkdale. He thought he had won the Ryder Cup after hearing a roar from the 17th green and thinking that Jacklin had beaten Nicklaus. Instead, Jacklin had drawn level, halved his match and the event ended in a tie for the first time.

Brian Huggett

Huke, Beverly

1951–. Born Great Yarmouth, Norfolk, England

A top amateur during the 1970s, with a Curtis Cup place in 1972 and English Champion three years later, Beverly Huke turned professional for the 1979 season. Since that time she has won seven events on the WPGA Tour and was in the top four money winners in 1983-1985.

Hunstanton, Norfolk, England

This links course lays claim to being the finest test of golf between the Humber and the Thames. It certainly ranks among the best, although nearby Brancaster is just as outstanding. Founded in 1891 with nine holes, it was later extended to 18, with first James Braid and then James Sherlock, the club's long-serving professional, making alterations to the course. More recently the 17th and 18th have been replaced by new holes.

Lying between the shore and the River Hun, a ridge of sandhills divides the course. After low-lying opening holes, the first notable ones are the sixth and seventh, the

Hunstanton Golf Club, Norfolk, England.

latter a par three from a raised tee across a chasm to a plateau green, leading to the best part of the links and finishing with the short downhill 16th, a long par four, again featuring a plateau green.

The course has been host to many amateur and professional events, including the English Ladies Championship in which Joyce Wethered won the third of five successive titles in 1922, the British Ladies, the English Amateur and the Brabazon Trophy. Doug Sewell's victory in the 1960 Amateur went to a record 41st hole against Martin Christmas. Sherlock, who died aged 91, played in the first professionals match against the Americans at Gleneagles in 1921, and also beat Harry Vardon in the Match Play Championship in 1910.

Hunt, Bernard

1930–. Born Atherstone, Warwickshire, England

Bernard Hunt achieved success after drastically modifying his swing. He was a long but wild driver, but then constructed a short flat swing and became a tournament winner from 1953. That year he won six events.

Bernard Hunt

Partly as a result of excellent iron play and good putting, Hunt was a tournament winner for 20 years and Vardon Trophy winner as leading player in 1958, 1960 and 1965. Apart from 1955 he was a member of the Ryder Cup team eight times from 1953 to 1969 and was non-playing captain in 1973 and 1975. He was third in the Open Championship in 1960 and leading British player in the Open in 1964, finishing in fourth place.

Hutchinson, Horace

1859–1932. Born London, England

Horace Hutchinson produced one of the very first instruction books, *Hints on Golf* (1886), which ran to 14 editions. A prolific golfing writer, he was the editor of *Golf*, now a collectors' item, published in the Badminton Library. His *British Golf Links* (1897) is much sought after, as is his autobiography, *Fifty Years of Golf* (1919).

Hutchinson began to write after being an excellent amateur golfer. He lost the final of the first Amateur Championship in 1885, but won the next two and was again a finalist in 1903. He was the first Englishman to captain the R and A, and he also did some work on course design, particularly at Brancaster, home of Royal West Norfolk.

Hutchison, Jock

1884–1977. Born St Andrews, Fife, Scotland

Jock Hutchison's best golf was played after he emigrated to the USA, where he made his mark before World War I. He won two major championships, the 1920 US PGA and the 1921 British Open. In the latter event, he tied with the amateur Roger Wethered but easily won the 36-hole play-off. In this event, great interest was caused by his play up to the flag because of the extreme backspin he was able to put on the ball.

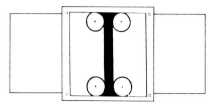

Inkster, Juli

1960–. Born Santa Cruz, California, USA

When Juli Inkster won the US Amateur in 1982 it was her third victory in a row, making her only the fifth woman to achieve the feat. She also took the individual prize in the World Amateur Team Championship that year.

On the LPGA Tour from August 1983, Juli Inkster won on only her fifth appearance, when she took the Safeco Classic. Before she had completed a year in professional play Inkster had added two majors, the Dinah Shore and the Du Maurier. In 1984 she was sixth in the money list. In 1986 she won four tournaments and was third in the money list.

Juli Inkster

Inverness, Ohio, USA: the 13th hole of one of the oldest clubs in the United States. Originally only nine holes it is now an 18-hole course.

Inverness, Ohio, USA

This course near Toledo takes its name from the Inverness club in Scotland, and a Scot, Donald Ross, redesigned it in 1919 after it had been established in 1903. After remaining unchanged for many years, the course was altered by Dick Wilson for the 1957 US Open and again by George Fazio for the 1979 US Open. In all, the course has staged four US Opens, the first in 1920 when Ted Ray became the second Briton after Harry Vardon to win the title. It has also staged the US Amateur Championship. Ray cut the corner at the short par four dog-leg seventh for a birdie in each of his four rounds, but this was one of four holes taken out by Fazio in his alterations. Ross designed small, fast and contoured greens, making downhill putts very difficult.

In the 1979 US Open won by Hale Irwin, Fazio's new eighth hole, a long par five, set the USGA a problem when Lon Hinkle decided

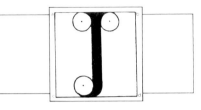

Jacklin, CBE, Tony

1944–. Born Scunthorpe, Lincolnshire, England

Tony Jacklin has taken his place among the greats of British golf. After turning professional in 1962, he really arrived with his victory in the 1967 Dunlop Masters, including a televised hole in one at Royal St George's. He first played the US Tour that same year and increasingly concentrated his efforts there: he won the Jacksonville Open in 1968, the first British winner in a full US Tour event since Ted Ray won the 1920 US Open.

Jacklin had no great US form behind him when he came to Lytham for the Open Championship in 1969. He immediately put himself in a strong position with an opening 68, which put him seven ahead of the favourite, Jack Nicklaus, and two behind the leader, Bob Charles. A 70 then kept him fully in contention, while another 70, to Charles's 75, gave him a two-stroke lead into the final round.

On that final day, he was paired with Bob Charles and for most of the afternoon the championship lay between them. But Jacklin held on to his two-stroke lead and came to the last hole with Charles needing a birdie three to tie if Jacklin faltered to a five. He did no such thing, banging a vast drive down the middle and then hitting a gentle seven iron comfortably to the green before two-putting. He had become the first British Open champion since Max Faulkner in 1951.

In 1970 Jacklin became a world superstar when he took the US Open, the first Briton to hold both Open titles simultaneously since Harry Vardon in 1899–1900. He

Hale Irwin was only the fifth man to pass $2-million winnings on the US Tour.

against the conventional route. He drove his ball through a gap in the trees on the left and on to the 17th fairway, cutting 70 yards off the distance and making a birdie. Other players took the same route, but during the night the USGA planted a tree in the gap, too small, however, to prove an obstacle and players continued to use the short cut. Now a grove of trees has been planted.

There was a sensational finish to the 1986 US PGA here when Bob Tway, who had drawn level with Greg Norman after being nine strokes behind after two rounds, holed a bunker shot at the final green, to win his first major title.

Irwin, Hale

1945–. Born Joplin, Missouri, USA

Consistency has been the hallmark of Irwin's game. In the 1975–1979 seasons he played 86 successive events before he missed a 36-hole cut, the third longest sequence known on the US Tour.

Irwin first won in 1971, in his fourth season, and has kept on winning. As he is not an especially good putter, his best results came on the more difficult courses. This was particularly true of the 1974 US Open at Winged Foot, where everyone was in difficulty. Irwin finished at seven over par but won by two. He won the title again in 1979 at Inverness. Going into the last round with a three-stroke lead, Irwin was six ahead after the first nine. His finish was one of the worst by a champion in recent times; he finished double bogey, bogey and that proved good enough.

The same year, Irwin led in the Open at Royal Lytham with two 68s and was still in the lead going into the final round but collapsed to finish in sixth place as Ballesteros won his first Open.

Irwin was only the fifth man to pass $2-million winnings on the US Tour. Besides his 17 US victories, he has also won several times overseas.

Tony Jacklin in 1969 winning the Open at Royal Lytham and St Annes.

led from start to finish, gradually pulling further away from his challengers. Jacklin opened with a flourish of birdies and completed his round in 71 to lead by two. A 70 to follow increased his lead to three, and another of the same on the third day put him four strokes ahead.

On the final day Jacklin dropped shots on the seventh and eighth and then on the ninth watched horrified as his long approach putt raced at the hole. It hit the back of the hole, skipped into the air and fell back in. He came up to the last with a six-stroke lead, hit the green in two and holed a long putt to win by seven.

Back in Britain at St Andrews a month later for the Open Championship, Jacklin played the first nine holes in 29 and seemed set to take the Old Course apart, when play was halted by a violent storm. With the momentum gone, he completed his round next day in 67 and followed with 70 to still be in

contention, but finished 73, 76, three strokes behind Nicklaus and Sanders, who tied, with Nicklaus winning the play-off.

Tony Jacklin at The Belfry after the Ryder Cup team's victory in 1985.

Jacklin continued to carry the flag for Britain in fine style in the Open Championship. In 1971 he was third, just two strokes behind Lee Trevino, the man who was to be his Nemesis at Muirfield the following year. The pair were level after two rounds and Jacklin then had a 67 on the third day. But Trevino had gone one better with a 66. On the last day, the title seemed to be Jacklin's as they played the 17th. Trevino, through the green in four strokes, chipped into the hole while Jacklin, just short of the green in two, pitched poorly and then three-putted to finish joint runner-up — with Nicklaus to Trevino.

Jacklin was never to feature in, much less challenge for, a major championship in the years ahead, although he continued to be a superb striker of the ball. His last win was the 1982 PGA Championship. This brought his number of European Tour wins to 14 and he won 10 events elsewhere, with his three US Tour wins still the most ever achieved by a British player.

In 1983, Jacklin captained the Ryder Cup team to the best performance ever in the USA, and two years later at The Belfry to the first win since 1957.

John Jacobs

Peter Jacobsen

Jacobs, John

1925–. Born Lindrick, Nottinghamshire, England

After a moderate tournament career with two victories and an appearance in the 1955 Ryder Cup, John Jacobs decided that his career lay in teaching. He became recognized as the best in Britain and extended his activities to the United States. His instructional books and videos have proved extremely popular.

In 1971 Jacobs was appointed Tournament Director of the PGA. He did a great deal to unify tournament golf in Britain and on the Continent, and to raise the levels of prize money. He was a non-playing Ryder Cup captain in 1979 and 1981.

Jacobsen, Peter

1954–. Born Portland, Oregon, USA

A consistent money winner since 1980, when he first won on the US Tour, Peter Jacobsen had his best season in 1984, when he won twice and was 10th on the money list. He has also won twice outside the USA and was a member of the 1985 Ryder Cup team.

James, Mark

1953–. Born Manchester, England

In a short amateur career, Mark James won the 1974 English Amateur, reached the final of the 1975 British Amateur and made a Walker Cup appearance. He turned professional at the end of 1975 and

two years later was in the Ryder Cup team, the first of three appearances. In the following three seasons, he won five times and was seventh, third and sixth in the money list. He won the Irish Open title in consecutive years, 1979–1980, and after a lean spell, came back as a tournament winner. He has often complained of poor putting but features well in the statistics. He was leading British player in the Open championship in 1976 (fifth), 1979 (fourth) and 1981 (third).

Jameson, Betty

1919–. Born Norman, Oklahoma, USA

The winner of 14 amateur titles, Betty Jameson's finest achievement before turning professional was to win the US Amateur in 1939 and 1940. When she won the US Open in 1947, her score of 295 was the first time a woman had played four rounds below 300. Altogether, she took 10 titles, and in 1952 she presented the Vare Trophy for the lowest scoring average on the LPGA Tour.

January, Don

1929–. Born Plainview, Texas, USA

One of the few golfers who have remained competitive on the US Tour into their late 40s, Don January was the oldest US player chosen for the Ryder Cup team when he played at Lytham in 1977 at the age of 48. The secret of January's longevity may be that he both swings and lives at a slow pace and was always prepared to take long rests from the US Tour when he felt he had earned enough. January even retired once and

Mark James

made a successful come-back in 1975. He won the Vardon Trophy the following year, when he took his last tour victory, the Tournament of Champions. It was 20 years after his first success — and his 12th title.

January then continued his tournament successes on the US Seniors Tour, winning more than 20 events.

Jockey Club, The, Buenos Aires, Argentina

Golf is not the only popular sport here, as the name implies, with horse racing and polo the other attractions adjoining the courses. They were laid out by Alister Mackenzie and completed in 1935, a year after his death. On flat land, almost at sea level, the main course, the Red, although relatively short, is quite testing, with the strategically placed mounds and bunkers created by Mackenzie, as well as lines of pine trees.

The World Cup was staged here in 1962 and 1970, providing memorable individual victories each time for the country's greatest golfer, Roberto de Vicenzo. Although finishing runners-up in 1970 to Australia's Bruce Devlin and David Graham, with Vicente Fernandez his partner, Vicenzo's 19 under par total of 269 gave him the individual title by a stroke from Graham. The course has also been the venue for the Argentine Open, won by Vicenzo for the first time in 1944 and on eight other occasions.

Johannesburg, Royal, South Africa

Although the first course was laid out in 1890 when Johannesburg was only a mining camp, it was not until 1906 that land was bought for a new course. In 1933 two courses were decided on, and the East championship lay-out was created. This in its turn was subject to change in 1955, resulting in its

Don January

present challenging design; Gary Player rates it as one of the best. In rolling, wooded parkland, it features a stream which affects several holes, as also do the trees, calling for accurate shots. As with most greens on South African courses, reading the nap needs great care and even courage to determine the right line.

The course has been host to the South African Open, one of the most memorable victories being in 1959 by amateur Denis Hutchinson over Gary Player, although Player returned to claim four of his 13 titles over the course. A final round of 65 for a record total of 272 earned Bobby Cole the title in 1974 after he had played a glorious second from the rough at the par five 11th, over stream and trees to the green for a birdie. Player matched his total when he won in 1981. Bobby Locke also won two Open titles here, the first in 1935 as an amateur, the second as a professional in 1946.

Jones, Bobby

1902–1971. Born Atlanta, Georgia, USA

The most remarkable feaure of Bobby Jones's career is that he achieved it all as an amateur. After a varied college education, with degrees in engineering, English literature and law, he became active as both businessman and lawyer.

A typical pattern for Jones's golfing year was little or no golf in the winter; Sunday fourballs in the summer; a very occasional tournament and the US Open and Amateur Championships. Unlike today's stars, he did not automatically travel to Britain for the two big events. It depended upon whether there was a Walker Cup match to be played. No wonder Jones found the British Amateur the most difficult title to win — he had only three opportunities to compete. He was knocked out in the fourth round in 1921, the sixth

in 1926 and won in 1930, the year he achieved his legendary Grand Slam.

On paper, Jones's record is more impressive in the British Open. In 1921, he lost his temper in the third round and picked up; in 1926 he won. He returned in 1927 although it was not a Walker Cup year, and won again; and again in 1930.

Although Jones was only 19 when he first appeared in Britain, he had been a star for five years in the USA, ever since his first entry for the Amateur at 14 when he had led the qualifiers after his first round and then won his first two matches.

Jones's second Amateur was delayed by World War I and then, aged 17, he was a finalist. The following year, 1920, he played his first US Open and finished eighth. In 1921, he moved up to fifth and in 1922 he tied for second, a stroke behind Gene Sarazen. At this point, he still had not won the US Amateur.

Although Jones was only 21 in the 1923 season, he felt like a failure. Most people seemed to think he was the best player in the country. Why couldn't he win?

That was corrected in the US Open. Jones was running away with it when, as he put it, 'I finished like a yellow dog.' As a result, Bobby Cruickshank caught him, but, in the play-off, Jones won in the end with a brilliant long iron from a poor lie over water to the 18th green.

This win set Jones off on a string of major successes in the space of a few years. In the US Open during the years 1922–1930 he only once finished out of first or second place. He won four, lost two play-offs and was second in another. The US Amateur was much the same story. From 1924–1930, he won five, lost one final and was knocked out in the first round in 1929.

In the years 1923–1930 he won a grand total of 13 major championships but 1930 was the climax

Bobby Jones wins the 1927 Open Championship at St Andrews.

Robert Trent Jones

when, over in Britain for the Walker Cup, he won both Amateur and Open and then hurried back to the USA to win the Open. There was a pause for a couple of months and then he completed the Grand Slam with the US Amateur. A few weeks later, he retired at the age of 28. He then devoted his energies to creating his own dream course, Augusta National, now home of the US Masters.

Jones, Robert Trent

1906–. Born Ince, Cheshire, England

A good amateur golfer, Robert Trent Jones must be one of the few university students to design his own course of studies. His chosen field was golf architecture, where he went on to be the leading practitioner of his time, and certainly the most widely known. As a result, he has produced over 400 courses in more than 20 countries (without counting his modifications to existing courses).

His best-known works are Peachtree, Oakland Hills (which Ben Hogan called 'a monster'), Baltusrol, Spyglass Hill, Firestone, Sotogrande, the vast 7516-yard El Rincon course at Bogota, Colombia, Hazeltine National, site of the 1970 US Open, Southern Hills, Royal Dar-es-Salam in Morocco

and Pevero in Sardinia, blasted through rock. His recent second 18 holes at Ballybunion is an exceptionally natural links lay-out, considered by many as one of the world's greatest.

Much of Jones's work contains his trademarks: vast tees to enable the length of the course to be much altered and save wear; big greens to allow a variety of hole positions; bunkers in irregular shapes; the concept of the 'heroic' shot, often involving a carry over water. In this last case, he often gave golfers a choice of route — safe or bold, with drastic punishment for failure.

Jones, Robert Trent, Junior

1939–. Born Montclair, New Jersey, USA

Robert Trent Jones joined his father's course architecture firm on leaving university but later set up independently. Much of his work has been carried out in the western USA, especially California, and he has also been very active in Japan. He believes a course should blend with the country in which it is set.

Jurado, José

1899–1972. Born Argentina

His country's best golfer during the 1920s and 1930s, José Jurado came close to winning the British Open. At Royal St George's in 1928, he was only a stroke off the lead going into the final round, but then he collapsed. Three years later, at Carnoustie, he led the eventual winner, Tommy Armour, by four strokes before the final round. The last two holes proved his downfall. On the 17th, he topped a 'safe' iron from the tee into the Barry Burn and came to the last, then a par five, needing a four to tie Armour. But Jurado did not know this and played his second shot safely short of the burn which crosses in front of the green. His 'safe' five gave him second place.

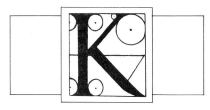

Kapalua Bay, Hawaii, USA

Arnold Palmer designed this fine course in the beautiful surroundings of the Hawaiian island of Maui. It was the setting for Sandy Lyle's first victory in the United States in the Kapalua International in 1984, seven months before he won the Open Championship at Sandwich. Although the Kapalua International did not become an official US Tour event until 1985, it attracted an international field in 1984, with Craig Stadler having a course record 62 on the first day; Lyle trailed by six strokes. The island course is subject to varying trade winds which Lyle found to his liking, going into a three-stroke lead after the third round.

In spite of even stronger winds, Lyle finished strongly with three birdies in the last four holes for a round of 65 and victory by eight shots from Bernhard Langer. In 1985, the Nissan Cup was held here with victory for the US Tour team over the European Tour, although Sandy Lyle took the individual honours with a four-round total of 267.

Kasumigaseki, Tokyo, Japan

English architect Charles Alison, who also designed Hirono, altered the original course, laid out by local player Kinya Fujita in 1929, and it became one of Japan's outstanding courses, sparking its golf boom. The then Canada Cup of 1957 provided a surprise win for Japan, with the home team of Torakichi 'Pete' Nakamura and Koichi Ono claiming victory from America's Sam Snead and Jimmy Demaret, with Nakamura the individual winner.

The course has also staged the

Japan Open and Amateur championships. A flat course, it is heavily bunkered, and among its best holes are the short 10th and the par five 18th. The former, a great par three, calls for a carry over water to a small, well-bunkered green, while the last hole, slightly dog-leg, presents a formidable second shot to carry large, deep bunkers at the entrance to the green. To the original East course, a West was added of shorter length.

Kawana, Ito, Japan

Of the two courses here, the Fuji of championship standard was built in 1936 by English architect Charles Alison, and was named after Japan's highest mountain, Fujiyama. The first course, Oshima, named after an island off the coast and built in 1928, is much shorter, with a ravine separating tee from green at the short sixth

Kawana, Ito, Japan: the sixth hole of the Oshima course with its daunting suspension bridge.

hole and with a daunting crossing for players over a swaying suspension bridge. The Fuji course is undulating, with several dog-leg holes providing the only intimidating features. It has been host to the Amateur, Open and Professional championships of Japan, and in 1962 staged the Eisenhower Trophy matches, won by the USA.

Kennemer, Zandvoort, Holland

One of the oldest clubs in the Netherlands, the Kennemer was established on its present site in 1928, although before that there had been a nine-hole course some miles away. It was designed by the English architect H S Colt and five

years after its opening it was the venue for the Dutch Open, marking the last occasion when the championship was decided over 36 holes.

With the German occupation during World War II, the course gave way to concrete fortifications; much work and effort was put into restoration before it regained championship standard. Colt's design was largely preserved, and the Dutch Open came back for the first time since Bobby Locke's victory in 1939 when Flory van Donck took the title in 1951. Among subsequent winners here have been Severiano Ballesteros in 1976 and Ken Brown in 1983. Kennemer has also staged the Dutch Amateur: the winner before war intervened in 1939 was Brigadier General A C Critchley. (Holland's oldest club is the Haagsche, The Hague, founded in 1889.)

Killarney, County Kerry, Eire

There can be no more glorious setting for the game of golf than is found here, among unrivalled scenery of mountains and lakes, and a quality of golf which comes close to matching the superb surroundings. Golf was played in Killarney from 1891, but it was in 1936 that Lord Castlerosse, later Lord Kenmare, engaged Sir Guy Campbell to design a course on his family's land at Lough Leane. It was completed in 1939, but it was only after the war that it gained its popularity.

In 1971 a second course, Killeen, was designed to follow the original course, Mahony's Point, holes from the two lay-outs intermingling to form completely new courses. Mahony's Point still retains Campbell's outstanding finishing trio of holes: the par five 16th stretches downhill to a green set against a backdrop of lake and mountains, the 17th runs alongside the lake, and the dramatic, daunting short 18th, where the lake extends to the edge of the green. Irish championships, men's and ladies, have been held here, as well as Home Internationals, and in 1975 the European Amateur Team Championship, for which a composite course was used.

King, Betsy

1955–. Born Reading, Pennsylvania, USA

After a good though not outstanding career as an amateur, Betsy King made no great impact during her first seven years on the LPGA Tour. All this changed in 1984 when she won three times and was leading money winner. She was sixth the following year and won twice on the US Tour; she also took the Ladies' British Open at Moor Park. In 1986 she won twice, was second on the US money list, and captured three US tournament titles in the first few months of 1987.

Kite, Tom

1949–. Born McKinney, Texas, USA

Outstanding as a tournament player, Tom Kite has on several occasions challenged for a major championship, but without success. He has worked his way into contention only to fall away during the last nine holes, especially in the Masters and the British Open. Indeed, Kite's claim to fame is not

Killarney, County Kerry, Eire: the 17th hole runs alongside the lake and unrivalled mountain scenery.

Tom Kite

as a winner of tournaments, either as an amateur or professional since 1972, but as an accumulator of money. Since 1974, his worst US Tour money list position has been 26th and he was five times in the top nine in the six years 1981–1986: he was leading money winner in 1981 and third in 1982. An example of his consistency came in 1981. In 26 US events, he was in the top 10 21 times and won the Vardon Trophy — yet he had just one victory, only the third in his 10 years on the US Tour.

Kite has stepped up his victory rate since then, winning six more in the years 1982–1986 but, even so, never more than two in any one year. As far as money is concerned, however, there is a different story. From 1976, he has always won more than $100,000 and has topped $250,000 each year from 1981, with four years over $340,000. In Britain, he was in position to win the Open in 1978, when he finished joint runner-up to Jack Nicklaus at St Andrews, and was leading at one stage in the final round of the Open at Royal St George's in 1985 before a disastrous hole ended his hopes.

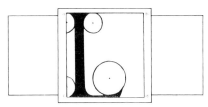

Lacoste, Catherine

1945–. Born Paris, France

During the second half of the 1960s, Catherine Lacoste proved herself the best woman amateur golfer in the world. Very powerful, she was one of the few women to be a superb one-iron player. Then she married and announced her retirement from serious golf, although she did return on occasion during the 1970s. Her last important win was in the 1976 Spanish Ladies.

Catherine Lacoste's two greatest years were 1967 and 1969. In 1967 she set all kinds of records in winning the US Open: first non-American, first amateur and the youngest. The same year, she also won the French Amateur Open, the first of her four wins in the event. In 1969, in amateur championships, she took the French, British and American titles. She became only the third woman to win British and US titles in the same year.

Lagunita, Caracas, Venezuela

Designed by Dick Wilson, one of America's best-known architects, and completed in 1962, Lagunita is the newest of three outstanding country clubs in the area. It has been host to the World Cup and the World Amateur Team Championships. The course is notable for its five testing par three holes, three of which are over 200 yards, all of which call for fine judgement.

In the 1974 World Cup only three players in the field of more than 90 finished under par for the four rounds: Bobby Cole, Hale Irwin and Masashi 'Jumbo' Ozaki. Cole and Dale Hayes won the event

for South Africa; Cole took the individual title with a total of 271, nine under par. Venezuela's Amateur Championship has been held here, and in 1986 the men's and ladies' World Amateur Team Championships were also staged.

Lahinch, County Clare, The Irish Republic

A course that takes its place among the best in Ireland, Lahinch is true linksland, with high sand dunes, natural hollows and plateau greens. Opened in 1893, it was laid out by Old Tom Morris. In 1927 it was reconstructed by Alister Mackenzie two years after he had left Britain for the United States, where he was first to make his name at Cypress Point. Two holes which remained unchanged were the fifth, Klondyke, and the sixth, The Dell, a par five and a par three. The Dell gives a blind tee shot to a green between two hills, both alien to today's design thinking but somehow quite acceptable in their natural setting.

The course has been the home of the South of Ireland Amateur Championship since 1895, and has hosted the Irish Amateur, Professional and Ladies Championship.

Laidlay, Johnny

1860–1940. Born East Lothian, Scotland

Johnny Laidlay laid the foundations of his golf game while a pupil at Loretto School, Edinburgh, absconding on moonlit nights to play and take lessons on Musselburgh links. He was at his peak from the late 1880s to the mid-1890s, winning the Amateur Championship in 1889 and 1891. In 1893 he was runner-up in the British Open.

Lamaze, Henri de

1918–. Born Trelissac, Dordogne, France

Probably the best French amateur

ever, Henri de Lamaze dominated the scene in his own country from a little after the end of World War II to the mid-1960s.

He won the Closed Amateur title 14 times between 1947 and 1971 and the Open Amateur title on 11 occasions in the years 1947 to 1960. In the 1950s, he also won the French Open three times. Overseas, he was less successful, once reaching the semi-final of the British Amateur in 1966 — the first Frenchman to do so.

Langer, Bernhard

1957–. Born Anhausen, Bavaria, West Germany

Germany had never produced a professional of near tournament-winning standard before Bernhard

Bernhard Langer

Langer arrived, and in spite of the much increased popularity of the game which his successes have helped stimulate he is still the only one.

Langer first attracted notice around 1976 for the quality of his long game — and poor putting.

Finding a putter he liked cured the condition — for a while. Putting marvellously, he won the 1980 Dunlop Masters. In 1981 he was leading money-winner on the European Tour, with two victories. The next season, his putting twitch returned. Otherwise, Langer seemed to be playing better than ever. His results were still good, but his money winnings were halved.

Langer practised his putting intensively, trying to find a method which gave him the confidence to defeat the twitch. He emerged with the reverse overlap grip for long putts, left hand below right for short putts and whichever felt right for the remainder. In 1983, he won three times in Europe and was third in the money list. There was further progress in 1984. He had four wins in Europe and was leading money winner for the second time. He also played a few times in the USA, making enough money to earn his Tour card without having to play in the qualifying school.

In 1985, Langer divided his time between Europe and the USA. In Europe, he won twice and was second money winner. In the USA he became a star, winning the Masters in fine style, with two 68s to finish, and followed with a tournament win the next week. By the end of 1985 he had won more than $270,000 in America.

In 1986, he won $379,000 and was tenth on the US money list. Although he did not win a tournament, he was proving one of the most consistent scorers and, even more remarkably, one of the best putters in the world. That year, he won twice in Europe and made the third most money in only seven appearances.

In recent years, Langer has been the most consistent of performers in the British Open and starts among the favourites. He has 24 worldwide victories. In the 1986 Sony World Rankings, he stood second to Greg Norman.

Lee, Robert

1961–. Born London, England

One of those thought most likely to succeed, Robert Lee has won considerable publicity for his disco dancing, and as a golfer he has attained an excellent standard. With 27 for nine holes during a round of 61 in the 1985 Monte Carlo Open, Lee equalled the world record. He also won the Cannes Open that year, and later the Brazilian Open.

Leitch, Cecil

1891–1977. Born Silloth, Cumbria, England

As one of Britain's outstanding women golfers, Cecil Leitch played the game in masculine style, hitting the ball with plenty of punch from the forearms. Before World War I, she was well-established as the best woman player and went on in much the same vein until she competed with Joyce Wethered. These two players then dominated women's golf in Britain, with Wethered usually holding the upper hand.

Leitch won the French championship five times, the English twice and the British four times. In her one Canadian championship. she took the final by 17 up with 16 to play.

Lema, Tony

1934 -1966. Born Oakland, California, USA

Just after competing in the US PGA, Tony Lema was killed in a plane crash. He had reached the top in world golf but was not given the time to establish himself in the history of golf as a truly major

Tony Lema

player, as it was predicted he would become.

Lema's greatest achievement was to win the 1964 British Open at St Andrews. With very little time to practise, he relied on his caddie to give him the line for the many blind tee shots and to club him for the shots to greens. After a 68 in the second round he was in the lead and, in spite of a Nicklaus 66 in the third round, Lema's second 68 left him seven strokes ahead of his main threat going into the final round. Here, a 70 left him with five strokes in hand. It was his first entry in the Open and he had had no previous experience of links golf.

Lema had won his first tournament in 1957 but experienced some very lean years afterwards. The turning point came in 1962 when he won three times. In 1963 he was fourth in the money list and second in the US Masters, a stroke behind Nicklaus, the best finish by a player making his first appearance for many years. He was again fourth in the money list in 1964 and had four US Tour wins.

Defending his Open title at Royal Birkdale in 1965, Lema led much of the distance but was eventually overhauled by Peter Thomson. Later that same year came the most memorable of encounters in the World Match Play. After 19 holes, Lema was seven up on Gary Player but lost on the first extra hole. In spite of these disappointments, it was a good year for Lema in the US, where he was second in the money list, achieving the rare feat at that time of winning more than $100,000.

By 1966 Lema was well established as one of the world's top four golfers — Player, Nicklaus and Palmer were the others. His swing had a graceful loop and was easy. A good putter, he was outstanding with the wedge and pitching clubs.

Bruce Lietzke

Lietzke, Bruce

1951–. Born Kansas City, Kansas, USA

Although he is not fond of tournament golf because he hates the nervous pressure, Bruce Lietzke has spent a dozen lucrative years on the US Tour and won 10 times. In 1977, when he was fifth in the money list and recorded his first two wins, it looked as if he would become a major player. Lietzke made over $200,000 that year. His best season was 1981, when he won three titles, well over $300,000, and was fourth on the money list. Perhaps his best performances have been to win the Canadian Open twice, in 1978 and 1982.

Although he is a long hitter, Lietzke manages to hit more fairways than most, relying on a fade. He has putted effectively with left hand below right for many years.

Lindrick, Nottinghamshire, England

This heathland course was the scene of a great home victory in the 1957 Ryder Cup when on the final day Dai Rees's team won six of the eight singles, with one halved, to rout the United States team and to gain only their third victory in the series. American captain Jackie Burke was generous in his praise of a course which he said was 'a golfing paradise — the turf is perfect, the greens flawless'. The praise was repeated by the ladies of the Curtis Cup in 1960, but this time it was the USA who triumphed.

Founded in 1891 as the Sheffield and District Golf Club, its fourth green on the borders of Nottinghamshire, Yorkshire and Derby was once the scene of cock-fighting. A long, blind second shot now greets the player, with a river beyond the green. Five holes are beyond a road which separates the main part of the course. The last of these is the par five 17th, where in the 1982 Martini International, Greg Norman, distracted by a photographer, hooked his drive into the trees. The hole cost him 17 strokes! Back over the road, the final hole is a long par three, sloping uphill, close to the clubhouse. Vivien Saunders won the Ladies British Open Championship here in 1977.

Little Aston, Staffordshire, England

One of the main championship courses in the Midlands, this parkland lay-out is one of the few attributed to the great Harry Vardon. It was founded in 1908, although subsequent changes were made by H S Colt, and by Mark Lewis, the club professional.

The setting of an old deer park offers peace and seclusion from the busy industrial life of nearby Birmingham. Three fine par fours, starting at the sixth, provide a testing sequence, followed by a short hole from among the trees into the open. The 17th is outstanding, tight from the tee, leaving a relatively short approach to a green sur-

Little Aston, Staffordshire, England: the clubhouse, set in an old deer park, offers peace and seclusion from nearby Birmingham.

rounded by bunkers, with water on the left. It has been the venue for the British Amateur and Stroke Play Championships, and for professional tournaments which include the Dunlop Masters.

Little, Lawson

1910–1968. Born Newport, Rhode Island, USA

No other golfer has matched Lawson Little's feat of winning the Amateur Championships of both the United States and Britain in consecutive years. He first attracted attention in the second round of the 1929 US Amateur. In the first round, the impossible had happened: Bobby Jones had been knocked out by Johnny Goodman. The glory was short-lived. Little defeated him after lunch.

In 1934 Little reached the semi-finals of the US Amateur and earned a Walker Cup place. He won his matches in dominant style. In the Amateur Championship final, he had an approximate 66 in the morning and began the second

round with four threes and a four. It was all over — by 14 and 13! He had little more difficulty in the US Amateur, taking that final by eight and seven. He was less awesome the following year, having a close tussle in the British Amateur final before winning the US Amateur more comfortably.

Lawson Little in 1935

Sally Little

At this period, Little showed what a revolution steel shafts had brought about. He was able to hit flat out from a shut-face position and many of his second shots only required a short iron.

Little turned professional in 1936, but it was not all a success story. He won the Canadian Open in 1936, and his greatest success came in the 1940 US Open which he won after a play-off with Gene Sarazen.

Little, Sally

1951–. Born Sea Point, Capetown, South Africa

After a good career in amateur golf, Sally Little went to America in 1971 to try her luck on the LPGA Tour. She made a modest name quickly and was Rookie of the Year. It was not until five years later that she became a leading player. In 1976, she won her first tournament and moved up to 13th place in the LPGA money list. That was her worst placing in the next seven years.

During this time, Little won two majors, the LPGA Championship

and the Dinah Shore, the latter with a 64 in the last round. By the end of 1982, a year when she won four events and was third in the money list, she had won 14 tour events. In 1983 she underwent knee and abdominal surgery and was out of golf for some time. In 1986 she came close to the US Open, losing to Jane Geddes after a play-off over 18 holes.

Littler, Gene

1930–. Born San Diego, California, USA

When Gene Littler first appeared, Gene Sarazen declared: 'Here's a kid with a perfect swing like Sam Snead's — only better.' Littler did not have the power of Snead but otherwise the judgement was correct.

Littler's golfing pedigree goes back to 1953, when he won the US Amateur. The following year, he won the San Diego Open and collected no money — he was still an amateur. This was the last tour win by an amateur until Scott Verplank won the Western Open in 1985.

Gene Littler

Littler turned professional; he took four events in 1955 and three in 1956. In his first three full seasons, he won the Tournament of Champions each year. Perhaps 1959 was his best season; he won five times and was second on the money list. Two years later he won the US Open by a stroke from Doug Sanders and Bob Goalby.

Littler tied for two more majors, the 1970 Masters, in which he lost the 18-hole play-off to Billy Casper, and the 1977 US PGA, where Lanny Wadkins beat him in sudden death after Littler had looked a certain winner with nine holes to go. After winning 29 US Tour events, Littler maintained his success on joining the US Seniors Tour, being a consistent winner.

Liverpool, Royal, Cheshire, England

Lying beside the estuary of the River Dee at Hoylake, the Royal Liverpool is one of the sternest tests of links golf, made even more challenging by winds which sweep in from the Welsh hills. At first glance, the flat stretch of land with banks or 'cops' to define out-of-bounds and sandhills in the distance seems unimpressive, yet it is true championship quality.

It starts with out-of-bounds along the right of the first hole and is ready to catch the unwary as the round continues. The short seventh, the 'Dowie', named after the first captain, has out-of-bounds a few yards from the green. At the 16th in the 1967 Open Championship, Roberto de Vicenzo saw his drive stop a few yards from the menacing bank. He then hit a courageous shot over the out-of-bounds to the heart of the green, to seal an emotional victory. Sadly, the Open has never returned, as it lacks the space to house the modern championship, although it continues to stage other important events.

Founded in 1869 (only Black-

heath and Westward Ho! in England are older), the Royal Liverpool staged the first Amateur Championship in 1885 and the first English Amateur in 1925. The first amateur internationals, England and Scotland in 1902, and Britain and the United States in 1921, were played here, and the inauguration of the Walker Cup followed in 1922. Hoylake was host to its first match in 1983, with a win by 13½-10½ for the USA.

In all, Hoylake has staged 16 Amateur and 10 Open Championships. When he won the Open here in 1930, Bobby Jones gained the second leg of his famous Grand Slam. The club celebrated its centenary in 1969 by hosting the Amateur, with Michael Bonallack claiming the fourth of his five titles. A popular Open win was that of Fred Daly in 1947. The club's fame

Royal Liverpool, Cheshire, England: the clubhouse, lying beside the estuary of the River Dee.

spread in its early years through three of its members, John Ball, Harold Hilton and Jack Graham. Ball and Hilton won three Open and 12 Amateur titles between them.

Locke, Bobby

1917–1987. Born Germiston, Transvaal, South Africa

Arthur D'Arcy (Bobby) Locke first appeared outside South Africa in the late 1930s. By that time, as an 18-year-old, he had already won the South African Amateur and Open. When he arrived in Europe, he found he was being out-hit by nearly everyone. This was primarily because Locke faded the ball

and also swung gently. As he did not wish to hit harder, he decided he had better learn to draw the ball because of the extra run he would achieve.

In due course, Locke emerged as the most extreme hooker ever but a player who could control his hook better than others could their fades. He would set himself up at almost 45 degrees to the target line and, even with the short irons, his ball swung back into play. Locke was one of the steadiest drivers ever and had superb judgement of distance. Even so, it was as a putter that Bobby Locke amazed the golfing world. Here again, he was unorthodox. He used an old hickory-shafted club with a discoloured steel blade and did not allow the face to open as he took the club back. Some said he hooked his putts, as well as every other shot. Although this was untrue, Locke did feel that cutting across the ball was fatal to good putting.

By the start of World War II, Locke had won the South African Open five times, and a host of other events. Overseas he won the Irish, Dutch and New Zealand Opens. Immediately after the war he became a star. Meeting Sam Snead at the 1946 British Open, Locke suggested a series of exhibition matches in South Africa over the winter. Snead agreed and was defeated 12-2. Snead felt that he went for the flag and as often as not took two putts; Locke, on the other hand, just seemed to go for the green and took one putt.

This experience prompted Locke to try his luck in America. He arrived in time for the 1947 Masters and not long after had won four events in five entries. He won three more events that year and was also third in the US Open.

The following season, he added three more wins. No foreign-based golfer before or since has done so well. Once he won by 16 strokes, still a record margin.

However, Locke preferred competing in Britain and there were also troubles with the US PGA. In 1949, he won his first British Open after a 36-hole play-off with Harry Bradshaw and came through again in 1950, his 279 beating the Open record. In 1952, he won with a new rival, Peter Thomson, only a stroke behind. These were really the Thomson years but Locke, at the age of 40, managed his fourth championship at St Andrews in 1957, leaving the Australian three behind.

For Locke, this was almost the end of a great career, during which he had won nearly 40 times in South Africa, 15 US Tour events and about 30 in Europe and elsewhere.

Henry Longhurst

Longhurst, Henry

1909–1978. Born Bedford, Bedfordshire, England

Longhurst came to golf through Cambridge University, whose team he captained in 1931. Although always troubled by a slice, Longhurst was good enough to do well in Continental amateur championships. He won the German title in 1936 and was runner-up for the Swiss and French titles — but that was the end of his success as a player.

As a journalist, Longhurst had a poor start, working unpaid for a small golf magazine. Soon he was more gainfully employed by both *The Tatler* and *The Sunday Times* — and by the latter for 40 years. He also wrote for the *Evening Standard* but his most important work was done for *The Sunday Times*, where his pieces appeared on the back page.

Longhurst began to commentate for BBC TV in the 1950s and his deep voice became nationally known. He also worked in the USA. His books have made a lasting contribution to the literature of golf.

Bobby Locke playing against Dai Rees in an exhibition golf match in 1939.

Nancy Lopez

Lopez, Nancy

1957–. Born Torrance, California, USA

After a good amateur career in which her outstanding achievement was to come second in the US Open, Nancy Lopez turned professional in 1977. In 1978, her first full season, she was at her best. She won nine tournaments, five of them consecutively, including one major, the US LPGA. She was news, and so was women's golf in the USA. Gates tripled. Lopez continued in the same vein in 1979, winning eight times. At one point she had entered 50 tournaments and won 17.

All this was achieved with a distinctly ponderous swing which contained several 'faults', the worst of which was her shut-face position at the top. However, for those two years it certainly worked.

Having two children interrupted her golf and by the end of 1986 she had only doubled the number of wins she had in her first two years. But she has remained a top player among the leading money winners. In 1985, she had another superb year: she won five times and was

leading money winner with over $400,000, beating her own 1979 stroke average record of 71.20 with 70.73. In 1986, though playing only four times, she still won $67,700 with an average of 70.29.

In Britain, she twice won the European LPGA Championship at Sunningdale in 1978 and 1979.

Love III, Davis

1964–. Born Charlotte, North Carolina, USA

After a good amateur career in which he was three times voted All-American winner of the 1984 North and South and a 1985 Walker Cup team member, Davis Love joined the US Tour in 1986. He was immediately successful, winning well over $100,000. Third in the Canadian Open was his best placing before winning in 1987.

Love attracted considerable attention because of his vast driving. Although tall, at 6ft 3ins he is no powerhouse 250lbs but gets his length more from rhythm and good striking.

Davis Love III

Lu Liang Huan

Lu Liang Huan

1936–. Born Taipei, Taiwan

A force in Asian golf for many years, with some 50 events to his credit, 'Mr Lu' is still a likely winner wherever he plays.

His greatest achievement was to chase Lee Trevino to the very end in the 1971 Open Championship at Royal Birkdale. Superbly consistent, Lu had rounds of 70, 69, 70 and 70. His second place was the highest achieved by an Asian golfer in the event and rivalled in the major championships only by Isao Aoki's similar finish in the 1980 US Open. Immediately after Birkdale, Lu won the French Open. He has seven wins in Japan and several on the Asian Circuit to his credit.

Lytham & St Annes, Royal, Lancashire, England

This is links golf in an urban setting. Although the course is enclosed by modern housing, with no coast or sea in view, it lacks nothing in terms of challenge or variety. Founded in 1886, the club settled here in 1897 and gained its Royal title in 1926. It opens with a

McCormack, Mark

1931–. Born Chicago, Illinois, USA

Mark McCormack first saw Arnold Palmer in 1950 at a college golf match in which they were both playing. They met in 1956, by which time McCormack was a graduate of Yale Law School. The meeting was to revolutionize professional sport, and golf in particular.

Working for a law firm, McCormack wanted to be involved in golf and hit on the idea of representing golfers. At the time, he intended to book exhibitions for them. Soon, his new firm was doing this work for Palmer, and a dozen or so other golfers. Some time later, Palmer asked McCormack to work for him exclusively.

Their partnership was the foundation of two fortunes. Palmer went on to make more money than any golfer before him; McCormack's International Management Group became the biggest commercial power in sport. McCormack soon had the Big Three in his stable: Palmer himself, Gary Player and Jack Nicklaus, although Nicklaus eventually left to set up his own organization. McCormack was quick to sign emerging talent. Players included Greg Norman, Ben Crenshaw, Bernhard Langer, Nick Faldo, Sandy Lyle, Tony Jacklin, Jan Stephenson, Laura Baugh and Nancy Lopez.

McCormack has also long been highly involved in promoting golf events (where the World Match Play Championship was an early and continuing success), TV events and negotiations and is also active in other sports. Today his firm has

par three, unusual in championship golf. A railway provides out-of-bounds along the right on four of the next eight holes, the eighth itself calling for an expert pitch to a pulpit green. The par four 17th produced one of golf's most famous shots in the club's first Open Championship in 1926 when Bobby Jones hit a mashie-iron from a sandy trap on the left of the dog-leg hole, drawing the ball in to the middle of the green to destroy the challenge of Al Watrous and gain the first of his three British Open titles. A plaque marks the spot where Jones played his shot and the mashie-iron is now a treasured souvenir in the clubhouse.

Bobby Locke in 1952, Peter Thomson in 1958 and Bob Charles in 1963 (the first left-hander to succeed) gained titles here, the last two in play-offs, then of 36 holes. In 1969 came Tony Jacklin's

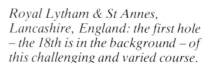

Royal Lytham & St Annes, Lancashire, England: the first hole – the 18th is in the background – of this challenging and varied course.

memorable victory, the first British win in 18 years. Gary Player, putting left-handed from the side of the clubhouse wall to the final green, won in 1974, followed in 1979 by Ballesteros's first Open success.

The Open of 1988 is Lytham's eighth, and it has been host to the Amateur Championship, the inaugural Ladies British Open on the original site in 1893, followed by two further championships, and the English Amateur and Ladies events. The Ryder Cup of 1961 saw an American victory, and in 1965 the club inaugurated its own major amateur event, the Lytham Trophy.

Mark McCormack

offices in many of the world's major cities. He has written his autobiography and a biography of Arnold Palmer. He has also produced *The World of Professional Golf* annually since 1967.

McDERMOTT, Johnny

1891–1971. Born Philadelphia, Pennsylvania, USA

Having lost a play-off for the US Open in 1910, McDermott became the first native-born American to win the very next year, after a play-off. He was then under 20 and he remains the youngest winner. He was champion again in 1912. He won three events in 1913, in one leaving the visiting Ted Ray and Harry Vardon many strokes behind. Several years later he had a nervous breakdown and competed no more.

Macdonald, Charles Blair

1856–1939. Born Niagara Falls, New York, USA

Charles Blair Macdonald learned to play golf at St Andrews University, where he competed against the leading figures of the day, including the Morrises, father and son. Although a US Amateur cham-

pion, he was far more influential as an administrator and golf architect. A founder member of the USGA, he later tried to unify the efforts of this organization with the R and A.

Macdonald designed the first 18-hole course in the USA but he had a greater ambition: to create a course with 18 outstanding holes, an almost impossible task. To this end, he studied British golf courses to make use of features he liked. The result was the National Golf Links of America. Opened in 1909, it attracted enormous praise and was the first course British architects studied for American effort. It had no blind shots, made the golfer think his way around and boasted what is thought to be the first hole set by a lake.

McEVOY, Peter

1953–. Born London, England

McEvoy's greatest feat was to win the Amateur Championship in both 1977 and 1978. At the same period, he was leading amateur in the Open Championship in 1978 and 1979. In 1978, he was also the first British amateur to play through all four rounds of the Masters.

In internationals, McEvoy had a tremendous record in the singles: at one point he had only lost one match out of 28 played for England. His omission from the 1987 Walker Cup caused a storm of controversy, renewed when the USA team gained a resounding victory at Sunningdale. McEvoy proved his ability as one of Britain's greatest amateur players by reaching the final of the Amateur Championship a week later.

Mackenzie, Alister

1870–1934. Born Yorkshire, England

Alister Mackenzie qualified as a doctor, but was enticed into golf

Peter McEvoy

architecture when he helped Harry Colt with the design of Alwoodley, near Leeds, where Mackenzie was secretary. Later, he became a full-time architect and was responsible for many British designs, most in the north of England.

His lasting fame was made with his work on three overseas courses: Cypress Point and Augusta National in the USA and Royal Melbourne in Australia. In a recent poll, each of these was voted among the top seven in the world.

The most famous hole Mackenzie ever designed was the 16th at Cypress Point, a par three where the tee shot either needs 200 yards and more of carry over the Pacific to the green, or can be played more conservatively by playing short of the green and reducing the carry.

Mackenzie died in 1934 before the first Augusta National Invitation Tournament, later called the Masters, and the course itself though not the basic design, has been modified several times. In 1920, he laid down some of the principles of golf architecture with which few would disagree today. They included no blind shots; all artificial features should seem natural; use of every club needed; different character in the holes; big

Mark McNulty

carries from some tees but with alternative routes; little ball searching.

McNulty, Mark

1953–. Born Bindura, Zimbabwe

With 18 wins in South Africa, including a phenomenal nine in 1986, Mark McNulty is likely to follow Bobby Locke and Gary Player as South Africa's premier player. McNulty had his best European season in 1986 when he was sixth on the money list, winning more than £100,000.

McNulty has tried the US Tour, but with no great success. He won the South African Order of Merit four times between 1980 and 1986. Outside his South African wins, which included the Sun City Challenge, he has won four times in Europe, and in 1987 won the Four Stars Pro-Celebrity, at Moor Park, beating Sam Torrance in a play-off to win all 13 tournament play-offs in which he has been involved.

Mahaffey, John

1948–. Born Kerrville, Texas, USA

One of the few players who has interested Ben Hogan, Mahaffey has been a leading American player since 1973, the year of his first Tour victory. He is a relatively short hitter by modern standards but very consistent. Twice he has come close to the US Open, losing a play-off to Lou Graham in 1975 when his putting let down better play through the greens, and again the next year when he was several strokes in the lead going into the last nine.

Two years later Mahaffey did win a major, the US PGA, after being seven strokes behind the leader, Tom Watson, going into the last round. His 66 pulled him level and he won on the second play-off hole from Watson and Jerry Pate.

Mahaffey had won eight Tour events by the end of 1986 and has been 12th or better on the money list five times. He played in the 1979 Ryder Cup team and won the World Cup individual in 1978.

John Mahaffey

Mangrum, Lloyd

1914–1973. Born Trenton, Texas, USA

World War II took away some of Lloyd Mangrum's best years for he emerged as a golfer in 1940. His record 64 in the Masters that year was not beaten until 1986. In 1941 and 1942 he was high on the money list, with five tournament wins.

Back in the USA Mangrum was in the top 10 money winners for the next nine years and took the 1946 US Open after a 36-hole play-off. In 1950, he tied for this title but lost the play-off to Ben Hogan. A consistent performer in the Masters, he was once second and twice third.

Leading money winner in 1951, Mangrum also won the Vardon Trophy that year and again in 1953. In 1948 he won eight tournaments. His 34 US Tour wins rank him eighth in the all-time listings, ahead of such great names as Tom Watson, Lee Trevino, Johnny Miller and Gary Player.

Mann, Carol

1941–. Born Buffalo, New York, USA

With 38 LPGA wins, Carol Mann is still ahead of all current players except Kathy Whitworth, JoAnne Carner and Sandra Haynie. Mann joined the Tour in 1960 and was at her peak in the years 1965–1969, although her years at the top really entended as far as the mid-1970s.

In 1968, Mann won 10 times, took the Vare Trophy and was second on the money list. Her stroke average of 72.04 stood until Nancy Lopez broke it in 1978. In 1979 Mann had eight wins and was leading money winner. She has not competed on the Tour since 1981.

Marsh, MBE, Graham

1944–. Born Kalgoorlie, Western Australia

Graham Marsh's first tournament

Graham Marsh, MBE

win came in New Zealand in 1970 when he also recorded his first European win. Soon Marsh was so internationally successful that there was little need for him to prove himself on the US Tour. However, he did so in 1977, winning the Hermitage Classic and being declared Rookie of the Year.

Marsh did not continue in the USA and since then his career has been confined to his home circuit, a few European events, Japan and Asia, where he has been at his most successful. He has won some 20 times in Japan with half a dozen more successes in Asia. He has been relatively unsuccessful in Australia: he took only one title up to 1982, when he made amends by winning three times. However, his career total is still only five, far fewer than his form elsewhere would suggest.

In Europe, Marsh has been a force since 1970 and has 13 wins to his credit, including the Swiss (twice), German and Dutch (twice) Opens. In Britain, Marsh's victories include the European Open, the Dunlop Masters and the Benson and Hedges International. In 1977 he won the World Match Play title,

beating Raymond Floyd in the final five and three. He was a member of Australia's winning team at St Andrews in the first Dunhill Cup in 1985.

Massy, Arnaud

1877–1958. Born Biarritz, France

The first non-British player to win the Open Championship, Arnaud Massy was also the last from Continental Europe until Ballesteros in 1979. Massy won the Open in 1907 by two strokes from J H Taylor. Four years later, he tied with Harry Vardon. He lost the play-off over 36 holes in an unusual way, conceding on the 35th green when several strokes behind.

Medinah, Illinois, USA

Although this course on the outskirts of Chicago has been the venue for only two US Opens, in 1949 and 1975, it has been the subject of plenty of controversy. Many assess it as one of the toughest in the world. All but two holes have dense woods edging into the fairways, there are nine dog-legs and three holes over water and

contoured greens, so it is indeed a formidable test.

The course was built in the 1920s for an Arabic Order known as the Shriners. A large lake, named Lake Kadijah after Mohammed's wife, cuts it in two, with a carry from the tee at the short second and again at a longer par three, the 17th, with the drive at the third over an inlet. Over the years the course has seen many changes. The most recent alterations were made by George Fazio for the 1975 Open, won by Lou Graham after a play-off with John Mahaffey.

Sam Snead's hopes of a US Open victory ended here at the 17th in 1949 when his one-iron tee shot cleared the water and missed the kidney-shaped bunker fronting the green. But instead of chipping he elected to putt through thick grass off the green, leaving the ball well short to drop a shot, and finish runner-up to Cary Middlecoff, a stroke adrift.

Medinah, Illinois, USA: the 17th hole of this course on the outskirts of Chicago, which many believe to be the toughest in the world.

Melbourne, Royal, Victoria, Australia

Twenty-five years after the course had been opened in 1901, British architect Alister Mackenzie was brought in to make major alterations. He had the assistance of an Australian Open champion, Alex Russell, who later laid out a second course, the East, to give the club an excellent addition to its main West lay-out.

Founded in 1891 on another site, the club is the oldest in Australia in terms of unbroken existence (both Royal Adelaide and The Australian had breaks in continuity). The present courses close to the sea were built on sandy dunes, giving excellent fairways and superb greens. For championship events a composite lay-out of the two offers

Royal Melbourne, Victoria, Australia: the fifth hole of Australia's premier course.

an outstanding challenge, with scores on the par 72 course ranging from 64 to 105 — the former by Hale Irwin. It provided Australia with a World (then Canada) Cup victory in 1959 by Peter Thomson and Kel Nagle from Sam Snead and Cary Middlecoff of the US, and when it was staged here again in 1972 Taiwan's team of Hsieh Min Nan and Lu Liang Huan were the winners.

In the Eisenhower Trophy in 1968, won by the USA from the Great Britain and Ireland team, Ronnie Shade found the task of getting down in two from just off the undulating green at the final hole more than he could manage.

Melbourne has been the venue for the Australian Open and PGA Championships on many occasions.

Merion, Pennsylvania, USA

Two of golf's legendary players, Bobby Jones and Ben Hogan, are linked with the history of this challenging course. It is ranked among America's best, and has been host to 14 US PGA championships — more than any other club. In 1916, Jones, aged 14, played here in his first US Amateur Championship, reaching the quarter finals; eight years later he returned to win the first of his five Amateur titles, and in 1930 he won the last of them here to complete his famous Grand Slam.

In 1950, a year after the car crash

which nearly cost him his life, Hogan defied constant pain in the US Open to finish in a tie with George Fazio and Lloyd Mangrum, winning the play-off the next day.

Founded as Merion Cricket Club in 1865, the golf club moved to its site at Ardmore in 1910. Its East course was laid out by a young member, Hugh Wilson, after he had been to Britain to study courses. Although short by championship standards, its lay-out, changed little over the years, demands the most accurate play, with narrow fairways, 120 bunkers containing clumps of dune grass, tight greens and a tough finishing stretch over a former quarry.

Merion's most famous hole, the 11th, saw Jones safely on the green over a creek to halve the hole and beat Eugene Homans eight and seven in 1930 for his Grand Slam. In 1950 Hogan hit a superb one-iron approach close to the pin at the 18th to force a tie. In 1981 Australian David Graham gave a superb display of accurate driving and iron play when he missed only the first fairway in his final round to return the lowest US Open total at Merion of seven under par 273. One of the distinctive features at Merion is the use of pear-shaped wicker baskets on top of flagsticks on the greens, an innovation Hugh Wilson brought back from England after seeing them at Sunningdale.

Merion, Pennsylvania, USA: the 17th hole of one of America's best courses which has played host to 14 US PGA Championships.

Middlecoff, Cary

1921–. Born Halls, Tennessee, USA

A qualified dentist in days when there were no real fortunes to be made on the US Tour, Middlecoff turned professional in 1947 after a moderately successful career as an amateur. He won in his first season and kept on winning until the early 1960s, becoming a name player with his victory in the 1949 US Open. That was the year Hogan did not compete because of his car crash. Hogan did not let anyone else win for some years after 1949, but Middlecoff won again in 1956. In 1957 he lost in a play-off to Dick Mayer.

Middlecoff's most impressive major championship victory came in the 1955 US Masters, which he

won by what was then a record seven strokes and included a round of 65. During this Masters he holed a putt at the 13th measured at 86 feet.

Middlecoff was an unlovely player to watch, taking an age to align himself for the shot and being one of the few golfers to stop at the top of his backswing. His slowness was such that Mayer scored psychological points by taking out a camping stool for their US Open play-off. He was, however, a formidable competitor and had a career

Johnny Miller

37 wins on the US Tour. After he retired, he began to write on the theoretical and instructional side of golf. His *The Golf Swing* is a minor masterpiece.

Mid Ocean, Bermuda, USA

Lying on the southern shores of this Caribbean island, Mid Ocean was laid out by Charles Blair Macdonald. Born in America of Scots descent, Macdonald went to St Andrews University. On his return he founded the Chicago

club, designed the National Golf Links of America, Long Island, and won the US Amateur Championship. He designed Mid Ocean in 1924 in its setting among pines, with the backdrop of the blue Atlantic. It is a fine test, made even more demanding by changes made in 1953 by Robert Trent Jones.

Mid Ocean opens with a testing par four, curving to the left, with cross bunkers across the fairway, appropriately named Atlantic for a hooked second shot could finish among the rocks. The fifth, a gentle dog-leg par four, is memorable, with a long carry over a lake: the bolder the drive, the closer to the green. In his later years, Archie Compston left England to become the club's popular professional.

Miller, Johnny

1947–. Born San Francisco, California, USA

Johnny Miller, tall and blond, was hailed as the possible successor to Jack Nicklaus when he produced a series of devastating performances in the early 1970s, demonstrating his superb iron play. After winning the US Open in 1973, he was supreme the next two years, during which he won 13 tournaments. Yet suddenly, after winning the British Open in 1976, the magic left him and he went four years before winning another tournament.

From being the US leading money winner in 1974, with a then record $353,000 and second the following year, Miller had slumped to 111th by 1978, winning a mere $17,400 that year. Miller himself was unable to explain the decline, and though he gradually emerged to become a tournament winner again in 1980 and in each of the next three years, he has never recaptured the superb form which put him among the world's outstanding players. In recent years, he has cut down drastically on his playing schedule, and after another

two years without a win from 1983, the magic returned in 1987 as he won the Pebble Beach National Pro-Am.

In his two outstanding US Tour seasons, Miller reeled off three successive victories at the start of 1974, ending the year with eight tournament wins; the next year, he won both opening tournaments, being 24 and then 25 under par to win by eight and nine strokes respectively. Two more tournament wins followed that year.

Miller's arrival as a star came with his first major title success in the 1973 US Open. Lying six strokes off the lead at Oakmont going into the final round, he produced a string of birdies for a record 63 to win by a stroke from John Schlee, with Weiskopf third, and Palmer, Nicklaus and Trevino sharing fourth place. Although rain had softened the course, making it a less severe test, Miller's round ranks as one of the outstanding performances in world golf.

A month later Miller finished runner-up behind Weiskopf in the British Open at Troon, was 10th at Lytham in 1974 and third at Carnoustie in 1975. He finally got his reward at Birkdale in 1976, resisting the challenge of a then unknown young Spaniard, Severiano Ballesteros, to add the British Open to his US Open title. Miller narrowly failed to win the US Masters, being runner-up three times. All told he has won 23 US Tour events.

Mize, Larry

1958–. Born Augusta, Georgia, USA

Larry Mize was the local boy who made good to the delight of thousands of his home fans in his native Augusta when he gained a sensational victory in the 1987 US Masters. Before that, he had won only one tournament, the 1983 Memphis Classic, in five seasons on the US Tour, but had been runner-

Larry Mize

up in three tournaments in 1986 and had finished fourth in the Bay Hill Classic only a month before the Masters.

At the start of the final day at Augusta National, Mize was two strokes off the lead, with half a dozen players separated by only two strokes, among them Ballesteros, Norman, Langer and Crenshaw, but he always remained in contention. A birdie on the final green tied him with Norman and Ballesteros on 285, three under par. The year before, Norman had squandered a chance to tie Nicklaus on the final green.

At the first extra hole, Ballesteros went out when he three-putted, and at the second — Augusta's 11th — Norman safely reached the green in two, with Mize way off the green on the right. Then Mize produced an amazing chip shot from 45 yards which landed just short of the green and rolled on and on before drop-

ping into the hole. Norman failed to hole from 30 feet and for the second time in a few months saw a major championship snatched from him. In the US PGA the previous August Bob Tway holed from a bunker to take the title.

With his father a scratch amateur player, it was perhaps appropriate that Larry should be given the second name of Hogan — no doubt the great Ben Hogan, winner of the Masters on two occasions, would be pleased. Larry also went on to Georgia Tech, the college attended by Bobby Jones, founder of Augusta National, and Mize was Number One on their golf team. He failed to join the US Tour in 1981, but qualified for the 1982 season. Both in 1985 and 1986 he finished 17th in the US money list, winning $314,000 in 1986. His Masters victory saw him pass the million dollar mark in Tour winnings.

Montreal, Royal, Quebec, Canada

Founded in 1873, Royal Montreal is the oldest club in North America. Its present site at Ile Bizard is its third. Its two courses — the Blue is the main championship lay-out — were designed by Dick Wilson and completed in 1959. It was established in the heart of Montreal, but in 1896 found a new location 10 miles away in Dixie, an area which took its name from a railway station. Here the Canadian Open and Amateur Championships were held, another move eventually becoming necessary through urban development.

Orville Moody

Dick Wilson's Blue course (the Red is equally demanding) is notable for massive greens and a testing finish: the last four holes have carries over a lake. At the 16th both the drive and the approach are over water. The 18th, a dog-leg left, offers a short route over the lake, but here in the 1975 Canadian Open, Jack Nicklaus drove into the water when in the lead and finished in a tie with Tom Weiskopf. At the first play-off hole, the 15th, Weiskopf's approach over the water finished two feet from the pin to give him the title and deprive Nicklaus once again of a championship he has never won. Lee Trevino's Canadian Open win in

1971 came after his victory in the US Open and was followed by his first Open win in Britain — three national championship successes within a month.

In 1973, the club marked its centenary by inviting the 'Royal' clubs of the world to take part in a tournament. It received its own Royal title in 1884.

Moody, Orville

1933–. Born Chickasha, Oklahoma, USA

Former American Army sergeant Orville Moody created a sensation when he won the US Open in 1969 at Houston. Moody was then 35, having served in the Far East, where he was able to play golf, to win the Korean Open and to come second in the Japan Open.

After leaving the Army in 1962, Moody joined the US Tour in 1967 and barely qualified for the 1969 Open. Yet Lee Trevino, who had seen him play in the Far East, tipped him to win. With two holes to go, Moody needed a par on each and kept his nerve to make them and win by a stroke from Al Geiberger, Deane Beman and Bob Rosburg, with Arnold Palmer sixth.

Fame and fortune did not follow. Although he won the World Series of Golf later in 1969, he never won another official US Tour event, but won overseas. He emerged again on the US Seniors Tour, winning twice in 1984 at the age of 50.

Moor Park, Hertfordshire, England

Laid out by H S Colt, Moor Park's championship High course, close to London, has been a popular venue for both professional and amateur tournaments. As well as being a severe golfing test, it is one of England's most attractive parkland courses.

Moor Park became a members' club in 1937, although golf was first played there in 1923 after Lord Leverhulme had bought the estate. Its history dates back to Roman times. Its owners have included Cardinal Wolsey, King Henry VIII and at least one of his wives, and its magnificent mansion, with Grecian-style portico, makes an impressive clubhouse. A plaque by the entrance marks its occupation by the Airborne Forces during World War II.

The High course opens with an uphill par four, followed by a sharp dog-leg left. It offers plenty of challenge, with the eighth guarded by a pond, and the short 12th over a valley to a two-tier green outstanding. It ends with a downhill par three where a missed green spells trouble. It staged its first PGA Match Play Championship in 1925, won by Archie Compston, and in 1976 Tommy Horton won the first Uniroyal International when Arnold Palmer was in the field. In 1985 the American Betsy King won the Ladies British Open, and it is the regular venue for the Four Stars Pro-Celebrity event. Sandy Lyle won the Youths Championship here, two years after winning the club's junior tournament, the Carris Trophy, in 1975.

Moortown, Yorkshire, England

Alister Mackenzie, secretary at nearby Alwoodley before gaining international fame in America as an architect, designed this fine moorland course in 1909, with its gorse, heather, streams, woods and springy turf. It calls for straight driving and provides a testing start with three long holes followed by an attractive par three set in woods. The eighth, another short hole, is the best of five par threes. Known as 'Gibraltar', the hole is built on rock, and anything off line is in trouble, with the green a sloping

Moor Park, Hertfordshire, England: the ninth hole of a course close to London, a popular venue for both professional and amateur events.

plateau. The par five tenth is one of the most testing holes, with heather and scrub a constant threat.

In 1929, George Duncan led his Ryder Cup team to victory over the US team, captained by Walter Hagen. It has also been the venue for the English Amateur and Ladies Championships. Michael Bonallack won the first of his five English titles here in 1962, and finished in a tie with Rodney Foster in the Brabazon Trophy in 1969. In appalling weather in 1976, the Americans beat the British team in the club professionals' PGA Cup match. The Car Care Plan professional tournament has also been held here, with two victories for Nick Faldo.

Morgan, Gil

1946–. Born Wewoka, Oklahoma, USA

After qualifying as a doctor of optometry in 1972, Gil Morgan turned to professional golf and progressed steadily and undramati

cally up the money-winning ladder until 1977, when he won his first tournament. Since then he has won five more times on the US Tour, won the 1978 Pacific Masters in Japan and played in the 1979 and 1983 Ryder Cup teams. Morgan's best years were 1978, when two victories and consistency made him second on the money list, and 1983 when he was fifth and won the two opening tournaments.

Gil Morgan

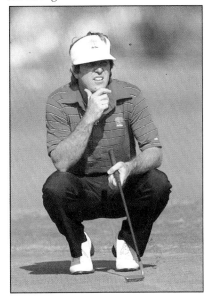

Morris, Tom

1821–1908. Born St Andrews, Fife, Scotland

Old Tom Morris, as he is usually known, was apprenticed when he was 18 to the best golfer of the time, Allan Robertson. He made feathery balls and clubs. He also developed as a player and took part in many famous challenge matches, often partnering Robertson.

In 1851, Morris became the first professional at Prestwick and in 1860 he was second to Willie Park in the very first Open Championship at Prestwick. Morris was then 39, and he won four times in the next few years. His last win in 1867 came when he was 46 and he remains the oldest winner of the championship.

A few years after Robertson's

Tom Morris was the oldest winner, at 46, of the Open Championship, and the first to design golf courses on a large scale.

death in 1859, Morris was invited to return to St Andrews and eventually became a much venerated figure.

Morris was the first to do design work on golf courses on a large scale, and he was particularly active in the 1890s. In those days no substantial changes could be made to the landscape, but Morris made use of the natural features. This meant picking out good sites for greens and devising a general route for the course. Almost all his work has since been obliterated over the years, though there are remnants remaining at such

famous courses as Lahinch, Prestwick, Westward Ho!, Royal County Down, Royal Dornoch, St Andrews New, Carnoustie and Muirfield.

Morris, Tom, Junior

1851–1875. Born St Andrews, Fife, Scotland

No wonder the Morrises are part of the folklore of golf. The father was the oldest winner of the Open Championship; the son, at $17\frac{1}{2}$ in 1868, the youngest. By the age of 22, Young Tom Morris had won four times and had made the Belt, the original trophy, his own property.

Young Tom Morris established a dominance over his rivals that has never been paralleled in Open Championship history. His first win was by two strokes, which increased to three in 1869, each time with the rest of the field well behind. His best performance came in his third consecutive Prestwick victory when he went round the 12 holes three times in 149, 12 better than Bob Kirk and Davie Strath in second place.

After the Belt, which the Earl of Eglinton had presented for the winner, became Young Tom's, it was replaced by the present trophy, the famous claret jug.

There was no championship in 1871 and it was renewed in 1872 when Young Tom won again, this time having his name inscribed on the trophy and being presented with a gold medal. He was placed third and second in the next two championships before his untimely death at the age of 24.

Muirfield, East Lothian, Scotland

The home of the Honourable Company of Edinburgh Golfers, the oldest golf club in the world, dating from before 1744, Muirfield's classic course has more of an

Muirfield, East Lothian, Scotland. Home of the Honourable Company of Edinburgh Golfers, Muirfield is the oldest golf club in the world.

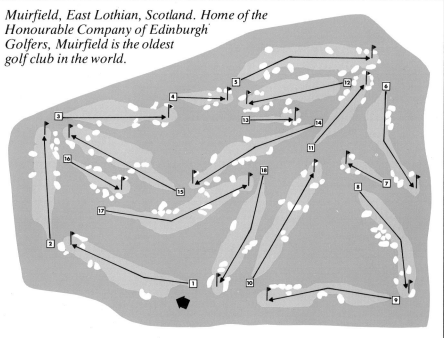

Card for the course		
Hole	**Distance**	**Par**
1	447 yards	4
2	351 yards	4
3	379 yards	4
4	180 yards	3
5	559 yards	5
6	469 yards	4
7	185 yards	3
8	444 yards	4
9	504 yards	5
OUT	**3518 yards**	**36**
10	475 yards	4
11	385 yards	4
12	381 yards	4
13	152 yards	3
14	449 yards	4
15	417 yards	4
16	188 yards	3
17	550 yards	5
18	448 yards	4
IN	**3445 yards**	**35**

inland flavour than traditional links, but is no less severe a test. From its first course at Leith, the club moved to Musselburgh in 1836, sharing the course with the Edinburgh Burgess and Bruntsfield Links societies, and then to Muirfield in 1891. A year later, the great amateur Harold Hilton won the Open here, the first time it had been played over 72 holes, and in 1896 Harry Vardon claimed the first of his six titles after a play-off with J H Taylor.

Alterations to the course have taken place over the years: the par five ninth hole was lengthened to make it even more testing for the 1987 Open, the 13th to be staged here. Laid out in two loops of nine, and with bunkers faced by neat layers of turf, it has no inferior holes, and in the first half, the fourth, the first of four short holes, and the eighth, a long par four, are really testing. In 1929 Walter Hagen drove far out to the right at the eighth for a short cut to the green to make birdies in the final two rounds and claim the title. Afterwards the planting of trees closed that route.

A cross wind can make the 10th formidable and the rough at this hole in 1966 ruined Arnold Palmer's chances, but Jack Nicklaus triumphed, in spite of waist-high rough, to complete victories in

Muirfield Village, Ohio, USA: the 12th hole of a course designed and financed by Jack Nicklaus.

all four major championships. The long 17th marked tragedy for Tony Jacklin in 1972 when Lee Trevino chipped in from the back of the green as Jacklin three-putted, and Trevino retained the title he had won at Birkdale the previous year. Luck was certainly with him, for that was the third chip he had holed during the championship. One at the 16th from a bunker had crashed into the flagstick and dropped into the hole.

Henry Cotton won his third Open at Muirfield in 1948 when King George VI wished him luck on the first tee. Cotton returned a record 66, but that did not last, and in 1980, when Tom Watson was the winner, his third round 64 was bettered by Isao Aoki with 63, eight

under par. Many internationals and championships have been held at Muirfield, among them the British and Scottish Amateurs, the Walker Cup, the Ryder Cup — the first to be held in Scotland — and the Curtis Cup.

Muirfield Village, Ohio, USA

This has been described as 'the course that Jack built' — referring to Jack Nicklaus, who lavished time, care and a great deal of money on creating this superb course, his pride and joy as an architect. In his design, mounds were built for spectators, the two halves start and finish at one point and lakes and creeks feature in the lay-out. When completed in the early 1970s, Nicklaus named it after the Muirfield course in Scotland, a favourite of his, where he won one of his three British Open titles in 1966 and played in the Walker Cup.

Bunkers are plentiful; the first hole gives an indication of what is to come, with its rolling fairway, numerous sand traps and contoured greens. The par five ninth sees the fairway narrow after the drive, and out-of-bounds follows on the left with a cluster of bunkers on the right. The short 12th calls for a carry over the largest lake to the smallest green, and towards the finish the 17th has a monster bunker on the left of the fairway.

Nicklaus inaugurated his own tournament, the Memorial, which each year honours a famous player. Bobby Jones was the first to be honoured in 1976, and Roger Maltbie the first winner. For the following year, the course had undergone some remodelling. Nicklaus celebrated by winning the event, and took the title again in 1984. He was host and captain of the US team for the 1987 Ryder Cup match over his own course. But his rival captain, Tony Jacklin, led the European team to victory.

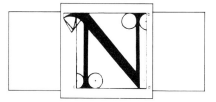

Kel Nagle

Nagle, Kel

1920–. Born Sydney, New South Wales, Australia

One of the great late developers, Kel Nagle only became a name to conjure with at the age of 40 when he won the Centenary Open Championship at St Andrews in 1960 by a stroke from Arnold Palmer, who was making his first appearance in the championship. Nagle began with rounds of 69 and 67, to be two behind de Vicenzo, but five strokes ahead of Palmer. De Vicenzo fell away on the final day's two rounds; Palmer came through with a 70 and a 68 but Nagle held on with two 71s.

With his 1960 success, Nagle's increased confidence led to his piling up victories and he was still winning when past his mid-50s. In 1965, he tied for the US Open but lost the play-off to Gary Player.

From being a player who seldom ventured beyond Australia and

New Zealand, Nagle became an international golfer. He won 10 times in Europe up to 1971, once in the USA and more than 20 times in Australia and New Zealand.

Nairn, Nairnshire, Scotland

Nairn was founded in 1887, designed by Archie Simpson and revised two years later by Old Tom Morris. Lying along the shores of the Moray Firth, this is true links-land with wonderful views, particularly in spring and autumn when the gorse and heather bloom. All the fairways, except the three from the 13th, run either east or west, with all the typical hazards of seaside golf. At the par four fifth, a sliced drive may land in the Moray Firth. A wind from the north calls for a drive partly over the sea, requiring iron nerve at this most testing hole. This the favourite hole of James Braid, one of the Great Triumvirate, who made alterations to the course.

Henry Cotton inaugurated Nairn's famous Golf Week each May, and the course has been the venue for Scottish Amateur, Professional and Ladies Championships. Jessie Valentine, a member of the Golf Week team, won two Scottish titles here. Eric Brown won the first of three successive Scottish Professional titles here in 1956, and eventually claimed eight.

Nakajima, Tsuneyuki

1954–. Born Gunma, Japan

Tsuneyuki Nakajima is one Japanese player who competes regularly overseas as well as in his own country, and plays for several months of the year on the US Tour, where he has yet to win.

In Japan, he has been a leading player since turning professional in 1975, two years after he had become the youngest winner of the

Tsuneyuki Nakajima

Japan Amateur Championship. Since then, he has won 36 tournaments in Japan and has taken over from Isao Aoki as leading player. In 1986, he retained the Japan Open and won five other tournaments. He has won the Japan PGA title four times. In the British Open at Turnberry in 1986, he was only a stroke behind leader Greg Norman starting the final round, but dropped two strokes at the opening hole to finish with a round of 77 for eighth place. In the 1978 Open at St Andrews he came to grief at the notorious 17th Road hole, where he took nine strokes — a few months after taking 13 at one hole in the US Masters.

National Golf Links of America, Long Island, USA

This is regarded as the first great golf course to be built in the US. It was the work of Charles Blair Macdonald, American-born of Scottish descent, who studied at St Andrews University and returned home to found and build the Chicago course at Wheaton. At Long Island he achieved his ambition to design a course which included replicas of holes he had seen on his visits to St Andrews, Royal St George's, North Berwick and Prestwick.

When completed in 1909 the course was immediately acclaimed. Bernard Darwin described it as 'a truly great course'. It is not a true links in the British sense — its fairways are softer — but it still has many characteristics, with dunes and scrub, big, deep bunkers and plateau greens. The par five seventh is modelled after the 17th Road Hole at St Andrews, without the road, and the par three fourth, the 'Redan', is a copy of North Berwick's famous hole. Macdonald's design makes the par four 14th possibly the most demanding, with a carry over water to a narrow fairway, and water again on the right. The green, apart from a narrow entrance, is almost completely ringed by bunkers.

It has been host to only one major event, the Walker Cup of 1922, the inaugural match between the amateur players of the US and of Great Britain and Ireland. It was held here at the invitation of the donor of the trophy, George Herbert Walker, a member of the 'National', and featured some famous players: Bobby Jones, Francis Ouimet and Jeff Sweetser, who helped the Americans to an eight to four victory against opponents who included Roger Wethered, Cyril Tolley and Bernard Darwin, who took over the captaincy through the illness of Robert Harris.

Nelson, Byron

1912–. Born Fort Worth, Texas, USA

Byron Nelson's name was established in golf history by his unequalled level of performance on the US Tour in the years 1944 to 1946. In 1944 he was money leader, won seven times and had a stroke average of 69.97.

Then, from 11 March to 4 August 1945 Nelson won every event he entered, 11 in all. By the end of the year he had 18 victories to his credit with a stroke average of 68.33. No one before had been below 71. Already a complete player, Nelson did not credit his success to any new secret.

Nelson went on winning in 1946 but there was a difference. Ben Hogan was back from the war and was winning even more often. Suddenly, Nelson had had enough of tournament golf. During the US PGA Championship, at the age of 34, he announced his retirement.

Nelson enjoyed the occasional return to the fields of glory. He won the Crosby in 1951 and the 1955 French Open, and competed in the Masters for many years. He played in two Ryder Cup teams, and captained the US team at Birkdale in 1965. He finished fifth to Henry Cotton in the Open at Carnoustie in 1937.

He won his first event in America in 1935 but really got going in 1937, when he had a famous Masters victory, and in 1939 won the US Open after a play-off with Densmore Shute and Craig Wood.

Byron Nelson

He won the US PGA in 1940 and 1945, and the remaining one of his five majors was the 1942 Masters, in which he beat Hogan in an 18-hole play-off.

On the US Tour, Nelson's 54 wins put him behind the victory totals of only Snead, Nicklaus, Hogan and Palmer.

Nelson, Larry

1947–. Born Fort Payne, Alabama, USA

Larry Nelson's is a remarkable story of a player who took up golf at the age of 21 and four years later in 1973 won his player's card for the US Tour after having previously played only one 72-hole event as a professional. It was 1979 before he broke through to win a tournament, but quickly followed with another win and that year won $280,000 to finish second in the money list. He was a tournament winner again in 1980 and 1981, and it was in 1981 that he claimed his first major victory championship success in the US PGA before a home crowd in Atlanta. With rounds of 70, 66, 66

Larry Nelson

and 71 he won comfortably by four strokes from Fuzzy Zoeller.

Nelson's second major title and the most satisfying came in the 1983 US Open at Oakmont. Opening rounds of 75 and 73 left him seven strokes behind the leaders, but a third round 65 brought him within a stroke of Ballesteros and Watson. It became a battle between Watson and Nelson in the final round until rain caused play to be abandoned for the day.

The next morning, Nelson's tee shot on the 226-yard 16th went far right, to the back of the two-tier green, 62 feet from the hole; with thoughts of possibly three-putting, Nelson hit a long curling putt which slowly inched its way across the green and dropped into the hole for a birdie two. It was the crucial stroke as he took the title with a round of 67 by a stroke from Watson, with Ballesteros fourth. Nelson's 10 under par 132 for the last 36 holes set a US Open record.

Nelson did not win again on the tour until the 1984 Walt Disney World Classic, but he won the 1983 Dunlop International in Japan, his second tournament victory in that country.

Nelson played in the Ryder Cup in 1979 and 1981, achieving the remarkable record of winning all his nine matches.

Neumann, Liselotte

1966–. Born Finspang, Sweden

Ten weeks after making her debut in 1985 as a professional at the age of 19, former Swedish amateur champion Liselotte Neumann became the youngest ever winner on the WPGA Tour. In front of her home crowd, she edged out Laura Davies to win the Hoganas Open at Molle and less than two weeks later won the IBM European Open at Kingswood to become the first tour player to win successive 72-hole events.

The talented newcomer had a

Liselotte Neumann

fine amateur record, winning the Swedish Championship in 1982 and 1983 and the country's match play title in 1984 before turning professional.

In 1986, after winning the German Open and four times finishing second and twice third in other events, she seemed set out to become the first non-Briton to head the WPGA order of merit with £37,000 in prize money, but in the last tournament of the season Laura Davies overtook her to go top by a mere £494.

Newton, Jack

1950–. Born Sydney, New South Wales, Australia

Jack Newton's golfing career ended tragically in 1983 when he walked towards an aeroplane in Australia and was struck by a propeller, severing an arm and causing internal injuries which almost cost him his life. Always a tough character, he survived and is still involved in the game in television and as a journalist.

Newton's greatest moment in the game came at Carnoustie in Scotland in 1975 when his big chance came to win the Open Champion-

ship. He was two strokes ahead with four holes to play, but dropped shots at the 15th, 16th and 17th and finished in a tie with Tom Watson, who was making his first appearance in Britain. In the play-off, the pair came to the last hole level and Watson's par on the 18th green gave him the title.

Nicklaus, Jack William

1940–. Born Columbus, Ohio, USA

The world's premier golfer of the modern era, Jack Nicklaus ranks among the greatest the game has known, among them Vardon, Jones, Hogan and Palmer. In terms of major championships won, Nicklaus stands supreme. Victory in the US Masters in 1986 at the age of 46 sealed his 20th major championship win; two US Amateurs in 1959 and 1961, four US Opens in 1962, 1967, 1972 and 1980, six US Masters in 1963, 1965, 1966, 1972, 1975 and 1986, three British Opens in 1966, 1970 and 1978, and five US PGA's in 1963, 1971, 1973, 1975 and 1980 are all to his credit. He is the only player to have won the four major championships twice.

Nicklaus has been leading money winner on the US Tour a record eight times, never lower than fourth until curtailing his tournament appearances in 1979.

Jack Nicklaus (left) in 1968, and (above) in 1986 at the Suntory World Match Play Championship. He is the world's premier golfer of the modern era.

On the tour, since starting in January 1962 — his first victory was the US Open — he had won 71 times until the end of 1986, and had an astonishing 58 second-place finishes. Into 1987, he was only a few thousand dollars short of $5-million in prize money won, nearly $1-million ahead of second-placed Tom Watson. While Palmer was first to win $1-million in 1968, Nicklaus was first to win $2-million in 1973, to win $3-million in 1977 and to win $4-million in 1983. He has been PGA Player of the Year five times.

Since the Tournament Players Championship started in 1974, Nicklaus won the event three times in the first five years, and the Mony Tournament of Champions five times. His other successes include being Australian Open champion six times, a member of six winning US World Cup teams, the winner of the 1970 World Match Play, the winner of World Series of Golf

four times, a member of six Ryder Cup teams, and the 1983 and 1987 Ryder Cup captain.

Among Nicklaus's most satisfying achievements have been to win the US Open for the fourth time in 1980, equalling the record of Willie Anderson, Bobby Jones and Ben Hogan; to capture his third British Open at St Andrews in 1978; and to win the Masters for the sixth time towards the end of his playing career, completing the last 10 holes of the Augusta National course in seven under par.

Before joining the US Tour, Nicklaus came close to winning the US Open in 1960 on only his second entry. He was just behind Arnold Palmer.

Nicklaus could have remained an amateur, but he wanted to test himself against the best players. In winning the 1962 US Open he shocked Arnold Palmer. They tied, played off for the title, and Nicklaus won with a round of 71 to Palmer's 74. At that time, Palmer was the darling of his army of supporters, while the Nicklaus of the 1960s was an unglamorous figure with crew-cut hair and bulging waist line. The crowd in that play-off tended to applaud his errors.

Nicklaus, however, was on his way and his sights were set on the majors. He wanted to be the greatest golfer ever. Like Jones before him, Nicklaus knew that only the majors count for history.

As soon as his second year, Nicklaus had won the three US majors. By the time of his first British Open in 1966, his total had risen to five. In 1967 he won his second US Open. Again Palmer suffered. Nicklaus went round Baltusrol in 65 to his 69 in the final round. They had begun level.

When he won in 1970 at St Andrews, Nicklaus captured his 10th major. He was still only 30 and Jones's record 13 was in sight. In 1972 he equalled the record when he won his third US Open, and he passed it the following year with the PGA Championship. By this time, Nicklaus cut a very different figure, with a modern hairstyle and a slimmed-down figure.

Rivals for his supremacy emerged, among them Miller, Weiskopf, Trevino, Player — but Tom Watson was a real threat and eventually did become the American and world Number One.

A lean spell for Nicklaus was broken at St Andrews in 1978, giving him his third British Open. In 1979 Nicklaus had a poor season in the USA, and, almost 40, he might have taken this as a hint to retire. Instead, he chose to take lessons on the short game, and with his former tour colleague, Phil Rodgers, he worked hard and long on his wedge play. It paid off with his success at Baltusrol in 1980. This was probably the last year Nicklaus still felt he had something left to prove. He continued to play well, but without winning, until capturing that 20th major by winning the 1986 Masters.

The qualities that have made Nicklaus such an amazing winner are mostly his dedication and application to the game, and a belief in himself and in his own ability. The secret is that when he is behind, he keeps trying. When in contention he says: 'I guess I fail a little less than the rest.'

In recent years, Nicklaus' many business interests have grown, and he has become involved in course design in America and overseas. He built his own course at a cost of $2-million near Dublin, Ohio — his home state — and because of his love for the Muirfield course in Scotland (he won the 1966 Open there) he gave his own course the name Muirfield Village. He inaugurated the Memorial Tournament there in 1976 and had the satisfaction of winning the event in 1977 and 1984. The course was the venue for the 1987 Ryder Cup, when Nicklaus captained the US team for the second time.

Nida, Norman von

1914–. Born Strathfield, Queensland, Australia

By the time World War II broke out, Norman von Nida had won a few titles in Australia and the Far East and set off to try his luck in the USA. He was then forced to return home by the war.

In 1946, with £17 in his pocket, von Nida sailed for Britain. Immediately he began winning money and ended the season second on the money list, with £1,330. The following year, he did a great deal better, having a sequence of three wins in four events and four in six. His seven titles and his £3,263 prize money was well above the previous record. He did almost as well the following year and won his last and 12th British event in 1951.

The title he most wanted had eluded him, however — the British Open, for which he started favourite on several occasions. He won the Australian Open three times and the country's PGA four times.

Noordwijk, The Netherlands

Built in the early 1970s by British architect Frank Pennink, who was twice English Amateur champion and a Walker Cup international, this seaside course has been a popular venue for the Dutch Open on several occasions since 1978, although the event that year was marred by a player's strike. On the first day, none of the European Tournament Players Division players competed because they objected to three young Americans in the field who they said were not eligible. A compromise was reached: the three Americans withdrew from the championship, although they still played and received prize money, and the event was decided over the final three rounds. Ironically, it was an American, the defending champion Bob Byman, who won.

Since then, Graham Marsh has won two Dutch Opens here, and in 1986 Ballesteros captured his third title, having previously won at Hilversum and Kennemer.

The club dates back to 1915, but the course suffered in the German occupation during World War II. A new site was obtained to the north; nine holes were completed in 1972, and the other nine followed soon afterwards. A tough duneland course, it presents a stern challenge with its links conditions. These were even more severe in the wind and rain of the 1986 Dutch Open.

Norman, Greg

1955–. Born Mount Isa, Queensland, Australia

Greg Norman established himself as the world's leading player in 1986, the year he broke through to win the British Open, his first major championship, as well as a million dollars in prize money. The year could so easily have seen him capture more than one major title, for in the three other champion-

Greg Norman: one of the longest hitters in golf.

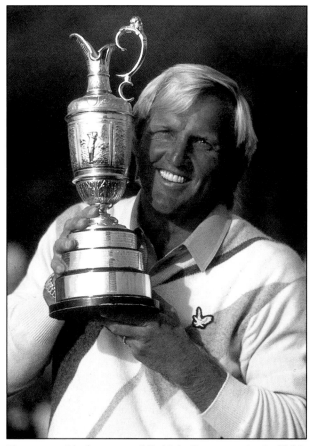

Norman with the coveted British Open trophy in 1986.

ships, the Masters, the US Open and the US PGA, he led going into the final rounds.

Two years earlier, he had tied for the US Open at Winged Foot, losing the play-off to Fuzzy Zoeller.

In June, Norman led by one after the third round of the US Open, but finished in 12th place. Then came the final blow at Inverness for the PGA Championship after Norman had convincingly won the British Open. Here his 65, 68 start gave him a four-stroke lead. He maintained it with a 69 in the third round and standing level on the final hole with Bob Tway, saw the American hole from a greenside bunker to take the title.

In the British Open at Turnberry, there was no real chance of his being pipped at the post. He equalled the Open record with 63 in his second round and had it won with several holes to play. His lead at the end was an impressive five strokes. Then came the European Open at Sunningdale in the autumn. He was in the 60s every round and won the play-off with Ken Brown on the first extra hole. In money terms, it meant £35,000 for winning, £50,000 for completing the 'double' with the Open Championship which earned him £70,000 as champion. In the Dunhill Cup at St Andrews, which Australia won for the second year, Norman received £69,000 as his share and passed the $1-million mark for the season, the first to achieve this. The following week he won the £50,000 first prize in the World Matchplay Championship at Wentworth, taking this title for the third time.

In America, he finished leading money winner for the first time with a record $653,296.

In Australia Norman won two tournaments to bring his total of victories in 1986 to 10 on three continents, to give him a career total of 45 world wide.

One of the longest hitters in golf, Norman has emerged as a great player, expert in every department of the game when he also learned to play the gentle shots.

His career goes back to 1976. In Australia, he won on only his fourth tournament appearance. He came to Europe for the first time in 1977 and a win in the Martini quickly established him. By the end of 1986, he had won 14 times in Britain and Europe and, with Ballesteros, the star attraction every time he played from 1980. He headed the money list in 1982, having been second in 1980. In Australia, he won the country's Open in 1980 and Australian Masters in 1981, 1983 and 1984.

North, Andy

1950–. Born Thorp, Wisconsin, USA

While Andy North has won two major championships, the 1978 and 1985 US Opens, yet he has won only one other event, the Westchester Classic in 1977.

In the first of his Opens, at Cherry Hills, North had a four-stroke lead with five to play, and only just made it. He needed a bogey to win and almost did not get it. He was bunkered in front of the green in three.

For the second victory Open at Oakland Hills in 1985 everyone faltered but North fulfilled the Nicklaus axiom that the champion is the man who fails the least. He played a fine bunker shot near the end and his 74 was good enough to win after Chen Tze-Chung had made a bid to become the first player from Taiwan to win an

Open. Leading by four strokes in the final round, Chen took eight shots at the fifth hole, being penalized for a double hit of the ball. He finished a stroke behind North.

In the Ryder Cup at the Belfry in 1985, North hit into the water on the final hole in his match with Sam Torrance and the Scot then holed the putt which gave the home team victory.

North Berwick,
East Lothian, Scotland

Although it dates back to 1832, the present course, the West links, was completed in 1895. There have been alterations and improvements since then. It is famous for two classic holes, the 14th — 'Perfection' — and 15th — 'Redan' — which have been copied in other parts of the world, notably America, though with some variations.

'Perfection', with a slight dog-leg to the right, calls for an accurate drive, followed by a blind approach shot over a ridge to a green with the sea behind. 'Redan' is a par three of 195 yards to a plateau green,

guarded by a huge, deep bunker and hidden from the tee by a high ridge. The first and 17th are both testing holes, with the greens on a hill sloping towards the sea.

Many Scottish events have been held here, among them the Boys Championship, Stroke Play and Ladies championships. It has been the venue for the Final Qualifying rounds of the Open Championship at nearby Muirfield, and the PGA Seniors Championship. A fine hotel flanks the course and there are wonderful views of the Forth estuary and the Bass Rock.

North Devon, Royal,
Westward Ho!, England

England's oldest links course, the Royal North Devon is steeped in tradition. In 1864, the Reverend I H Gossett of Northam founded the course at Westward Ho!, named after Charles Kingsley's novel. The club's most famous player was John Henry Taylor, one of the great triumvirate of Vardon, Braid and Taylor, who learned the game as a caddie and went on to win five Open Championships. In 1957 the club elected him president, and he lived in his native village until his death in 1966 aged 92.

Old Tom Morris designed the

Andy North who won the US Open Championship in 1985. He beat Chen Tze-Chung by one stroke.

North Berwick, East Lothian, Scotland: host to many Scottish events since 1895.

Royal North Devon, Westward Ho!, England: a view of Northam Burrows.

course, which was rebuilt in 1908 by Herbert Fowler. It has been little changed since then. The opening holes go out to Pebble Ridge, and the fourth, famous for its huge and intimidating 'Cape' bunker, leads to sandhill terrain. While the course is mainly flat, its greens are fast, and apart from bunkers, its hazards include sea rushes, so sharp and tough they can pierce a ball.

Drives at the 10th and at the 11th — considered the toughest hole — have to clear stretches of them. The 18th provides a testing finish, with a burn in front of the green awaiting the second shot. It has been the venue for Amateur and Ladies championships, but not in recent years because of its remoteness. It staged the Martini International in 1975. In its first Amateur Championship in 1912, John Ball won his eighth title when he beat Abe Mitchell at the 38th hole.

Northumberland, Tyneside, England

Golf had been played among the Freemen's cattle on the Town Moor for many years before a group of players formed this club in 1898 and laid out the course in and around a racecourse in an 18th-century deer park. The present course, re-designed by H S Colt in 1911 with further changes by himself and by James Braid contains many of the original features; the racecourse continues to affect play on at least eight holes.

The course is a fine test of golf; length and accuracy are important, especially in a westerly wind which makes for a tough finishing stretch. Only a short distance from the industrial heart of Newcastle-upon-Tyne at High Gosforth Park, it is parkland at its best, with established trees and small oak bushes interspersed with heather. A dog-leg short par four first hole is barely

reachable at 315 yards by even the long hitters, but in the Newcastle Brown 900 Open in 1980, Greg Norman who finished joint runner-up to Des Smyth, made his par in an unorthodox way. With his first ball unplayable, he drove the green and holed his putt. In that event, Tommy Horton equalled the course record with 65, one set by Tony Jacklin.

One of the most demanding holes is the shortish par four 12th, with its sloping green, heavily bunkered. The 18th is one of the most scenic across the racecourse. Many championships have been held here: the English Close in 1929, the Brabazon Trophy, the English Amateur, the British Ladies Open, won by American Debbie Massey in 1973, the English Ladies Stroke Play, and a number of professional tournaments, including the Daily Mail and Senior Service events. It will be the venue in 1991 for the Ladies' Commonwealth Tournament.

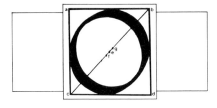

Oak Hill, New York, USA

Oak Hill takes its name from the hill on which the clubhouse stands overlooking the course and its oak trees. It was designed by the immigrant Scot Donald Ross in the early 1900s and it remains a tribute to his ability. It was changed in more recent times by Robert Trent Jones, who added length and bunkers to the lay-out. Its closing three holes provide one of the most testing finishes in championship golf: all are long par fours, and the 17th proved fatal for Ben Hogan in the 1956 US Open as he avoided intimidating bunkers but went through the green and lost to Cary Middlecoff.

One of the best holes is another long par four, the sixth, which has a creek running along the right and then cutting in front of the green. It also cuts across five other holes. Lee Trevino won his first US Open here in 1968 before coming to Britain for the first time to play in the Alcan Golfer of the Year event at Birkdale, where he was to win his first British Open three years later.

Oakland Hills, Michigan, USA

Ben Hogan called this course a 'monster' and with some justification, for in the 1951 US Open, Robert Trent Jones, then relatively unknown, at the bidding of the US PGA transformed the original Donald Ross lay-out of 1916 into the severest of tests. Bunkers lined the edges of fairways and surrounded greens; the fairways themselves were menacingly narrow, setting the most demanding driving test that many of the players had ever experienced.

On the first day Hogan dropped shots at five of the first nine holes and finished six over par on 76, but he improved each round with 73 and 71 to take a two-stroke lead. He then produced what has been described as the best single round played in a championship to return 67. Clayton Heafner, whose final 69 was the only other sub par round played, was second, two strokes away. Afterwards Hogan said, 'I am glad I brought this course, this monster, to its knees.'

Ten years later in 1961 with less demanding conditions, Gene Littler won the fourth US Open played here: the first two were staged in 1924 and 1937. Littler's total of 281 was six strokes better than Hogan. In 1972 in the US PGA Championship Gary Player produced a memorable shot under pressure at one of the course's most famous holes, the 16th, to make certain of his second title. After

Oakland Hills, Michigan, USA: Andy North won the US Open there in 1985. The course is demanding.

slicing his tee shot behind weeping willows on the dog-leg hole, he faced a blind shot of 150 yards over the trees and a lake bordering the green. He hit a towering shot with a nine-iron to within four feet of the hole for a birdie.

In 1979, Australian David Graham won a sudden death play-off against Ben Crenshaw to win the PGA and his first major title. The US Open returned here in 1985 when Andy North became the 15th player to win the title more than once: his first success was at Cherry Hills in 1978. Chen Tze-Chung made a bid to become the first player from Taiwan to win a US Open when he held a four-stroke lead after two holes of the final round. But he then dropped four strokes at the par four fifth hole, where he had a double hit in play-ing his ball from the rough. He finished runner-up, a stroke behind North.

Oakmont, Pennsylvania, USA

This course is regarded as one of the toughest in championship golf and some of the greatest players have triumphed over it. Among them are Tommy Armour, Bobby Jones, Ben Hogan, Jack Nicklaus and Johnny Miller — and all have testified to its qualities. This is a tribute to its designer, Henry C Fownes, in 1903, aided by his son William, a US Amateur champion and a president of the USGA.

Oakland Hills, Michigan, USA: the 17th hole of a course which is the severest of tests.

Although the course has been lengthened, its design has remained unchanged, and is noted for its almost unbelievably fast greens. Its fearsome Church Pews bunker, ready for a hooked drive at the third and fourth holes, gets its name from seven grassy ridges running across its 60 yards length. For its sixth US Open in 1983, the fairways were so narrow and the rough so intimidating, that direction was all important; Ballesteros resorted to 1-irons off the tees except at the par fives. Forty-one players shot rounds in the 80s on the first day, with George Burns running up a 10 at the 18th for 83 and quitting the tournament. Storms interrupted the event, and the final round was completed on the fifth day. The title went to Larry Nelson with a remarkable

run of 11 under par for the final 32 holes.

On the first hole of the morning, the 226 yards 16th, Nelson was 62 feet from the hole with his tee shot, but holed the curling putt to take the lead from Tom Watson. The US Amateur and PGA Championships have also been held here, and notable in the US Opens have been the victories of Ben Hogan in 1953, the year he won the Masters and the British Open, of Jack Nicklaus in 1962, who beat Arnold Palmer in a play-off, and of Johnny Miller in 1963, with a record last round 63, when a violent storm had taken some of the terror from the greens. Bobby Jones won the Amateur here in 1925, and Sam Snead the PGA in 1951.

O'Connor, Christy

1924–. Born Galway, County Galway, Ireland

With 24 wins in Britain and Europe from the mid-1950s to the early

Oakmont, Pennsylvania, USA: the third hole uphill and the fourth downhill.

1970s, Christy O'Connor was one of the outstanding European golfers of the post-war period, and one of Ireland's greatest.

His best days came in the 1960s when he was second in the money list seven times. Perhaps his finest achievements were the 1957 PGA Matchplay and two Dunlop Masters. One of the best players not to win the Open Championship, he came close in 1965, finishing second, and he was third in 1961. Perhaps his best chance was in 1958. He led the Open after two rounds and at the last hole bunkered his tee shot, taking five when a par four would have given him a tie. He finished third.

O'Connor made a record 10 consecutive Ryder Cup appearances in the years 1955–1973. He and Harry Bradshaw won the World Cup for Ireland in 1958, the only success by any of the four home

countries in that event.

O'Connor had a relaxed swing which he maintained when qualifying for Seniors golf at 50. He won the British PGA Seniors title a record six times in eight years from 1976 and the World title in 1976 and 1977.

Christy O'Connor

Mac O'Grady

O'Grady, Mac

1951–. Born Minneapolis,
Minnesota, USA

It took Mac O'Grady 17 attempts
to qualify for the US Tour, from
autumn 1971 to November 1982.
Although he was not an instant
success, he secured third place in a
tournament his first year and
finished third three times in 1985.
He also attracted much publicity
when he was in dispute with the US
Tour Commissioner, and fined.

After four years of trying, he
won his first tournament, the 1986
Greater Hartford Open, shooting a
brilliant final round 62 to tie Roger
Maltbie and won the play-off. His
second win came in the Mony
Tournament of Champions in 1987.
He played on the European Tour in
1982 before winning his US player's
card and finished 52nd in the money
list, his best performance being
third in the PGA championship at
Hillside.

O'Grady's playing style is highly
individualistic. He plays right-
handed and putts left.

Okamoto, Ayako

1951–. Born Hiroshima, Japan

One of Japan's top women players,
Ayako Okamoto joined the US
LPGA Tour in 1981 and had her
best season in 1984 when she won
three tournaments and captured
the Mazda-LPGA Series award of
$125,000. She was a runaway
winner in the 1984 British Ladies'
Open by 11 strokes from her
LPGA colleague Betsy King and
Britain's Dale Reid. Her 1985 US
campaign was limited to 18 events
due to a back injury: even so, she
had six top-10 finishes, as well as
being runner-up in one event.

Okamoto made a comeback in
1986 with two victories for her
second-best year on the tour,
finishing ninth in the money list
with $198,362; in 1984 she finished
third with $251,108. While playing
the Japanese tour in 1981 she set a
record for single-season winnings
of $130,000. Okamoto made a suc-
cessful start to the 1987 season,
winning three tournaments.

Olazabal, José-María

1966–. Born San Sebastian, Spain

José-María Olazabal came into

Ayako Okamoto

José-María Olazabal

professional golf late in 1985 with
one of the best amateur records of
recent times. In Britain, he has won
the Amateur Championship, the
Boys and the Youths — and while
still a junior, the Spanish and
Italian Amateur Championships.

He won the Tour School qualifying event and ran Ballesteros very
close in the Spanish PGA. He came

Olympic, California, USA: the eighth hole of a course planted with thousands of majestic trees.

to the European Tour with a steady, long game and a mastery of wedge and putter. He had a remarkable start to his European Tour career in 1986, winning the European Masters in Switzerland and then the Sanyo Open in his native Spain, again finishing ahead of Ballesteros. While Ballesteros finished as Epson Order of Merit leader, Olazabal finished second, his official winnings of £136,775 being three times what any other first-year Tour professional had earned.

Olgiata, Rome, Italy

Designed by the British architect C K Cotton, this course lies some 12 miles north of Rome. It was completed in 1961, and has two loops of nine holes, out and back to the clubhouse. In a spacious layout, it features several raised greens in its opening half, starting at the par four first and the short second. The ninth, a dog-leg left, is the

longest hole of 555 yards. Few holes offer completely straight fairways; many are bordered by trees, and most of the greens are well bunkered.

Olgiata was the venue for the World Amateur Team Championship, the Eisenhower Trophy, in 1964, when the British team of Michael Bonallack, Rodney Foster, Michael Lunt and Ronnie Shade triumphed after a late scare from Canada's Keith Alexander, who needed birdies over the last five holes to put the countries level — and after four in succession failed at the last.

In 1968 Canada's team of Al Balding and George Knudson won the World Cup (which formerly bore their country's name) from the United States team of Julius Boros and Lee Trevino, then US Open champion. Balding played

the decisive shot at the 17th, a slight dog-leg to the right, where his second shot on this par five found a bunker right of the green. He holed his shot for an eagle for a victory which also gave him the individual honours on 271, 17 under par.

In 1987, Olgiata was the venue for the European Final of the Dunhill Nations Cup, and provided the French team with their victory over the host country, Italy.

Olympic, California, USA

Thousands of majestic trees — as many as 40,000 eucalyptus, pine and cypress — which the club planted after buying the Lakeside site in 1922, are the outstanding feature of the Olympic. In the moist climate, and with fog often rolling in towards evening, the trees keep it playing long, with a string of par fours presenting a formidable test. Lying west of San Francisco, between the Pacific and Lake Merced, the Lake course is out of sight of the sea, in contrast to the Ocean lay-out on the seaward side. Its third hole, a long par three, gives a glimpse of the Golden Gate bridge from its high tee, stretching down to a small green protected by five bunkers — although bunkers are notable by their absence on all but one fairway. The fourth hole, a narrow dog-leg with trees encroaching, is just one of the demanding two-shot holes, many with uphill shots.

The Lake course has hosted two of the most dramatic US Opens in history, in 1955 and 1966, and was again the venue for the 1987 Open. In 1955, Ben Hogan, seemingly sure of his fifth title, having finished with a 287 total and clear of the field, was shocked by an unknown club professional from Iowa, Jack Fleck, who birdied two of the last four holes to tie, and although given no chance in the play-off next day, took the title with a round of 69 to Hogan's 72. At the 18th Hogan's foot slipped as he drove and the ball flew into deep rough on the left. He took three strokes to get the ball back on the fairway.

In 1966, 11 years after Hogan's defeat, it was the turn of Arnold Palmer, then at the height of his fame, to suffer a shock defeat. Seven strokes ahead of Billy Casper with nine holes to play, he dropped six strokes in seven holes, and lost the 17th with a five to a four to finish in a tie. In the play-off, Palmer was again ahead as he played his natural attacking game, but after having a two-stroke advantage with nine holes to play, again paid dearly for his boldness to finish with 73, as Casper's 69 earned him his second Open title. In 1987, Scott Simpson, a 31-year-old Californian, who had won only two tournaments in eight years in the US Tour, gained a shock Open win over Tom Watson. With some

remarkable putting over the last nine holes, he won by a stroke. The US Amateur has also been held here; Charles Coe won in 1958, and in 1981, Nathaniel Crosby, son of the famous Bing, took the title at the 37th hole.

O'Meara, Mark

1957–. Born Goldsboro, North Carolina, USA

After a good amateur career, during which he won the 1979 US title, Mark O'Meara made the transition to the US Tour with apparent ease: he was 55th in the money list and Rookie of the Year. For two seasons he then made no real progress but became a name player in 1984. He won for the first time and was second five times. He was eight times in the top three and 15 times a top 10 finisher — the best on the Tour that year. He won some $465,000, only a few thousand behind leading money winner Tom Watson.

In 1985 O'Meara won consecutive tournaments. Although his results in both 1985 and 1986 were

Mark O'Meara

Peter Oosterhuis

good, he failed to add to his three US Tour wins. However, he did win the 1985 Kapalua International, a Japanese event the same year and the 1986 Australian Masters. He played in the 1985 Ryder and Nissan Cup teams.

Oosterhuis, Peter

1948–. Born London, England

A major figure in European golf, Peter Oosterhuis moved on to the US Tour in 1976 after being order of merit leader on the PGA Tour for four consecutive years from 1971. In his last season in Europe in 1974 he won three tournaments and was runner-up at Lytham in the Open Championship, but has had little success in America. He won only one US Tour event: the 1981 Canadian Open. His best year came in 1981 when he was 28th in the money list and won $115,862. In 1985 he finished 130th and lost his card.

In his early days Oosterhuis was a magnificent scrambler, who always seemed able to get down in two from anywhere around the green. He was also a fine putter, but liable to push his drives.

When Oosterhuis went to the USA, he had achieved six wins in South Africa, 10 in Europe and three elsewhere. He had tied and lost a play-off for a US Tour event, finished second in the Open Championship and led the US Masters with a round to go. In six Ryder Cup matches, he achieved a record 14 wins, and was undefeated in singles until 1979. As well as being Open runner-up in 1974, he finished joint second to Tom Watson in the 1982 Open at Troon.

Open Championship

The Open Championship was by no means open to all when it began in 1860 at Prestwick in the west of Scotland. Few golfers of the day even knew about it and no amateurs took part. This, the first of golf's open championships was really a gathering of a handful of the best Scottish professionals to round off an autumn club meeting at Prestwick golf club. It took place as late in the golf year as 17 October over three rounds of the 12-hole course. It was won from a field of 12 by Willie Park of Musselburgh. Park returned 174, Tom Morris (Prestwick) 176, Andrew Strath (St Andrews) 180, Bob Andrew (Perth) 191, Daniel Brown (Blackheath) 192, Charlie Brown (Prestwick St Nicholas) 195, Alex Smith (Bruntsfield) 196, William Steel (Bruntsfield) 232.

The club's records of the event seem casual, but it was undeniably a true championship. The best golfer of the day, Allan Robertson, had recently died and Tom Morris and Willie Park were his closest rivals — Bob Andrew and Andrew Strath were also leading players and featured well in the championship for some years.

The following year amateurs entered, becoming the first true 'Open'. There was a Colonel J O Fairlie of Prestwick, who had helped out as a marker in 1860, and

J H Taylor, the first English professional to win the Open.

one other, Robert Chambers of Prestwick.

The early years were dominated by Willie Park and Tom Morris. Park won in 1860, 1863, 1866 and 1875; Morris in 1861, 1862, 1864 and 1867. Then came the first of the great golfers, a man so dominant in his own times that he may well have been the equal of the great champions who followed. This was Tom Morris junior, who won the Championship Belt presented by the Earl of Eglinton in 1868, 1869 and 1870. He was 17 at the time of his first victory and his third in a row won him the belt outright. The championship was in abeyance in

George Duncan, another Open champion, playing at Troon in 1923.

Bobby Jones winning the Open at St Andrews with a record score of 285.

1871 while money was collected by Prestwick, the R and A and Musselburgh for the silver claret jug which is still the trophy today. In 1872, Morris won again. His four consecutive wins have never been equalled and his scoring, always at Prestwick, was unparalleled.

With the participation of Musselburgh and St Andrews, the championship began to grow and there were 82 entrants by the time of the 1891 championship at St Andrews. In the meantime, two players, Jamie Anderson and Bob Ferguson, had distinguished themselves by each taking the title three years in a row: Anderson 1877–1879 and Ferguson 1880–1882. John Ball, of Royal Liverpool, was the first amateur winner in 1890.

In 1892 the championship was played over 72 holes for the first time. Ball's amateur colleague, Harold Hilton, won at Muirfield, a new course the competitors thought inferior. The year 1894 was even more momentous. The championship went to England for the first time and the first great player of a new age, J H Taylor, won at Sandwich, the first English professional to do so.

These victories signalled not so much the decline of Scotland as a golfing power but the rise of England and, in due course, other countries. Willie Auchterlonie, 1893 champion, was the last Scotsman resident in his homeland to win.

When Taylor won again easily in 1895 at St Andrews, a course he disliked, he seemed to have established himself as the greatest player of the day. His pre-eminence did not last. The following year he was beaten in a 36-hole play-off by a little-known Channel Islander, Harry Vardon, who went on to win in 1898 and 1899. Taylor returned with a comfortable victory in 1900. He beat Vardon by eight strokes to level the score at three apiece.

In 1901 the third member of what was soon to be known as 'the Great Triumvirate' arrived, the Scotsman James Braid, based in England throughout his playing career. This was the last championship won with a gutta percha ball. In 1902, Sandy Herd made a late decision to use Coburn Haskell's invention of a rubber core ball with wound thread — and beat Vardon and Braid into joint second place. The guttie was dead.

Braid was the dominant player over the following years and by 1910 he had become the first man to win five Open Championships. Arnaud Massy, a Basque Frenchman, became the first overseas winner in 1907. By 1909 Hoylake and Deal had been added to the championship venues. Taylor won his fifth Open at Hoylake in 1913 and the next year Vardon gained a record sixth Open, fittingly at the

Bobby Jones receiving the Open Championship trophy in 1927.

Gene Sarazen, Hoylake, 1924.

Jim Barnes wins the Open at Prestwick in 1925.

original venue, Prestwick. His six wins have still to be equalled.

Shortly after World War I, the R and A took over sole responsibility for organizing the championship. The day of the triumvirate, all born some 30 years before the turn of the century, was over. Their apparent successors were George Duncan and Abe Mitchell, born in 1883 and 1887 respectively. Mitchell was to be the greatest player never to win the Open. One of his best chances came in that first post-war Open at Deal. He began with rounds of 74 and 73 to a pair of 80s from Duncan. His lead evaporated in the third round as Duncan finished in 71; Mitchell, then starting his rounds, collapsed to 84 and Duncan went on to win with a 72 in the final round.

In 1921, the trophy went to the USA for the first time when it was won by Jock Hutchison, an expatriate Scot. A year later Walter Hagen won at Sandwich — the first American-born player to do so. He was to win three more titles during the 1920s. In the years 1921–1933, the title was won by Britain only once by Arthur Havers in 1923 at Troon.

Besides Hagen, Bobby Jones was the outstanding figure. As a mature golfer, he won every time he entered — 1926, 1927 and 1930 — an unequalled success rate. Other transatlantic champions were Jim Barnes, Tommy Armour, Gene Sarazen and Densmore Shute, who dominated the championship from 1922 to 1933.

It was Henry Cotton who ended

Lee Trevino at the Open Championship at St Andrews.

the American domination at Sandwich in 1934 when he became the first British winner since Havers in 1934. Three years later he won again at Carnoustie. The title stayed in British hands until World War II.

Sam Snead won the first post-war Open at St Andrews in 1946, but it was two Commonwealth players, Bobby Locke of South Africa and

Bob Charles at the 1969 Open Championship at Lytham St Annes.

A second Open title for Severiano Ballesteros in 1984

Peter Thomson of Australia, who made the most impact. Locke took four titles in the years 1949–1957 and Thomson, in 1956, became the first man this century to win three titles in a row, 1954–1956. He won his first Open at Birkdale in 1954 and captured his fifth title also at Birkdale in 1965.

During this period there was a lack of American interest; Snead did not bother to defend his title after his win in 1946.

Ben Hogan played for the first time in 1953 after winning the Masters and US Open that year. He was urged by Americans with a feeling for golf, including Hagen, that to win the British Open on a links course would crown his' career. He was persuaded to make the journey to Carnoustie four years after the car accident which nearly cost him his life, came two weeks early to get to know the course, won by four strokes and never returned.

Arnold Palmer restored American interest in the championship when he played for the first time in the Centenary Open at St Andrews in 1960, losing by a stroke to Kel Nagle of Australia: Palmer then won in 1961 and 1962. By then, Jack Nicklaus, already US Open Champion, was in the field.

From that time, American interest has consistently increased, with the R and A qualifications for entry to the championship designed to attract a top international field, more so than the other three major championships.

Five-times winner Tom Watson

Tony Lema, champion in 1964, and Nicklaus, became the men to watch. Lema was killed in an air crash in 1966; Nicklaus won in 1966, 1970 and 1978.

During the 1960s, Palmer, Thomson, Nagle, Bob Charles, Lema, Roberto de Vicenzo and Gary Player took the title overseas. Then the trend was ended with a thrilling win in 1969 by Tony Jacklin, only the fourth success by a British golfer since the war. Fred Daly, Henry Cotton and Max Faulkner were the others.

Lee Trevino won consecutive titles in 1971 and 1972, Tom Weis-kopf in 1973 and in 1974 Gary Player increased his total to three.

Since 1975 Tom Watson has been the dominant player. He won on his first appearance at Carnoustie in 1975. Two years later, having won his first Masters, he gained a thrilling win over Jack Nicklaus at Turnberry, setting a scoring record of 268. He won again in 1980, 1982 and 1983 to match the five victories in the modern era of Peter Thomson.

After Tony Jacklin's 1969 victory no home player looked likely to

Winner in 1969: Tony Jacklin

Sandy Lyle wins the 1985 Open

win except Jacklin himself who was third in 1971 and 1972. Then in 1979 at Lytham, Seve Ballesteros became the first European player since Arnaud Massy in 1907 to win the championship. In 1985 at Royal St George's, Sandy Lyle became the first Scottish winner since Tony Jacklin. In 1987, Nick Faldo claimed the title for England.

The story of the Open Championship has been one of almost continuous growth, though limited in the post-World War II period 1946 to 1960. Total prize money

A triumphant Nick Faldo in 1987

has risen from a few pounds in 1860, to £1,000 in 1946, £10,000 in 1965, £102,000 in 1977, £250,000 in 1982 and £650,000 in 1987. The eight entries in 1860 had risen past 100 for the first time in 1901, 300 in 1934, 600 in 1974 and totalled 1,407 in 1987. The highest entry was 1,413 at St Andrews in 1984.

As an attraction, the Open has grown just as dramatically. As late as 1896, when Vardon won his first Open, it is said only a handful followed his final round, but by 1925 unruly fans cost Macdonald Smith his victory at Prestwick. Crowd control has steadily improved and in 1987 even the traditional rush towards the final green after the final tee shot was checked. The biggest attendance at an Open was 193,126 at St Andrews in 1984, when gate money was £1,050,000.

Only links courses have ever been used for the championship, but the playing qualities have changed with automatic watering of greens and fairways in recent years.

A total of 14 courses have been used. Some have been removed from the rota, mainly through lack of required facilities. The present rota is St Andrews, Muirfield, Royal St George's, Royal Lytham, Royal Birkdale, Royal Troon and Turnberry. Carnoustie, last chosen in 1975, is a likely candidate for a return in the 1990s.

Otago, Dunedin, New Zealand

Golf was introduced to New Zealand in 1871 at Dunedin by a Scot, Charles Ritchie Howden, from Edinburgh, who became the first captain. The club went out of existence until 1892 when it was formed as the Otago club, moving to its present site three years later and retaining links with the original club.

Its undulating course at Balma-

cewen has been altered over the years to give it greater length and championship quality, with testing holes. Among them is the 11th with its high tee shot down to a fairway lined by gorse and trees, and the final hole which calls for an accurate approach to an elevated green.

Otago has been the venue for a number of New Zealand Open championships. Its winners include Bobby Locke in 1938 and Peter Thomson in 1953 for the third of his nine titles, the Australian claiming the New Zealand Professional title here the same year.

Ouimet, Francis

1893–1967. Born Brookline, Massachusetts, USA

America's first native-born golfing hero, amateur Francis Ouimet surprised everyone by defeating Harry Vardon and Ted Ray for the 1913 US Open at The Country Club, Brookline. First he caught them by finishing two under for the last six holes, having taken 43 to the turn followed by a five on the par-three 10th; then he confronted them the next day in an 18-hole play-off. No-one gave 20-year-old Ouimet a chance. But he held them over the first nine, took the lead on the 10th and held it the rest of the way. The outcome was settled when Ouimet had a birdie three on the 17th to Vardon's five. The final scores were Ouimet 72, Vardon 77, Ray 78.

Although that was far and away Ouimet's greatest achievement in golf, he took the US and French Amateurs the following year. In 1920, he was a US Amateur finalist and was joint third in the 1925 US Open. When Bobby Jones retired, Ouimet won the US Amateur for the second time in 1931. He was a member of every US Walker Cup team from 1922 to 1934, and was non-playing captain in 1936, 1938, 1947 and 1949. In 1951 he became the first non-Briton to be elected captain of the R and A.

Palmer, Arnold

1929–. Born Latrobe,
Pennsylvania, USA

Arnold Palmer has been the most exciting player the game of golf has known. With a charisma few players have ever approached, and a bold, dashing style, he has commanded the devotion of fans world wide. Wherever Palmer played the fans rolled up. So enthusiastic did they become that they formed themselves into spectator battalions and were given the title at the US Masters of 'Arnie's Army'.

Palmer's thrilling golf and tremendous personality was a major factor in the growth of the game in the United States. His appearance in Britain in 1960 for the Open Championship at St Andrews soon brought all the top American players following his lead, and resulted in the growth of the championship after a decline.

Since the days of Hagen and Jones, Americans had not bothered to come to Britain. It was the same in 1961 but US entries increased every year afterwards until, by the mid-to-late-1960s, the best Americans knew it was a championship they needed to win. For that, the main credit must go to Palmer.

In 1961, in generally foul and sometimes extreme weather, Palmer won at Royal Birkdale. The following year, at Troon, he gave one of the most dazzling performances of his career. He won by six strokes in a new championship record of 276.

Palmer was expected to win many more Opens, but strangely he never really featured again; yet this is paralleled by what happened to him in the US major championships. His first was the 1954 US Amateur. He turned professional shortly afterwards. In 1957 he won four events but his real arrival was the winning of the 1958 Masters, and 1960 was his greatest year. He won eight American events, the most since Sam Snead's 10 in 1950 and only equalled since by Johnny Miller in 1974.

Probably more important than the number of victories, however, was the fact that two of the wins were the Masters and the US Open. The Masters did something to create the Palmer legend of his being the man who could produce the great shots when he needed to. Although he had led throughout he came to the last holes needing a birdie at one of them to tie Ken Venturi. Instead, he birdied both. The US Open at Cherry Hills made him a legend. Palmer went into the last round seven strokes behind, and, stung when he was told he had no chance, told a journalist that a 65 could win — and that was indeed his score.

The Masters proved to be Palmer's best event. He won again in 1962 and 1964, bringing his total to four. In 1962 he won after an 18-hole play-off. In 1964 his performance was of the calibre of Troon. He had the same margin of victory, six strokes, and the same score, 276.

Although only 35 at the time, Palmer was to win no more major championships. He threatened at times, and in the 1966 US Open at the Olympic Club, he dropped seven strokes to Billy Casper over

Arnold Palmer (inset), and at the Bob Hope Desert Classic in 1982. A thrilling golfer and personality, Palmer has been the most exciting player the game of golf has known.

the last nine holes of the final round to end in a tie and lost the play-off next day.

Palmer's achievements, of which his eight major championships were just a part, have been of immense value to golf. Snead and Hogan, the great stars who immediately preceded him, had been admired for their brilliance. Palmer was loved. His determination, joy or disbelief that a putt could miss were all allowed to show through.

Palmer always played the game with great boldness. He went for the long drive, not the safe iron; the flag, not the widest part of the green. His putting was probably the boldest aspect of his game. In tournament play, in spite of his failure in the majors after 1964, Palmer was a winner up to 1973 when he took his total to 61, the fourth highest total in Tour history. He also won 19 overseas titles, including in Britain the PGA Championship over a windswept Royal St George's. He played in six Ryder Cup matches between 1961 and 1973 and captained the US team in 1963.

Palmer was US leading money winner in 1958, 1960, 1962 and 1963. From 1957 to 1971 he was never out of the top 10, and for 11 of those years he was never worse than fifth. In recent years he has competed on the Senior Tour where he has won nine events. He was the first player on the US Tour to win $1-million in prize money in 1968.

In Britain Palmer won the first World Match Play Championship at Wentworth in 1964 and he won the event for the second time in 1967. In 1965 he also won the PGA Championship in a gale at Royal St George's. His affection for the British Open has never diminished; he competed at Muirfield in 1987 and the following week played in the inaugural Seniors British Open at Turnberry.

Palmer, Sandra

1941–. Born Fort Worth, Texas, USA

Having played the LPGA Tour for over 20 years, Sandra Palmer was still good enough to win the 1986 in her mid-40s. She joined the Tour in 1964 and enjoyed a remarkable 10-year spell in 1968–1977, when she was never worse than ninth in the money list. Her first win came in 1971 and most of her 21 wins came in the seven years up to 1977. She has also won three 1980s events. In her best year, 1975, she was leading money winner and won the US Open. Her victory in the Mayflower Classic in 1986 made her the LPGA's 13th millionaire in prize money won.

Panton, Cathy

1955–. Born Bridge of Allan, Stirlingshire, Scotland

Daughter of John Panton, one of Scotland's best known professionals, Cathy Panton was a Scottish international as an amateur and British champion in 1976. She turned professional in 1978 and

Cathy Panton

became a member of the WPGA Tour on its formation in 1979, won two tournaments and ended the year as leading money winner with £2,495, a small sum compared with the subsequent growth of the tour. In 1986 Laura Davies, leading player for the second year, won £37,500.

Panton qualified to play the LPGA Tour in America and competed for two seasons in 1983–1984. Back in Europe, she won again on the WPGA Tour in 1987, to bring her total of WPGA victories to 13.

Panton, John

1916–. Born Pitlochry, Perthshire, Scotland

One of Scotland's outstanding professionals, John Panton, along with Eric Brown, dominated tournament golf in their country for nearly 20 years. Panton won the Scottish Professional title eight times, the Northern Open seven times and a string of other Scottish events.

In European golf, he won nine events, including the British PGA Match Play in 1956. He was a Ryder Cup player in 1951, 1953 and 1961, and a World Cup player for Scotland in four consecutive years from 1957.

After reaching the age of 50, he won the PGA Seniors Championship in 1967 and 1969, and beat Sam Snead three and two in the World Seniors final at Wallasey in 1967.

Park, Willie

1834–1903. Born Musselburgh, East Lothian, Scotland

With Old Tom Morris, Willie Park was the best golfer of his generation. In 1860, he won the first Open Championship at Prestwick and had three more wins, the last in 1875. He was also second four times.

Even more important then were the challenge matches for high stakes. Park had several famous encounters with Old Tom and for 20 years kept a standing offer open to play any man for £100. He was renowned for his putting.

Park, Willie, Junior

1864–1925. Born Musselburgh, East Lothian, Scotland

An even better putter than his father, Willie Park Junior coined the phrase: 'A man who can putt is a match for any man.' No one doubted he was the best putter of his time but an almost equally poor driver, hitting a low hooky ball that frequently found trouble. A putting lapse when he missed from about a yard cost him the 1898 Open, won by Harry Vardon.

Park had won the 1887 and 1889 championships and became active on the commercial side of golf. His clubs were particularly successful, especially his 'bulger' driver (a club with convex face) and his patented wry-necked putter, even today a serviceable implement.

In the long run Park's work as a golf course architect was far more influential. He designed two of the first good inland courses in the British Isles, Huntercombe and Sunningdale Old, as well as a host of other courses, often working inland rather than on the traditional linksland. In the mid-1890s, he became active in the USA and Canada and lived there for most of his final years. Golfing folklore has it that he overworked himself and returned to Scotland to die.

Pate, Jerry

1953–. Born Macon, Georgia, USA

When still a few months short of his 23rd birthday, Jerry Pate had done just about everything that could be expected of a young

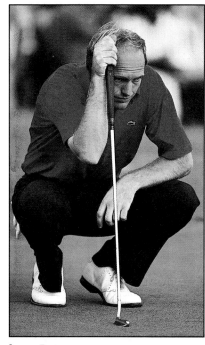

Jerry Pate

golfer. He had won the 1974 US Amateur. He followed this in his first year as a professional with the 1976 US Open, and then the Canadian title. His winning shot in the Open at the Atlanta Athletic Club was one of the most dramatic to win a major championship. Pate hit a five-iron 190 yards from the rough over a lake to within two feet of the flag. He won the Canadian Open with a last round 63.

In 1976 Pate competed in the British Open at Birkdale, but in the third round, he had an 87, which included an eight and three sevens on the second nine. He was not alone, for defending champion Tom Watson was in the 80s and both went out of the championship.

Pate continued to be a great success on the US Tour. By the end of 1982, he had increased his total of US Tour wins to eight, and also had a couple of wins overseas.

He was the youngest man on the US Tour to win a million dollars.

Then Pate tore a cartilage in his left shoulder, and after operations

in 1985 and 1986 has missed many tournaments.

In his amateur days he was in the US Walker Cup team in 1975. The previous year, he was individual winner in the Eisenhower Trophy, won by America. He played in the 1981 Ryder Cup match at Walton Heath.

Pavin, Corey

1959–. Born Oxnard, California, USA

Corey Pavin had a successful amateur career. He won the outstanding college player for 1982 award, the 1977 World Junior title and the North and South and Southwest Amateurs in 1981, the year in which he made the Walker Cup team. Pavin played overseas in 1983 as a professional, winning the South African Open and two European events.

When Pavin joined the US Tour in 1984 he challenged in his second event and won during his first season, setting a money-winning

Corey Pavin

Pebble Beach, California, USA: the 18th hole of one of the most spectacular courses in the world.

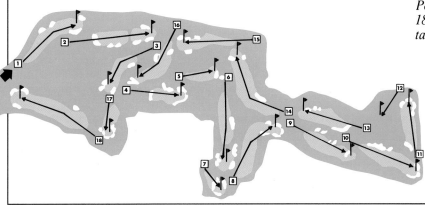

Card for the course		
Hole	**Distance**	**Par**
1	385 yards	4
2	507 yards	5
3	368 yards	4
4	325 yards	4
5	180 yards	3
6	515 yards	5
7	120 yards	3
8	425 yards	4
9	450 yards	4
OUT	**3275 yards**	**36**
10	436 yards	4
11	380 yards	4
12	205 yards	3
13	400 yards	4
14	555 yards	5
15	406 yards	4
16	400 yards	4
17	218 yards	3
18	540 yards	5
IN	**3540 yards**	**36**

record for a first-year player of $260,000. In 1985, Pavin had the most top 10 finishes on the tour and won the Colonial National Invitational with a record score of 266 with rounds of 66, 64, 68 and 68. He was sixth on the money list, his best season's performance, winning $367,500. In 1986 he won the Hawaiian Open and Greater Milwaukee Open, and early in 1987 retained the Hawaiian Open title, after winning the Bob Hope Classic.

Pebble Beach, California, USA

One of the most spectacular courses in the world, built in 1918 on the Monterey Peninsula, Pebble Beach is a tribute to the design of

two Californian Amateur champions, Jack Neville and Douglas Grant, who created a superb layout, with eight of its holes lying along the rocky shore of Carmel Bay. They start at the fourth, with the fairway along 50 feet high cliffs, and then from the sixth to the tenth, with the short seventh down to a tiny green bordered on three sides by foaming sea and well bunkered. The par four eighth is even more spectacular. The next two are equally intimidating, both long par fours along the edge of the cliffs, calling for accurate shots with the ground sloping towards the beach. The 18th is one of golf's great finishing holes: a par five curving left, with the beach always menacing below.

It was at the 17th, a long par three, with the green close to the rocky shore, that Tom Watson played a memorable shot in the 1982 US Open to give him the one title he had waited so long to claim. Needing pars at the last two holes to tie Jack Nicklaus, who had

Pebble Beach, California, USA: the short seventh leads down to a tiny green bordered on three sides by the rocky shore of Carmel Bay.

already finished, Watson's tee shot at the 17th finished in thick grass between two bunkers, and about 18 feet from the hole. 'Get it close,' said his caddie, but Watson replied 'I'm going to make it.' He plopped the ball on to the green with a sand wedge, saw it hit the flagstick and drop for a birdie two.

Playing the 18th conservatively, he left his third shot 20 feet past the pin, lagged the ball to the hole, and had the bonus of another birdie as it took a last roll into the hole. It deprived Nicklaus of his second US Open title at Pebble Beach, for he had won here in 1972, 11 years after he had won the US Amateur, the only player to win both championships over the same course.

In the 1929 US Amateur, the first championship to be played here, Bobby Jones lost in the first round, the only occasion he failed

to reach the final over a span of seven years, and the championship returned in 1947. In 1936 Bing Crosby inaugurated his National Pro-Am here, with rounds later having to be spread round adjoining Cypress Point and Spyglass Hill courses, and Nicklaus won the event three times. In 1977, Lanny Wadkins beat Gene Littler in a play-off in the US PGA Championship.

Peete, Calvin

1943–. Born Detroit, Michigan, USA

Peete did not join the US Tour until 1976 when he was nearly 33. He had little success until he won a tournament in 1979. He then faded into the background again until 1982, when he won four times and was fourth in the money list. He held this position the following year, has continued to win an event or two each year and was third in the money list in 1985 with $384,489.

Peete's greatest achievement came in 1985 when after first winning the Phoenix Open, he added the Tournament Players Championship, giving him 10-year exemption on the tour. He followed this in 1986 by winning the Mony Tournament of Champions and the USF & G Classic. He is noted for his accurate driving and approach shots to the green. Peete has played in two Ryder Cup matches.

Peete comes from a family of 19 and did not try his hand at golf until the age of 23. He has succeeded in spite of not being able to straighten his left arm, the result of falling out of a tree as a child.

Penina, Algarve, Portugal

The first course built on the Algarve in 1966, Penina was designed by Henry Cotton and with tees 100 yards long it can be stretched to nearly 7,000 yards. Although flat, as it is laid out on a rice paddy field, as many as 360,000 trees and shrubs were planted to lend character to its testing lay-out. It calls for accurate shots over water hazards and around doglegs, and it has large, true greens to

Calvin Peete

Penina, Algarve, Portugal

hold approach shots.

Penina has been the venue for the Portuguese Open on several occasions, with Howard Clark and Sam Torrance among the winners. Hal Underwood was the first American to take the title in 1975. The European Amateur Team Championships were held here, with victories for the England ladies in 1967 and the men in 1973. Penina and its hotel were home for many years for Henry Cotton, but with new owners and changes made to the course, he has moved away from the area.

Pennink, Frank

1913–1983. Born Delft,
The Netherlands

English Amateur champion in 1937 and 1938, Frank Pennink was one of the few who could claim to have played in a winning Walker Cup team, that of 1938, a year when he also won the Royal St George's Challenge Cup.

Later Pennink became an influential committee member of the R and A and joined a golf architecture firm in the mid-1950s. Afterwards, he carried out remodelling work on such Open Championship courses as Royal St George's, Hoylake, and Royal Lytham.

He has produced many new courses: among the best known in

Britain are Saunton, Frilford Heath and Ross-on-Wye. Equally active overseas, he had the distinction of having designed two of Libya's three courses and even nine holes in Warsaw! He has worked in Europe, Africa and the Far East, and some of his best work has been done in Portugal. He was president of the English Golf Union in 1967.

Picard, Henry

1907–. Born Plymouth,
Massachusetts, USA

In 20 years of a playing career from 1925, Picard was outstanding, especially in the 1930s, and was noted for his fine swing. Winner of 27 events on the US Tour, Picard was leading money winner in 1939, and won six times. He took two major championships, the 1938 Masters and the 1939 US PGA, when he beat Byron Nelson in the final. He played in the 1935 and 1937 Ryder Cup matches. He was sixth in the British Open in 1935 and fifth in the US Open in 1936.

Pinehurst, North Carolina, USA

This famous resort can boast five courses, but it is the No. 2 that has gained world-wide fame. A Boston pharmacist, James W Tufts, chose this area of sandhills to establish a

Pinehurst, North Carolina, USA: the internationally famous No.2 course built by Donald Ross.

winter retreat from the bitter weather of New England. A nine-hole course soon appeared, but in 1900 it was the arrival of Donald Ross, from Dornoch, as professional, that shaped its future. By 1907 Ross had built the course he called his masterpiece. He continued to make improvements: in the mid-1930s he extended it to 7000 yards and skilfully blended mounds and slopes around the greens.

Each hole is virtually enclosed by the tall pines and only at the 16th is water encountered. It starts with a big two-shot hole, then an even bigger par four with a plateau green, and another at the par three third, with the fourth and fifth on a hilly part of the course. The ninth is a fine par three on top of a ridge, and the tenth is typical of Ross's skill, with again an elevated contoured green.

In a testing finish, the par three 17th, enclosed by trees, has a green sloping away to bunkers around it, at the 18th, after a drive uphill, the approach is again to a plateau green. Densmore Shute won the US PGA Championship here in 1936. In the Ryder Cup match in 1951, Ben Hogan and Sam Snead both won their two matches as the United States beat Great Britain nine matches to two. The No. 2 course has also been the venue for the US Amateur in 1962, the first World Open in 1973 and the Colgate Hall of Fame Classic in 1977. In 1974 President Gerald Ford opened the World Golf Hall of Fame here, commemorating the names of famous players.

Pinero, Manuel

1952–. Born Puebla de la Calzada, Badajoz, Spain

A former caddie, Pinero has played the European Tour since 1971 and first won in 1974. He now has nine wins to his credit, among them three wins in the Madrid Open in 1974, 1981 and 1985. Perhaps his best performances came in winning the 1977 PGA Championship and the 1982 European Open with a brilliant final round of 63, having a run of birdie, eagle, par, birdie from the 13th.

Pinero was fourth in the money list in 1976 and 1977 and fifth in 1981 and 1982. In 1976 Pinero and Ballesteros won the World Cup at Palm Springs for a first win by Spain in the event. In 1982 he and José-María Canizares won the event again in Acapulco. In 1985 he played a vital role in the Ryder Cup at The Belfry: with Ballesteros they won three foursomes and fourballs and in the singles he beat Lanny Wadkins three and one, as Great Britain and Ireland beat the USA for the first time in 28 years.

Pine Valley, New Jersey, USA

Although regarded as the toughest inland course in the world, Pine Valley has never been host to any major championships or tournaments because of lack of space for spectators. Its most notable events were the Walker Cup matches in

Pine Valley, New Jersey, USA: the 15th hole. The course has a reputation for severity but fairness: it rewards the well-placed shot.

Manuel Pinero

1936 and 1985. Victory went to the United States on both occasions: on the first, the Great Britain team was overwhelmed by nine matches to nil, but on the second, only the final singles series decided the result by the narrow margin of 13-11.

Great players, who have played the course, among them Arnold Palmer, testify to its severity but also its fairness. It dates from 1912 when George Crump, a hotelier from Philadelphia, laid it out to his own design in the pine-covered sandhills at Clementon, with later help from H S Colt of Sunningdale fame. When Crump died in 1918 with four holes still not completed, it was finished by Hugh Wilson, of Merion fame, and his brother Alan. With vast sandy stretches, thick forest, never more than two consecutive holes in the same direction and carries over water at four holes, it is a penal course, but there are always rewards for well-placed shots.

The par three third hole has sand all the way from tee to green, while the par five seventh is dominated by 'Hell's Half Acre', a virtual desert of sand and scrub to be cleared by the second shot, with the green ahead an island surrounded by sand. The tenth is one of four superb short holes, with a small green full of slopes, and a steep bunker in front, from which it is only possible to play out backwards.

Byron Nelson and Gene Littler played a match here in the early 1960s. Arnold Palmer came here after winning the US Amateur in 1954 to play with members, and his round of 68 earned him $800 in bets — a welcome windfall as he was about to be married. The favourite Pine Valley story is of a local amateur, Woody Platt, who started birdie three, eagle two, hole in one and birdie four — six under par — after which his party decided it called for a drink. They went into the clubhouse, never to reappear.

Player, Gary

1935–. Born Johannesburg, South Africa

One of the 'Big Three' of world golf in the 1960s — the others are Palmer and Nicklaus — South African Gary Player takes his place among the all-time greats of the game. His international record of successes around the world of more than 130 championship and tournament victories is unsurpassed. In the last three decades, he has played top-level golf in countries far and wide, and, although maintaining his home in Johannesburg, he has done what no one has achieved — he has won 21 events in the United States without being

Gary Player, one of the world's smallest, fittest, and greatest golfers, playing at Sun City in 1982.

permanently based there. He was one of the first players to be inducted into the World Golf Hall of Fame in Pinehurst.

With his small stature — Player is 5 feet 7 inches tall and weighs just over 10 stone — he set out to compete with more powerful golfers by sheer dedication to the game and to physical fitness. His record proves how well he has succeeded.

Player won nine major championships — three Masters in 1961, 1974 and 1978, three British Opens in 1959, 1968 and 1974, two PGAs in 1962 and 1972 and one US Open in 1965. Only Nicklaus, Jones and Hagen have won more. Player has won the South African Open 13 times since 1956, the Australian Open seven times, the World Match Play five times and the World Cup individual title in 1965

and 1977. In winning the 1974 Brazilian Open, he scored 59, the first time 60 had been broken in a national championship. He was the first overseas player for 45 years to win the US Open, and the third man in history to win all four major championships. He was leading US money winner in 1961.

In the 1984 US PGA Player had a tournament record of nine under par 63 in the second round at Shoal Creek, and finished joint runner-up with Lanny Wadkins to Trevino. He was the oldest player in 1978 at the age of 42 to win the US Masters before Nicklaus took the title in 1986 aged 46.

On reaching 50, Player joined the US Seniors Tour in 1986, winning the first tournament in which he played. In 1987, he won the Seniors Tournament Players Championship and followed the same month by winning the Seniors Open. In Britain he competed in the first Seniors British Open at Turnberry after appearing in the Open at Muirfield.

Player won his first tournament in Britain in 1956. He first played in the USA in 1957 and was a winner the following year. He finished second in the US Open, and took the British Open at Muirfield in 1959. Two years later, he won the Masters, then the US PGA in 1962. He completed the Grand Slam of each of the four professional titles in 1965, winning the US Open after a play-off with Kel Nagle. Player's swing was never rhythmic and his short game was probably the key.

Pohl, Dan

1955–. Born Mt Pleasant, Michigan, USA

One of the longest drivers in the US Tour, Dan Pohl's power game cost him an early victory in his professional career. His approach shots finished through the green at the last three holes of the Western Open in 1979 and he finished third.

Dan Pohl

In 1982 he had the chance to win the Masters when Craig Stadler bogeyed the final hole and finished in a tie with Pohl. Stadler won the play-off at the first extra hole.

Pohl finished third in the 1981 US PGA and third in the 1982 US Open. He broke through for his first tournament win in the 1986 Colonial and went on to win the World Series, finishing fifth in the money list, with $463,630.

Porthcawl, Royal,
Mid Glamorgan, Wales

This championship course, one of the few where the sea is visible from every hole, is basically a links layout, but inland holes rise to a plateau and feature bracken, heather and thick gorse. It is the premier course of Wales, founded in 1891 with nine holes, extended to 18 in 1895, and then rebuilt three years later, with the original nine discarded.

Laid out in a triangle, the first three holes run along the shore, then turn inland at a fine short hole and climb uphill to the fifth green on the plateau. The ninth hole, a

shortish par four, calls for a drive over a big dip, and then an approach to a well-bunkered green. The 13th, back towards the sea, can be a real test with its exposed fairway swept by winds, while the 18th gives a superb finish, downhill to the sea.

Porthcawl was given its Royal title in 1909 and has been the venue for countless Welsh championships. It staged its first British Ladies Championship in 1934. It was again the venue in 1953 and 1974, and it has hosted the British Amateur on four occasions, with victories for Michael Bonallack in 1965 and Welshman Duncan Evans in 1980.

The Curtis Cup was played here in 1964 and professional tournaments have included the Dunlop Masters and Coral Classic, with victories in the former for Peter Thomson in 1961 and in the latter for Sandy Lyle in 1980.

Portmarnock, County
Dublin, Eire

One of the greatest of links courses — certainly the Irish would claim the greatest and there are many who support that view — Portmarnock has all the qualities of a true seaside course: crisp turf, no unfair carries from the tees and perfect greens. It owes its existence to two enthusiasts, J W Pickeman and George Ross, who rowed from Sutton across the estuary to a peninsula of duneland, bracken and natural bunkers in 1893 and at once set up a club.

In the early days, players reached the course by boat or horse-drawn cart at low tide. The first four holes go out along the estuary and sea, and the sixth, a new hole which followed the building of a nine-hole lay-out, is a monster. Stretched to 600 yards in tournaments, calling for two wood shots, with water on the left for the second and a pitch to a high green with bunkers left

Portmarnock, County Dublin, Eire: one of the greatest of links courses with crisp turf and perfect greens, set up in 1893 by Pickeman and Ross.

and right, not even Ballesteros has been tempted to reach it in two.

The ninth comes back to the clubhouse, and an outstanding hole is the 14th, a par four, with the scenic Ireland's Eye as the line, and a fairway curving to the left and bunkers to the front and right of a sloping green. It cost Henry Cotton seven strokes here in the Irish Open in 1927, the year that George Duncan in a gale had a superb 74, the only player to break 80 and to take the title.

The British Amateur has been held only once in Eire when in 1949 the powerful Max McCready of Northern Ireland, one down with four to play, won the next three to beat American Willie Turnesa. In the 1959 Dunlop Masters, which developed into a battle between two of Ireland's greats, Christy O'-Connor birdied the toughest par four, the 17th, in each of the final two rounds to take the title from Joe Carr with a last round 66.

In 1960 Arnold Palmer and Sam

Snead won the World (then Canada) Cup for the United States by eight strokes. The Dublin firm of P J Carroll revived the Irish Open in 1975 after a lapse of a few years, and among its winners at Portmarnock have been Americans Ben Crenshaw and Hubert Green, Irishman John O'Leary, Mark James on two occasions, Severiano Ballesteros and Bernhard Langer, who in 1987 gained an outstanding victory by 10 strokes over Sandy Lyle, finishing on 269, 19 under par.

Portrush, Royal, County Antrim, Northern Ireland

This great seaside course has been the venue for the only British Open Championship to be held in Ireland. Appropriately, it provided a

popular British champion in Max Faulkner in 1951. The Amateur Championship was also held here in 1960, with an equally memorable victory for Ireland's Joe Carr.

Founded in 1888, on a beautiful stretch of the Antrim coast in wonderful dune country, it has seen many changes. The present challenging lay-out is the work of H S Colt. It received its Royal title in 1893, and in 1895 it staged the first professional event in Ireland. The same year it hosted the first British Ladies Championship outside the mainland, with the event returning on six further occasions; its winners included Joyce Wethered, Pam Barton, Jessie Valentine and Catherine Lacoste.

Three years earlier, the Irish Open Amateur had been inaugurated here. With most of the holes curving or dog-legged, it is a tight driving course, with mounds and hollows more than bunkers providing the hazards round the greens. Its fifth hole is spectacular, a fine dog-leg downhill to a green on the edge of the Atlantic, while the par three 14th, the notorious 'Calamity Corner', is daunting, with nothing but rough between tee and green. It has been home to many famous players, notably the Hezlet family, Charles and his sisters, May and Florence, Rhona Adair, twice British champion and Irish champion four times in a row, and a young caddie, Fred Daly, who became the only Irishman to win the Open.

Prairie Dunes, Kansas, USA

Golfing history was made here in the 1986 Curtis Cup match when the visiting Great Britain and Ireland Ladies became the first team from Europe to win on American soil, a triumph which had eluded men's teams in both Walker Cup and Ryder Cup matches. Led by captain Diane Bailey, herself a former Curtis Cup player, the

team, a blend of youth and experience, beat the United States for the first time since 1956. The 13 matches to five victory marked the last international appearance at the age of 50 of the great Scottish player Belle Robertson on her retirement from competitive golf; she and Mary McKenna, of Ireland, making her record ninth consecutive match appearance, formed a successful foursomes partnership.

The Prairie Dunes course near Hutchinson, with its narrow fairways, unyielding rough, rolling sand dunes and natural beauty was designed by Perry Maxwell, who was also responsible for Southern Hills, Tulsa, and Colonial, Fort Worth. It was opened with nine holes in 1937, and completed by

Royal Portrush, County Antrim, Northern Ireland: a great seaside course founded in 1888. It has been the venue for the only British Open Championship to be held in Ireland.

Maxwell's son Press in 1957. A prevailing south wind and intense heat make it an exhausting test, as the British team discovered, but they played superbly over a course characteristic of Scottish links, although away from the sea.

Two of its outstanding holes are the par four dog-leg eighth, demanding two great shots, and the short 10th, where the green is protected by a deep bunker in front and thick yucca grass all around. In 1958 teenager Jack Nicklaus beat Deane Beman in the Trans Mississippi Amateur, and Nicklaus and Palmer played an exhibition match here in 1962. It was the venue for the US Ladies Amateur in 1964 and again in 1980 when Juli Inkster won the first of three consecutive titles.

Prestwick, Ayrshire, Scotland

A superb links course, founded in 1851 when 12 holes were laid out,

Prestwick was the venue for the first British Open Championship in 1860, won by Willie Park. It was held here every year until 1870 when Young Tom Morris, having won three in a row, became the proud possessor of the Championship Belt. After a lapse of a year, it was revived with the Cup as the trophy, with Young Tom the first winner, again at Prestwick, but it then alternated with St Andrews and Musselburgh as the venue.

Its last Open was in 1925, won by Jim Barnes, who had emigrated from Cornwall and become a naturalized American, but the event is remembered for the disaster that overcame Macdonald Smith, a Scot who had also emigrated to the United States. Holding a five-stroke lead as he started his final round, he was virtually engulfed by an excited crowd, who destroyed his chances. Made aware of its limitations, the R and A removed Prestwick from the Open rota.

The Amateur Championship, first won here in 1888 by John Ball, has continued to be held over these challenging links, nine times in all until 1952. It was once again the venue in 1987. While retaining many old-time characteristics, hidden greens, blind shots and bunkers lined with wooden sleepers, it remains an outstanding course. The third hole is famous for its vast sleepered Cardinal bunker to be cleared with the second shot and the Pow Burn along the right and continuing to be a threat at the fourth, especially by the green. Here J H Taylor came to grief in the 1914 Open, giving Harry Vardon his sixth title.

The last four holes finish in a loop; the 16th, the 'Cardinal's Back', has a small green perched by the end of the vast Cardinal bunker. The Amateur of 1934 saw

Prestwick, Ayrshire, Scotland.
It was the venue for the first British Open Championship in 1860.

the biggest victory margin achieved by American Lawson Little, who defeated Scottish hope Jack Wallace, 14 and 13. Young Tom Morris's Championship Belt is now treasured by the R and A at St Andrews.

Price, Charles

1925–. Born Philadelphia, Pennsylvania, USA

A columnist currently for *Golf Digest,* much of Charles Price's golf writing was done for *Golf,* whose editor he was from its beginnings. He has also worked for *Collier's* and for the *Saturday Evening Post.* His history, *The World of Golf* is sharply and authoritatively written and a post-war classic. More recently, his *Golfer-at-Large* takes a fresh and often hilarious look at some of the game's great figures.

Price was a good amateur and tried for a time without success on the US Tour after World War II.

Nick Price

Price, Nick

1957–. Born Durban, South Africa

Nick Price had a major championship in his grasp and then saw it slip away. He was three strokes in the lead with six holes remaining, in the 1982 Open at Troon. He finished second to Tom Watson. However, on the US Tour the following year he won the World Series.

Price's victories in South Africa include the Masters, and in Europe he won the Swiss Open in 1980 and the Lancome Trophy in 1985. His third round 63 in the 1986 Masters was a record.

Prince's, Kent, England

Of the trio of famous links courses at Sandwich, Prince's is the youngest. Founded in 1904, it has been subject to great changes as a result of two world wars. After being used as a battle training area in World War II, it was completely redesigned in 1948 by J S F Morrison and Sir Guy Campbell. Many of the old features were destroyed, and a new lay-out of 27 holes created, the championship Blue and the nine-hole Red. Although flatter, it still retained the shallow valleys and links terrain to give a testing course with plateau greens and many bunkers.

With the course restored, the English Ladies Championship returned here in 1953; its first visit had been in 1912, followed in 1922 by the British Ladies and a first victory for Joyce Wethered. In 1956 Prince's hosted the Curtis Cup, with victory for the British ladies by five matches to four. In the same year, a Great Britain v. Commonwealth and Empire professional match was held, notable for a great win for the 1951 Open champion Max Faulkner by four and three over Peter Thomson, winner that year of his third successive Open title. It resulted in another home victory by seven to five.

Further change came in 1985 with the opening of a new clubhouse some distance from the existing one, resulting in the lay-out numbering being altered. The three nines of the 27 holes were re-named Himalayas (after the range of sand-hills at the far end of the old course), the Shore and the Dunes. Before the war, Prince's was host to its only Open Championship, with victory going to Gene Sarazen with a record score of 283, equalled two years later by Henry Cotton at adjoining Royal St George's. Sarazen who led all the way and won by five strokes, had won his second US Open that year. Walker Cup player Laddie Lucas, who was born in the old clubhouse (his father was secretary of the club) and who was a fighter pilot in the RAF during the war, put his knowledge of the course to good effect when he was able to land there with a damaged Spitfire during the Battle of Britain.

Puerto de Hierro, Madrid, Spain

Established in 1904, Puerto de Hierro is Spain's oldest course, host for many years to the Spanish Open and also the Madrid Open. Winners in recent years of the latter event include double successes for home favourites Severiano Ballesteros and Manuel Pinero and also for Britain's Howard Clark. The Spanish Ladies Championship has also been held here.

Lying in a private estate, the course suffered during the country's Civil War, but was afterwards restored to championship standard. Located high above the Spanish capital, with outstanding views, its two lay-outs of 18 holes, the Number One being the championship test, are on hilly terrain, with bridges spanning the small valleys, and tree and bush-lined fairways. The World Amateur Team Championship for the Eisenhower Trophy was held here in 1970. Victory went to the United States from New Zealand; the American team included Tom Kite and Lanny Wadkins.

Quinta do Lago, Algarve, Portugal

Designed by American Bill Mitchell, Quinta do Lago is one of a number of excellent courses of championship quality, which at the same time are attractive to the handicap player, and which have made the Algarve so popular for holiday golf. Only a short drive from Faro, the course is one of great beauty. It has wide fairways, where there are always good lies, and each hole is virtually isolated from the others.

In 1984 Quinta do Lago became the venue for the Portuguese Open, with the course stretched to over 7000 yards and a par of 72. It was the scene of two outstanding rounds by South African David Frost, who first returned a record 65 and the next day bettered that with 64, but was still only able to finish third behind Tony Johnstone of Zimbabwe. The following year, it marked a popular first win in professional golf for former English Amateur champion and Walker Cup player, Warren Humphreys.

Rafferty, Ronan

1964–. Born Newry, Northern Ireland

Since turning professional in 1981, Ronan Rafferty has improved his position in the European Tour order of merit every year. He moved into the top 10 for the first time in 1986 when he finished in ninth place, with his highest prize money of £96,331. He came close

Quinta do Lago, Algarve, Portugal: venue for the Portuguese Open in 1984.

Ronan Rafferty

to his first tournament victory in Europe when he tied fellow Ulsterman David Feherty in the 1986 Italian Open, but lost the play-off.

Rafferty was something of a prodigy in his amateur days. A boy international at 14 and youth international at 15, he became the youngest player at the age of 17 to play in the 1981 Walker Cup match at Cypress Point. He won the British Boys, Irish Youths and Ulster Youths titles in 1979 when he was 15, and a year later won the Irish Amateur and tied for the English Amateur Stroke Play. He made many international appearances. In his first full year as a professional, he won the Venezuelan Open in 1982.

Rankin, Judy

1945–. Born St Louis, Missouri, USA

Judy Rankin's career dates back to 1959 when, as a 14-year-old, she won her state title. The following year she was leading amateur in the US Open. By 1962, she was a professional; two years later she was showing signs of being a leading player. She first won in 1968 and, with a win in 1979, her last victory, had won every year since except 1969. Her total is 26.

In money winnings, Rankin was ninth or better 11 times and was leading money winner in 1976 and 1977. In 1976 she was the first to break the $100,000 barrier with $150,734 — over $70,000 more than anyone had won before. In 1973 and 1976 she won the Vare Trophy, and was also declared Player of the Year in 1976. By the end of 1979, she stood second in the all-time money winners' list.

A slight figure of 5 foot 3 inches, Judy Rankin plays with a very strong left-hand grip, which partly accounts for the low, drawn flight she gets on her long shots.

Rawls, Betsy

1928–. Born Spartanburg, South Carolina, USA

An LPGA Tour player during the

Judy Rankin

years 1951–1975, Betsy Rawls won 55 events, ranking her behind only Mickey Wright and Kathy Whitworth. She won at least one event every year from 1951 to 1965 and her last victory came in 1972. Eight of those wins were in major championships and include the US Open four times and two LPGA titles. In 1959, she had 10 wins (out of 26 entries) and was leading money winner for the only time: her $27,000 broke the previous record by several thousand dollars.

On her retirement, Rawls became tournament director for the LPGA and was the first woman to serve on the rules committee for the (men's) US Open.

Ray, Ted

1877–1943. Born Jersey, Channel Islands

An unorthodox and self-taught swinger who swayed back from the ball and then well-nigh threw himself at it, Ted Ray was a long hitter and very powerful at recovery play.

Ray first came to the forefront in 1903, when he reached the final of the Match Play Championship. He was to do so twice again, although he never won. In the British Open between 1908 and 1925 he was five times in the top three and won in 1912. He then went on a tour of the USA with Harry Vardon, and while there tied with Vardon and Ouimet for the US Open. The American won. Ray and Vardon were there again in 1920 and this time Ray won a closely-contested championship. Until Raymond Floyd in 1986, he remained the oldest winner. He was the last foreign player to win until Gary Player in 1965 and the last Briton until Tony Jacklin in 1970.

Ray played against the USA in 1921, 1926 and 1927. The last of these was the first Ryder Cup match, when he captained the team.

Rees, CBE, David James (Dai)

1913–1983. Born Barry, South Glamorgan, Wales

One of the greatest triumphs of Dai Rees, the little Welshman with a great fighting spirit, came in the Ryder Cup at Lindrick in 1957. The Great Britain team had not won a match since 1933 at Southport and Ainsdale, although they had a great chance at Wentworth in 1953, before going down five and a half to six and a half. It did not look promising when in 1957 the United States led the foursomes three to one, but Rees, the playing captain, inspired his men to a famous victory, with the team winning the singles six and a half to one and a half for overall success seven and a half to four and a half. Rees won both his matches, having a seven and six victory over Ed Furgol in the singles.

Rees played in nine Ryder Cup matches between 1937 and 1961 and was playing captain in five successive matches from 1955 to 1961 and non-playing captain in

Dai Rees

1967, an all-time record.

He was one of the outstanding British players unlucky never to win the Open Championship. He finished runner-up three times, and was third once. In 1946, he finished fourth after being level with the eventual winner Sam Snead, but took 80 on the last day at St Andrews. In 1950 he was again level after three rounds at Troon, this time with Bobby Locke, but finished in third place behind the South African. In 1953 at Carnoustie he finished joint runner-up, four strokes behind Ben Hogan; in 1954 at Birkdale, needing a par on the last hole to tie Peter Thomson, he took three from just through the green, and was again runner-up, a stroke adrift; in 1961, again at Birkdale, he went into the last round a stroke behind Arnold Palmer, and both finished with 72s to leave Rees second once again.

Rees won the PGA Match Play Championship four times between 1936 and 1950, one of his victories being over Henry Cotton, the PGA Championship in 1959 and the Dunlop Masters in 1950 and 1962. He had more than 20 tournament wins, and when 60, finished runner-up in the 1973 Martini International. He followed Harry Vardon as professional at the South Herts Club, remaining there until his death in 1983.

Riviera, California, USA

At Riviera in 1948, Ben Hogan captured the first of his four US Open titles, winning by two strokes from Jimmy Demaret. He set a new Open record with an aggregate of 276 which stood for 19 years until beaten by a stroke by Jack Nicklaus at Baltusrol in 1967. That year Hogan had already won the US PGA, and was strong favourite for the title, for he had won both the 1947–1948 Los Angeles Opens over the course, which was being called 'Hogan's Alley'. Rounds of 67, 72,

68 gave him a record three-round total of 207 for him to lead by two strokes, and a final 69 ensured his victory.

The exclusive Riviera club, whose members include many famous film and show business stars, was opened in 1926. The course, designed by George Thomas, underwent reconstruction in 1974 to restore a stream, which over the years had turned into a ravine. The course was brought back to its former superb condition. It is a testing one, with tight fairways and an elaborate arrangement of bunkers, especially at the short sixth hole. Hogan claimed that the par four second, which calls for an approach shot over undulating fairway to a tightly bunkered green, was one of the finest holes he had played.

A few months after his Open victory at Riviera, Hogan's car was involved in a crash with a bus which so nearly cost him his life. With incredible courage, he made his golfing comeback in 1950, less than a year after the accident. The venue was the Riviera club for the Los Angeles Open. In spite of being in constant pain, Hogan tied Sam Snead for the title, but lost the play-off. A few months later, he won his second US Open at Merion.

Robertson, Allan

1815–1859. Born St Andrews, Fife, Scotland

The first golfer to be widely accepted as the best of his time, Allan Robertson had a golf workshop at St Andrews where, with Old Tom Morris and others apprenticed to him, he turned out feathery balls and clubs. The two became formidable as a foursome partnership in the challenge matches, then the most important form of competitive golf.

Robertson played with a long, easy swing and light clubs. He was

Belle Robertson

an excellent all-round player: a good driver and putter but at his best in the little shots from 50 yards in. He is also said to be the first to play longer approaches with an iron, rather than the wooden baffy.

Robertson may have been the first man asked to design golf courses. He made changes to St Andrews: some think he built the notorious 17th green — or at least decided to make use of the features already there.

Robertson, MBE, Isabella (Belle)

1936–. Born Southend, Argyll, Scotland

One of the greatest players in women's amateur golf, Scotland's Belle Robertson has won virtually every honour in the game in a career which lasted from the end of the 1950s until her retirement at the age of 50 after the 1986 Curtis Cup. In that historic match at Prairie Dunes in Kansas, in temperatures over 100 degrees, she and Mary McKenna in foursomes partnership played a vital role in the first victory by the Great Britain and Ireland team for 30 years. It was

Mrs Robertson's seventh appearance against the United States, and she was also team captain in 1974 and 1976.

She won the British Ladies Stroke Play title three times, in 1971, 1972 and 1985, but after appearing in her first final in the Ladies British Amateur Championship in 1959, the title eluded her. She finished runner-up three times until achieving the ultimate crown in ladies amateur golf, winning in a play-off at Conwy in 1981.

Mrs Robertson was dominant in Scottish golf, winning the Amateur title seven times from 1965 to 1986 and a string of other national events. In the Ladies British Open, in a strong field of professionals, she was runner-up and leading amateur in 1980 and 1981. As well as many international appearances in this country and overseas, in Vagliano Trophy, Commonwealth Tournament, European and World Team championships, she won the New Zealand title in 1971, and was leading qualifier in the US Amateur Championship in 1978. She won the Avia Watches International Foursomes four times,

Chi Chi Rodriguez

being partnered on the last two occasions in 1984 and 1986 by Mary McKenna. She was named Avia Woman Golfer of the year in 1985 for the third time. She was also Scottish sportswoman of the year four times from 1968 to 1981.

Rodriguez, Chi Chi

1935–. Born Bayamon, Puerto Rico

Chi Chi Rodriguez came into golf as a shoe-shine boy and graduated to being a caddie boss. He was a good golfer by the age of 17, when he joined the army.

In 1960, he joined the US Tour and competed until he became eligible for the Seniors Tour at the end of 1985.

He won his first tournament in 1963 and his best year was in 1964 when he won two events and moved to ninth in the money list. On Tour he had his eighth and last win in 1979, and reached a million dollars in career prize money. He made one Ryder Cup appearance in 1973 and represented Puerto Rico on 12 World Cup teams. As a Senior, he had three Tour wins in his first year.

Rogers, Bill

1951–. Born Waco, Texas, USA

When Bill Rogers won the British Open at Royal St George's in 1981, the members of his club at Texarkarna in Texas flew the Union Jack in celebration. And throughout 1981, it flew every time he was home. It was a year to remember for the popular and likeable Rogers, but just as suddenly as he had emerged as the outstanding player of that year, he suffered a complete loss of form which sent his game into an almost total decline.

During that year, he won seven tournaments, three on the US Tour, and as well as his victory in the British Open, he won the Aus-

Bill Rogers

tralian Open and other events in Australia and New Zealand. Constant travelling and playing continuously undoubtedly took its toll; from being named US Player of the Year in 1981 and being fifth in the money list, he had slumped to 131st in 1986.

Rogers only success since 1981 was to win the US F and G Classic in 1983. He won the World Match Play at Wentworth on his first appearance in 1980, and was in the US winning team in the Ryder Cup at Walton Heath in 1981.

Ross, Donald

1872–1948. Born Dornoch, Sutherland, Scotland

Once apprenticed to Old Tom Morris at St Andrews, Donald Ross went to the USA in 1898. Before that he had been at Dornoch as greenkeeper and professional for five years.

For a time, Ross was greenkeeper-professional at a Boston, Massachusetts club. He was asked to work the winters at a new resort the Tufts family was developing at

Pinehurst, North Carolina. Ross accepted and the move brought him fame. He planned and changed the courses at Pinehurst and visitors liked the magnificent work he was doing. His name spread throughout the growing American golf scene and he was much in demand as an architect.

Ross preferred to use the natural contours of the ground and to create subtle rolls on his greens. Estimates vary as to the number of courses he designed, but the total is somewhere between 500 and 700. So successful was he that six Opens in the years 1919 to 1926 were played over his designs. His highest rated courses are: Pinehurst Number 2, Seminole, Oakland Hills, Oak Hill, Inverness, Brae Burn, Scioto, and Broadmoor, but many more are of high repute.

Runyan, Paul

1908–. Born Hot Springs, Arkansas, USA

A good putter, with great variety in his short game, Paul Runyan was leading US money winner in 1933 and 1934. He won the US PGA in 1934 and 1938, in the latter year beating Sam Snead by a record eight and seven in the final.

Runyan played in the 1933 and 1935 Ryder Cup teams and in 1959, 1961 and 1962 he won the US PGA Seniors. He took the World title in 1961 and 1962.

The Ryder Cup

In 1913, Johnny McDermott, Mike Brady, Tom McNamara and Alex Smith, in Europe for the British and French Opens, played Arnaud Massy, Louis Tellier, Jean Gassiat and Pierre LaFitte at Versailles. It was a sort of USA versus France match and the American team lost every game.

This could be said to be the forerunner of the Ryder Cup, which dates not from the presentation of

a cup by Samuel Ryder but from the idea of international golf matches. This seems to have been the first between teams from opposite sides of the Atlantic. The first time a team of American and British professionals met was at Gleneagles in 1921. That same year a team of US amateurs played against Great Britain at Hoylake and won by nine matches to three.

The story was reversed at Gleneagles. Britain took six singles to three, with one halved and the foursomes went much the same way — three and a half to one and a half.

By 1926, golfers from America had begun to win the Open Championship — Walter Hagen in particular — but the second match at Wentworth between the teams went even more emphatically to Great Britain. Again, there were 10 singles, and they went to Great Britain eight and a half to one and a half.

On the suggestion of British captain George Duncan and Abe Mitchell, his personal professional, Sam Ryder presented his gold trophy, and the first Ryder Cup match was played in Massachusetts in 1927, with victory to the Americans, nine and a half to two and a half. It was a biennial event and two years later at Moortown it was a different story, for the cup returned to Britain seven to five. The result in Columbus, Ohio, in 1931, seemed to establish a pattern; Britain could not cope in the USA and lost nine to three. This was confirmed when the pendulum swung back in 1933 at Southport and Ainsdale but by a narrow margin.

Until World War II, USA teams were totally dominant on home soil but the British usually managed to struggle through when their turn came round again — though not in the 1937 match, lost eight to four. Overall, however, honours were even at four matches each.

The Ryder Cup began as a competition between Britain and America's best professional golfers. Above: the American Sam Snead practises before the competition. Above right: J H Taylor, Sam Ryder and Walter Hagen at the 1933 match. Below right: the US Ryder Cup team in 1983. They won by a single point.

After the war, it was a different story. The USA were successful in front of their own spectators (though few bothered to come) and won by commanding margins. Over the years, the format and number of games changed. Since 1979, it has been a four-match foursomes and fourball formula for the first two days, then every team member playing in the singles, bringing the number of these matches to 12.

Matches on the British side of the Atlantic have always been more closely contested and 1949, for instance, was extremely encouraging. After humiliation at Portland, Oregon, the USA only just won at Ganton seven to five and then at Wentworth in 1953 six and a half to five and a half. Eventual victory came as a surprise at Lindrick in 1957 when, after the US had taken a three to one lead in the foursomes, the British team led by Dai Rees won the singles six and a half to one and a half.

This was a lone success, although in one of the most exciting matches, in 1969 at Royal Birkdale, the teams were level after two days and the British team then took the singles on the final morning, five to three. When the USA reversed that result in the afternoon, the match was tied, Nicklaus generously conceding a three foot putt to Tony Jacklin on the final green.

The next two matches in Britain went to the USA comfortably, and there came pressure for change from the Americans after 1977 and the Great Britain and Ireland team was strengthened to include players from the Continent. Ballesteros and Garrido were the first to be selected — for the 1979 match in West Virginia. In 1981, Pinero, Langer and Canizares made the team at Walton Heath, and the gulf between the two teams was virtually removed in 1983 at the PGA National in Florida, when the teams went into the 12 singles of the final day level. Throughout, one side then the other held the lead, with the USA winning by a single point.

Hopes of a European victory were high at The Belfry in 1985.

The European Ryder Cup team in 1985 at The Belfry, captained by Tony Jacklin. It was the first European victory for 28 years.

The USA took a three to one lead the first morning but at the end of the day it was three and a half to four and a half. At lunch on the second day, the teams were level and a three to one result in Europe's favour in the afternoon's foursomes gave a useful lead for the 12 singles the third day. Of the first eight matches out, the USA obtained only one win and a half. The Ryder Cup was out of American hands for the first time in 28 years, after a brilliant achievement, from a team inspired by their captain, Tony Jacklin. In 1987, the match moved to Nicklaus's Muirfield Village course in Ohio, with Jacklin and Nicklaus the respective captains, as in 1983.

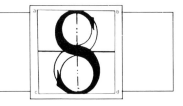

St Andrews, Fife, Scotland

The home of golf and the most famous course in the world sum up simply the history and renown of this famous links and the grey granite headquarters of the Royal and Ancient Golf Club of St Andrews overlooking the first tee of the Old course. The earliest evidence of golf here was a licence in 1522 to allow the public to rear rabbits on the links and 'play at golf, futball, schuteing' and other pastimes. For more than 400 years, any golfer has been able to play over this famous strip of land, and today they flock from all over the world to achieve this ultimate ambition.

Not all the great players have taken to the course on first viewing — among them Bobby Jones and Tom Watson — and only later have they come to admire and respect it. Jones said, 'If I had had to select one course on which to play the match of my life, I should have selected the Old course.' With its fearsome, natural bunkers and changing winds, it can be frustrating, yet a fine shot is always rewarded.

Its first hole, with wide open fairway, seems innocuous, yet many players have misjudged their approach to the green and had to fish their ball out of the Swilcan Burn. Of all its holes the 17th, the notorious 'Road' hole, has been the one where championship hopes have foundered, notably Arnold Palmer's in the 1960 Centenary Championship, won by Kel Nagle, and by Tom Watson in 1984. His approach bounded over the green and the road to clatter against the stone wall and end his hopes of a

St Andrews, Fife, Scotland: the home of golf and the most famous course in the world. Golf was played here as early as 1522; today, more than 400 years later, playing here becomes the summit of golfing ambition.

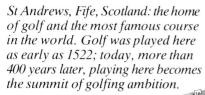

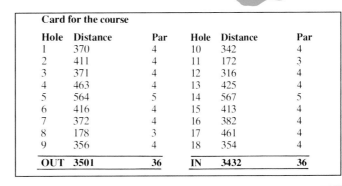

Card for the course

Hole	Distance	Par	Hole	Distance	Par
1	370	4	10	342	4
2	411	4	11	172	3
3	371	4	12	316	4
4	463	4	13	425	4
5	564	5	14	567	5
6	416	4	15	413	4
7	372	4	16	382	4
8	178	3	17	461	4
9	356	4	18	354	4
OUT	**3501**	**36**	**IN**	**3432**	**36**

St Andrews, Fife, Scotland: home to four municipal courses and to the Royal and Ancient Club.

sixth title at the one venue where above all others every player dreams of winning the Open.

In 1984 it was Severiano Ballesteros who claimed the distinction, and Jack Nicklaus has twice had the joy of accepting the Claret Jug trophy here, in 1970 and 1978. The first occasion was a tragedy for Doug Sanders, who missed a putt of about three feet on the final green to deprive him of victory and then lost the play-off the next day by a single stroke.

The first Open at St Andrews was played in 1873 and won by local player Tom Kidd. Since then, champions here have included J H Taylor, James Braid, Bobby Jones, Peter Thomson, Bobby Locke, Sam Snead and Tony Lema. Jones won the Amateur Championship here for the first stage of his famous Grand Slam of 1930, and in 1971 there was a home victory in the Walker Cup for the first time since 1938. In the 1970 Open, defending champion Tony Jacklin covered the first nine holes in 29. He seemed set at least to equal the 65 set by Neil Coles earlier when a violent thunderstorm ended play for the day. Jacklin was unable to complete his round the next morn-

ing with the same magical touch, and his hopes of retaining the title faded away.

St David's, Royal, Gwynedd, Wales

With a background of Snowdon and the Harlech Castle of King Edward I looking down on this links course like 'a broody sentinel' as Tom Scott wrote, the setting of St David's is incomparable for natural golf, with flat holes and those among dunes and hillocks, and no two fairways parallel. Dating from 1894 when golf was first played on the 'Morfa', a sheep grazing area below the castle, the course opened with John Ball winning a special competition and his equally famous amateur colleague Harold Hilton tied for the Harlech Town Bowl in 1902.

In 1912 St David's received its Royal title and in 1935, the Prince of Wales (later the Duke of Windsor) played himself in as captain. It staged its first championship in 1926 when Cecil Leitch won her fourth British Ladies title. It has

also hosted Welsh championships, has been the venue for further British Ladies events, with the championship once again here in 1987, and Home Internationals have also been played here.

Off the fairways, tough rushes and dog roses punish the wayward shot, and the course has tough finishing holes. The 15th is possibly the best on the course, slightly dog-leg right through sandhills, with a hollow short of the green and often into a prevailing wind.

St George's, Royal, Kent, England

One of the great links courses of Britain and the venue for the first Open Championship outside Scotland in 1894, St George's saw many outstanding championships up to 1949, the year of Bobby Locke's victory, when it went out of favour. After a lapse of 32 years, the Open returned in 1981 with traffic problems eased by a by-pass round the town of Sandwich. It was such a success that it was back again in 1985 when Sandy Lyle became the hero by claiming the first British victory since Tony Jacklin in 1969.

Five years after the founding of St George's in 1887, John Ball won the Amateur Championship here. Its great Open champions include Harry Vardon, Jack White, Walter Hagen and Henry Cotton, the latter in 1934 opening with record rounds of 67, 65 before finishing with 283, one stroke more than Sandy Lyle 51 years later.

St George's is a course which features big sandhills and deep valleys, giving the player a sense of solitude. It can become even more of a fearsome test when the wind sweeps across the links, as it did in the 1975 PGA Championship. Only Arnold Palmer was able to master it as he battled to a final 74 and a two-stroke win.

For both the 1981 and 1985 Opens, changes were made, the par

Hole	Distance	Par	Hole	Distance	Par
1	445 yards	4	10	375 yards	4
2	376 yards	4	11	216 yards	3
3	214 yards	3	12	362 yards	4
4	466 yards	4	13	443 yards	4
5	422 yards	4	14	508 yards	5
6	156 yards	3	15	467 yards	4
7	529 yards	5	16	165 yards	3
8	415 yards	4	17	425 yards	4
9	387 yards	4	18	458 yards	4
OUT	**3410 yards**	**35**	**IN**	**3419 yards**	**35**

Card for the course

Royal St George's, Kent, England: a course which can become a fearsome test when the wind sweeps across the links.

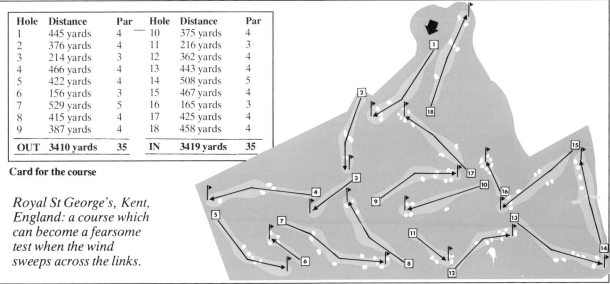

three third having a new green visible from the tee, and new tees built at the eighth, 12th and 14th. The latter, the 'Suez', with a canal to be crossed by the second shot, saw Henry Cotton's approach go out-of-bounds here in 1938, letting in R A Whitcombe. In 1928 Gene Sarazen took seven here as Hagen claimed the title. The 10th hole saw Tom Kite's hopes founder in 1985

when he failed to find the green on its high dune and took six, while Lyle conjured up crucial birdies at the 14th and 15th to earn his victory. Locke's title in 1949 came in a play-off with Harry Bradshaw, victim of a bizarre incident in the last round when his ball finished in the base of a broken bottle and he smashed bottle and ball when he could have had a free drop, and

took six.

St George's has hosted the Walker Cup and the European Team Championship, and among the winners of its own Grand Challenge Cup appears the name of J W Nicklaus in 1959. In 1967, Tony Jackin's hole in one at the 16th on his way to victory in the Dunlop Masters was the first to be seen live on British television.

St Mellion, Cornwall, England

The parkland course, the venue for the 1979 Benson and Hedges International three years after its opening, and for the 1983 and 1984 Tournament Players Championship, now takes second place to a magnificent new lay-out created by Jack Nicklaus and completed in 1986. Just over the border into Cornwall from Plymouth, the courses are the brainchild of two brothers, Martin and Hermon Bond, who after the success of the first lay-out invited Nicklaus to design a course to compare with the best in the country.

Built at a cost of over £2 million, it stretches over 7000 yards. More than a million cubic metres of earth have been moved to create an American-style lay-out, featuring streams and lakes, and undulating greens, with natural viewing galleries for spectators. Water is a domi-

St Mellion, Cornwall, England: the parkland course was given a magnificent new lay-out created by Jack Nicklaus in 1986 and built at a cost of over £2-million.

nant feature at a number of holes, notably the par four fifth, with a carry from the tee over a lake. The par five 12th has similarities with the notorious 13th at Augusta National, with a ditch in front of the green. The 18th, the last hole of the original course, now has the lake on the left of the green. The ladies were given the first chance to show their skills over the course in its first championship, the Ladies British Open in 1987, won by Alison Nicholas.

Sanders, Doug

1933–. Born Cedartown, Georgia, USA

Doug Sanders was nearing the end of his career when he missed a putt of about three and a half feet for

the 1970 Open Championship at St Andrews. He had the championship in his grasp after he had managed to get down in two from the notorious bunker on the 17th 'Road' hole and a par at the last would have given him victory. After a good drive at the 18th, he sent his approach racing to the back of the green and then left his first putt short. As he stood over the ball, he suddenly bent down to pick up an object, either real or imaginary, on his line. Instead of walking away and then settling himself again, he resumed his stance and rolled the putt past the right side of the hole. The tap-in bogey left him in an 18-hole play-off with Nicklaus, who had already finished his round for a 283 total. Nicklaus won his second Open with 72 to Sanders's 73. Sanders had been runner-up a stroke away four years earlier, again to Nicklaus at Muirfield.

Sanders won the 1956 Canadian

Open as an amateur and turned professional soon afterwards. On the US Tour his best year was 1961 when he was third in the money list and won five events. By the time he retired from the US Tour, he had won 20 tournaments, but the majors eluded him. In the 1961 US Open at Oakland Hills, he needed a birdie on the 18th to tie Gene Littler, but only parred the hole.

Sanders, a colourful character in his brightly-coloured clothes, was noted for the shortest back swing in golf. On the Seniors Tour he won the 1983 World Seniors Invitational.

Sandwich *See* St George's, Royal, England

Sarazen, Gene

1902–. Born Harrison, New York, USA

Among the greatest shots by players which have led to major championship victories, one by the legendary Gene Sarazen will always be remembered. Playing for the first time in the US Masters in 1935, his four-wood second shot on the par five 15th hole carried the

Gene Sarazen

Doug Sanders

lake and ran into the hole for an albatross. He finished in a tie with Craig Wood and won the play-off.

It was Sarazen's only Masters victory in one of the longest golfing careers on record. At the age of 20,

he won the US Open in 1922, and his last round 68 was then the lowest by a champion. He won the US PGA the same year, beat Walter Hagen in a 72-hole challenge match and in 1923 again beat Hagen to win the US PGA title for the second time. He captured it again in 1933.

Sarazen was runner-up in the British Open in 1928. He claimed his only victory in the championship in 1932, the same year he won his second US Open; he is one of the few players to win the British and US Opens in the same year. They brought his total of major titles to seven. He played in the first Ryder Cup match in 1927 and completed a run of six consecutive matches in 1937.

In the 1932 Open at Prince's, Sandwich, he started favourite, led throughout and his 283 was a championship record that stood until 1950. Back at Fresh Meadow for the US Open, Sarazen's start of 74, 76 left him well behind. Halfway through the third round he trailed by seven strokes, but he changed from defensive play to fire at the flag; it gave him rounds of 70, 66, the latter a record which stood until Palmer's 65 in the 1960 US Open. It was his last Open victory, although in 1940 he tied with Lawson Little at Canterbury, Ohio, but lost the play-off 70 to 73.

To Sarazen is attributed the introduction of the modern sand wedge. He certainly added lead to the sole of a club behind the leading edge to produce excellent bunker shots, although versions of sand wedges had appeared before his modified club was used in his Open victories of 1932.

Sarazen was invited to the British Open in 1973 when he was 71. He completed two rounds partnering former champion Max Faulkner and had the satisfaction of a hole in one at Troon's famous short eighth hole, the 'Postage Stamp'.

Sawgrass, Florida, USA

Designed by Pete Dye, this course at Ponte Vedra and named the Tournament Players Club became the home of the Tournament Players Championship in 1982. It was notable for the conclusion of the first event there, when the winner, Jerry Pate, carried out his vow that if he won he would throw into the lake not only the designer but the Tour Commissioner Deane Beman — which he did. He then followed them in himself for a victory swim.

After previous years playing at nearby Sawgrass, the players found the new stadium-type course, with water everywhere, small greens, and three fearsome finishing holes really daunting. By 1984, Dye had made some concessions to its layout, particularly at the spectacular 17th par three, just 130 yards over water to an island green, where on one windy day 64 balls finished in the lake.

Demanding as it is, Tom Watson tamed it in 1982 when he strung together six birdies in a row for 67, only for Fred Couples to do even better with 64 as he went on to win the event which the Commissioner has hopes of becoming a fifth major championship. In 1987 there was a memorable first British victory for former Open champion Sandy Lyle. His opening rounds of 67, 71 left him five shots adrift at halfway. He then shot 66 to be 12 under par but still two shots behind the leaders. He tied for first place with a final 70, for a total of 274, to take the title and his biggest ever prize in golf of $180,000 when he won the play-off with Jeff Sluman.

Sawgrass, Florida, USA: designed by Pete Dye, this daunting course became the home of the Tournament Players Championship in 1982.

Seminole, Florida, USA

The great Ben Hogan chose Seminole as one of his favourite courses, and with good reason. While it has never hosted the top professional tournaments, it is undoubtedly a superb test. Hogan in his heyday became a member, choosing to practise here before going on to the Masters. When he cut down on his tournament appearances after the car accident which nearly cost him his life in 1949, he usually began his season by playing in the Seminole Pro-Am tournament.

Opened in 1929 in a magnificent setting by the Atlantic Ocean, north of Palm Beach, the course was designed by Donald Ross. It is a true linksland among the Florida sand dunes and palm trees, with some fine dog-leg holes, a large lake covering the centre of the course, and masses of bunkers.

During World War II, the course

barely survived, but with the wealthy set returning to Palm Beach, one of its residents, Christopher J Dunphy, restored the course to its former glory. Its exclusive membership prefers to host its own tournaments, rather than widen its appeal to professional events. Its annual pro-am, which attracted a number of leading professionals, was discontinued in 1960. Claude Harmon, a former Masters champion, was the club's professional for a number of years; during his stay he returned a course record of 60.

Sheehan, Patty

1956–. Born Middlebury,
Vermont, USA

Patty Sheehan joined the PGA Tour with a fine amateur record, and established herself among the top professionals. She had won several state titles, reached the final

of the 1979 US Amateur, won the National Collegiate Championship and played in the 1980 Curtis Cup team. She went straight to the top on the Tour, winning in her first season when she was Rookie of the Year.

Since then, she has been a consistent winner, taking her tournament haul to 17 titles by the end of 1986, including two LPGA Championships. In these five years, she has always passed $200,000 and her worst money list ranking has been seventh. In both 1983 and 1984 she was second.

Shinnecock Hills, New York, USA

Located in the resort of Southampton on Long Island and adjoining

Shinnecock Hills, New York, USA: founded in 1892, this club is among the oldest in the United States, and takes its name from a tribe of Indians.

the National Golf Links, Shinnecock Hills, dating from 1892, is among the oldest clubs in the United States. The course, less of a links than its neighbour, lying more inland, owes its championship layout to Dick Wilson, who lengthened and improved it in 1931.

The second US Open came here in 1896 and again two years later it was the venue for the Open, with the US Amateur also held two years previously. It was then ignored until 1986 when Raymond Floyd captured his first US Open title. In 1977 it staged the Walker Cup; victory went to the United States.

The club took its name from a tribe of Indians who lived on the island and who helped to build the course in the early 1890s. Today their descendants are still employed by the club. The long 16th was a crucial hole for Floyd in 1986 and after two shots he was still short of

the green on this par five hole; but in spite of being distracted by photographers, he coolly wedged to 10 feet and holed the putt for a birdie that clinched his title.

Siderowf, Richard

1937–. Born New Britain, Connecticut, USA

Dick Siderowf became only the third American in history in the 1970s to win the British Amateur Championship more than once. He equalled the two wins of Lawson Little (1934–1935) and Frank Stranahan (1948 and 1950) at Porthcawl in 1973 and at St Andrews in 1976; in the latter he was taken to the 37th hole by John Davies, of Surrey.

Although failing to win the US title, Siderowf won the Canadian Amateur in 1971. He played in the Walker Cup four times and was non-playing captain of the US team in 1979.

Sigel, Jay

1945–. Born Berwyn, Pennsylvania

One of the outstanding players in

Jay Sigel

American amateur golf, Jay Sigel has an impressive record in Britain, as well as his own country. It was at Hillside in 1981 that he gained his first major success, beating countryman Scott Hoch three and two to win the British Amateur title. He won the US Amateur in consecutive years 1982 and 1983, and also won the US Mid Amateur.

Sigel has been a member of the US Walker Cup team in six consecutive matches from 1977, and was playing captain in 1983. He won three matches as the US team gained an overwhelming victory at Sunningdale in 1987. His total of 14 match wins is the highest by an American player.

Simpson, Scott

1955–. Born San Diego, California, USA

In eight seasons on the US Tour, Scott Simpson had won only two tournaments by the start of 1987: the Western Open in 1980 and the 1984 Westchester Classic. A steady, consistent player, finishing each year between 22nd and 41st in the money list, he did not come into the reckoning for the 1987 US Open played at the Olympic Club in San Francisco, although the signs were there that he was in top form. He had finished fourth to Sandy Lyle in the Tournament Players Championship in March and the next week won the Greater Greensboro Open.

At the Olympic Club he proved how good he is, when in spite of the pressure in the final round of knowing Tom Watson, Ballesteros, Langer and Crenshaw were all in contention, he stayed cool to hole crucial birdie putts at 14, 15 and 16 — from four feet, 30 feet and 15 feet. Then at the 17th, he played a fine bunker shot and holed from eight feet to save his par. When Watson failed with a 45-foot putt on the final green, needing a birdie

Scott Simpson

to tie, Simpson was Open champion by a stroke. His final 68 gave him three under par 277.

Simpson had a fine amateur record, winning the National Collegiate titles in 1976 and 1977 for the University of Southern California and gaining Walker Cup selection in 1977, before turning professional in 1977. He twice failed to qualify for the US Tour before making it in 1978 and joining the US Tour the next year. He won the Hawaii State Open in 1979 and 1981 and in Japan in 1984 won the Chunichi Crowns and Dunlop Phoenix titles.

Sindelar, Joey

1958–. Born Fort Knox, Kentucky, USA

Joey Sindelar followed a trio of former Ohio State University students on to the US Tour, and no doubt the example of the three, Jack Nicklaus, Tom Weiskopf and Ed Sneed has been an influence on his career. He was a member of the NCAA Championship team for

Joey Sindelar

Ohio State, won 10 collegiate titles, was three times All-American and 1981 Ohio State athlete of the year.

Sindelar joined the US Tour in 1984 and won the Greater Greensboro Open and BC Open in 1985. He finished 12th in the money list, and although he did not win in 1986 he finished runner-up in two events and won $341,000 dollars, his highest total, for 14th position. He also won the statistics categories in birdies and eagles during the season.

Smith, Alex

1872–1930. Born Carnoustie, Angus, Scotland

The originator of that piece of putting wisdom 'Miss 'em quick', Smith won the US Opens of 1906 and 1910 and lost a play-off in 1901. On another five occasions he was in the top three.

Smith, OBE, Frances

1924–1978. Born Liverpool, England

An outstanding player to emerge in British women's golf after World War II, the former Bunty Stephens won the English Ladies title in 1948, 1954 and 1955 and reached four finals of the British Ladies', winning in 1949 and 1954.

She is best remembered for her Curtis Cup performances, in which she was never beaten in singles. Two of her wins were especially decisive. In the last match on the course in 1956, her one-hole victory over Polly Riley clinched the Curtis Cup; and in 1958, in the USA, she beat Polly Riley by two holes for Great Britain and Ireland to retain the cup in a tied match. It was the first British team not to lose on US soil.

Smith, Horton

1908–1963. Born Springfield, Missouri, USA

Appearing, it seemed, out of nowhere, Horton Smith won nearly all the titles on the 1928–1929 winter tour in the USA. He had a beautifully slow swing and a putting stroke to match.

Smith went on to win some 30 US events and won the first Masters in 1934. He won again in 1936. He played in the 1929, 1933 and 1935 Ryder Cups and was selected for the 1939 and 1941 teams, which did not play because of the war.

Smith is thought to have been the first man to use a sand wedge in competition. His had a concave face, a type which was later banned.

Smith, Macdonald

1890–1949. Born Carnoustie, Angus, Scotland

One of a famous trio of golfing brothers (Alex and Willie were the others) Macdonald Smith was the best. Yet he never managed to win a major championship.

Smith tied for the US Open when he was 20, but lost the play-off to brother Alex. This was the nearest he came to a major title in a quarter of a century at the top. Twenty years later, in 1930, he was second to Jones.

One of his losses is legendary. He took a five-stroke lead into the last round of the 1925 British Open at Prestwick, but was engulfed by an enthusiastic crowd and took 82 when a 78 would have been good enough.

Snead, J C

1941–. Born Hot Springs, Virginia, USA

After joining the US Tour in 1968, Jesse Carlyle Snead, a nephew of the famous Sam Snead, decided to be known by his initials rather than first names, saying 'Jesse Carlyle hasn't been playing worth a damn!' It did not take him long to refute that statement, as he won two tournaments in a three-week period at Tucson and Doral in 1971. He had his highest finishes in a season in 1974 and 1976, taking sixth place in the money list, and by 1981 he had won seven events.

He failed to win again until capturing the West Chester Classic in a play-off with Ballesteros in 1987. He won the Australian Open in 1973 and played in three consecutive Ryder Cup matches from 1971.

Snead, Sam

1912–. Born Hot Springs, Virginia, USA

Sam Snead, of the classic, flowing swing, with 135 victories during an outstanding career, will be remembered as the great player who never won the US Open. He came close to gaining the coveted title on a number of occasions which would have given him the grand slam of all four major titles, but it was not to be.

Snead nearly won the US Open the first time he played. In 1937 he

Sam Snead

finished his last round at Oakland Hills with an eagle for 283 total, and led the field. But Ralph Guldahl, who still had nine holes to play, had just eagled the eighth; with birdies at 12 and 13 he needed only pars the rest of the way, and he made no mistake. Forty years later Snead played in his last Open, his dream unfulfilled.

Two years after being so close at Oakland Hills, Snead needed a par five for victory at Philadelphia, but thinking a birdie was necessary, went for risky shots which cost him eight. In 1940, he started the last round at Canterbury, Ohio, a stroke off the lead, but took a disastrous 81. Snead came closest in 1947 at St Louis. He showed no nerves as he holed an 18-foot putt on the last green to tie Lew Worsham. In the 18-hole play-off, they stood level on the last green, both with putts of about 30 inches after three shots. Snead moved to putt first, but was stopped by Worsham who asked for the distance of the putts to be measured. Snead had been right: his was marginally farther from the hole, giving him the right to putt first. The delay was

fatal. Snead missed his putt and Worsham holed for the title.

Snead was second twice more. In 1949, he needed a birdie on the last hole at Medinah to tie Cary Middlecoff after making up five strokes, but could only par the hole. In 1953 he finished six strokes behind Hogan.

In 1946 Snead won the British Open at St Andrews. He was a stroke behind Henry Cotton after two rounds, but was level going into the last round and won by four strokes from Locke and Johnny Bulla, his last round 75 giving him a 290 total. Cotton's 79 left him in fourth place. It was Snead's second major championship victory — in 1942 he had won the US PGA, a title he won twice more in 1949 and 1951.

Snead had to wait for his first Masters title, which also came in 1949. In 1939, he set a new scoring record with 280, only for Guldahl to foil him for the second time in a major as he completed Augusta's last nine holes in 33 to win by a stroke. Then 10 years later, Snead made no mistake. With everyone struggling in the wind on the first two days, he kept in contention, and cruised away with two 67s to win by three strokes.

In the Masters in 1952, Snead went into the lead with rounds of 70 and 67. Then the winds got up and Snead took 77, but no one did much better and a 72 gave him the title by four strokes. Perhaps Sam's most satisfying victory was the Masters of 1954. The previous year, Hogan had swept all before him — Masters, US Open and British Open. Hogan's reputation was still at a peak, but Snead tied him at Augusta and beat him in the 18-hole play-off.

This was Snead's last major title but he kept on winning tournaments until 1965 when, at the age of 52, he became the oldest player to take a tour event. It was his 84th Tour victory, 13 better than the

next man on the all-time list, Jack Nicklaus.

Sotogrande, Cadiz, Spain

This was the first European course to be designed by the famed architect Robert Trent Jones. It was opened in 1965 ahead of the rash of courses which sprang up all along the Costa del Sol, and stands comparison with any that have appeared since. With 10 dog-leg holes, cleverly placed bunkers and excellent positioning of water, the Old course, as it became known when Trent Jones designed a second course nearby, was the venue for the Spanish Open, won by Roberto de Vicenzo, a year after its opening. One of the finest holes is the long par four seventh, with a drive into a narrow fairway and out-of-bounds on the left, while the approach to the green slopes towards a bunker and water.

Southern Hills, Oklahoma, USA

At a time when golf clubs were going out of existence in the American depression of the 1930s, a group of Tulsa golfers banded together to build this course and chose the Oklahoma architect Perry Maxwell to design it. The result is a course where the drive is the key feature, with most of the course flat parkland. Ten of its 12 par fours and its two par fives curve either right or left, and trees line the fairways.

The course claimed attention when the US Open was played here in 1958; Tommy Bolt, in brilliant form, won by four strokes on 283 from Gary Player. In 1965 Bob Murphy won the first stroke play US Amateur Championship, and the 1970 US PGA title went to Dave Stockton after a superb round of 66 on the third day.

The US Open returned in 1977 when Hubert Green was told halfway through his final round that a

Southern Hills, Oklahoma, USA: designed by architect Perry Maxwell, most of the course is flat parkland with tree-lined fairways.

death threat had been telephoned, saying he would be killed on the 15th green. He chose to play on and safely negotiated the hole, carrying on for a gallant win under great pressure. No attempt on his life was made.

Hollis Stacy

Stacy, Hollis

1954–. Born Savannah, Georgia, USA

One of only two players to take the US Girls' title three years in a row, Hollis Stacy has always been in the top 20 money winners in the years 1976–1986. She also had at least one victory in the period 1977–1985 to total 17, including the US Open three times — 1977, 1978 and 1984 — which makes her one of four with three wins. She has also taken the 1983 Peter Jackson Classic.

Stadler, Craig

1953–. Born San Diego, California, USA

Craig Stadler first came to prominence when he won the 1973 US Amateur and played in the 1975 Walker Cup team before turning professional. He made no great impact on the US Tour until 1980 when he won twice and finished the season eighth in the money list.

Stadler maintained much the same pace in 1981 but became more of a household name in 1982

Craig Stadler

when he won four times. It was the Masters in April 1982 that brought him world recognition, not only for leading the event but for his portly figure and walrus moustache. Although he faltered towards the end and dropped into a tie with Dan Pohl, he won the play-off at the first extra hole for his major success. He finished the year leading money winner with $446,462. He also won the World Series that year.

Winner of eight US events up to 1986, Stadler won the European Masters in Switzerland in 1985. He played in the 1983 and 1985 Ryder Cup teams, missing a tiny putt at The Belfry which was a turning point in the match won by the home team in 1985.

Stephenson, Jan

1951–. Born Sydney, New South Wales, Australia

One of the best Australian junior golfers ever, Jan Stephenson captured three national titles. In 1973, she turned professional and played the limited Australian tour, win-

Jan Stephenson

ning the LPGA and Open among other titles.

In 1974, she began to play the LPGA Tour in the USA and immediately more than paid her way. In 1976, she won twice and moved to eighth on the money list. She has been a star ever since.

Stephenson's scoring has been consistent, particularly since 1981, and in that year, and also in 1983, she had three wins. She has 13 US victories, three of which rank as major titles — the 1981 Peter Jackson Classic, the 1982 LPGA Championship and the 1983 US Open. She has had several more victories outside the USA, which include a second Australian Open, in 1977, and the 1985 French Open.

Stephenson is the first professional woman golfer to design golf courses.

Stewart, Gillian

1958–. Born Inverness, Highlands, Scotland

As an amateur, Gillian Stewart was one of Scotland's outstanding players. She won the 1975 Scottish Under-19 title and was British

Girls' champion in 1976. She was Scottish champion three times, in 1979, 1983 and 1984, and won the 1984 European Open as an amateur. She played in the 1980 and 1982 Curtis Cup teams and was surprisingly omitted from the 1984 team at Muirfield, when the home team went down by a single point.

Turning professional for the 1985 season, she won her first event, the Ford Classic, and won again in 1987.

Stewart, Payne

1957–. Born Springfield, Missouri, USA

Payne Stewart, one of the US Tour's most consistent players, has seen many tournament titles slip away. In three seasons 1984–1986, his winnings exceeded $1-million without a victory, and after finishing in a tie for first place in three events, he lost the play-offs.

On the Asian circuit, Stewart won the 1981 Indian and Indonesian Opens and in Australia in 1982, he won the Tweeds Head Classic. He broke through in America to win the 1982 Quad

Payne Stewart

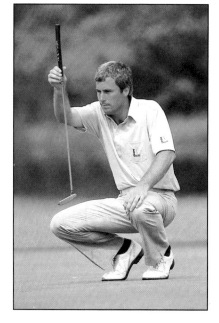

Cities Open. He won the Walt Disney Classic in 1983 and the Bay Hill Classic in 1987.

Stewart challenged for the British Open in 1985 when he finished runner-up to Sandy Lyle, and again in 1987 when he was fourth to Nick Faldo. He made himself a favourite with the fans with his stylish dress of pastel shades in plus twos, stockings and cap.

Strange, Curtis

1955–. Born Norfolk, Virginia, USA

One of the most successful and consistent players on the US Tour, Curtis Strange's search for a major title seemed about to succeed in the 1985 Masters. Then the notorious 13th in Augusta National's so-called 'Amen Corner', where many hopes have foundered, ended his dream. Three strokes ahead of the field, he decided to go for the green on this par five hole, only to see his second shot end in the creek in front of the green. Rather than drop out under penalty, a choice that could still have given him a chance of making par, he tried unsuccessfully to hit out of the creek. The hole cost him seven and let in Bernhard Langer for the title.

Strange won a record $542,321 on the US Tour in 1985 for first place in the money list, with victories in three tournaments, including the Canadian Open which he won again in 1987.

In his amateur days, Strange won a number of events, including the NCAA Championship, and was unbeaten in the Walker Cup match at St Andrews in 1975. His first US Tour win was the 1979 Pensacola Open and in 1980 he moved up to third in the money list with two victories. By the end of 1986 he had won 11 times and had been placed four times in the top 10 money winners. He has twice played in the Ryder Cup.

Curtis Strange

Streit, Marlene Stewart

1934–. Born Cereal, Alberta, Canada

A dominant force in Canadian amateur golf, Marlene Stewart, later Streit, won the country's Closed title nine times, but after she had taken seven in a row in the years 1951–1957, the event went into abeyance for a couple of years. She had two more victories up to 1968, the last year the event was staged.

Streit's record in the Open Amateur is even better. She reached 13 finals and only lost twice, the last of these being in 1982, when she was nearly 50. In the USA, she won the 1956 North and South and reached two national finals, beating the brilliant JoAnne Carner in 1956 and losing to her in a marathon on the 41st hole in 1966.

In 1953 she won the British Ladies' title, beating Ireland's Philomena Garvey seven and six. She is one of only two players to have won the British, US and Canadian titles and the only woman golfer to have this combination and the Australian

Championship, which she won in 1963.

Suggs, Louise

1923–. Born Atlanta, Georgia, USA

Winner of five regional amateur titles, Louise Suggs went on to win the US Championship in 1947 and the British the following year. She also won two LPGA events as an amateur, the 1946 Titleholders and the 1947 Western Open.

Suggs had little difficulty in adapting to professional golf. In 1949, she took the US Open in amazing style, beating Babe Zaharias into second place by 14 strokes. Her 291 set a scoring record. Thereafter, with the exception of 1950, she won every year up to 1962 and at that point had 50 wins, a total bettered by only three other players to date. Eight of these wins were majors, including the Open in

Sunningdale, Berkshire, England: the 10th hole of the Old course, noted for all that is best in heathland golf.

1949 and 1952. Her peak year was 1953 when she had eight victories and was leading money winner, a position she also occupied in 1960.

No longer a serious competitor after the mid-1960s, Suggs still made the occasional appearance. She continued to do so until 1985, the only player to compete for this length of time on the LPGA Tour.

Sunningdale, Berkshire, England

Sunningdale's Old course is one of the most famous in a stretch of country in Berkshire noted for all that is best in heathland golf. It has been a splendid venue for some outstanding championships, both amateur and professional, men's and women's. Founded in 1900, it was laid out by Willie Park and improved by H S Colt, who was the club's first secretary and designer of the later New course, more exposed but equally testing.

The Old winds through fir trees, with many scenic holes, and glorious views from high tees and

greens, notably from the green of the par three fourth, with the par four fifth sweeping away to a green guarded by a pond, and the sixth another downhill drive in the same direction. At the 10th, with the drive down to a wide fairway, James Braid in the PGA Match Play of 1903 hit a superb long iron out of a bunker on the left on to the green and holed the putt for a birdie, finally beating Ted Ray for the title. The final three holes provide a testing finish, with an uphill approach to a green in the shelter of a magnificent oak at the 18th.

One of the most memorable performances came from the great Bobby Jones when the Open qualifying rounds were held here in 1926, returning 66 to break the course record by six strokes and then having 68. He went on to win his first Open at Lytham. In 1956 Gary Player won the Dunlop Tournament for his first major professional success.

In recent years it has been the

Royal Sydney, New South Wales, Australia: now in the centre of urban development, this course retains its seaside characteristics and is a fine championship test.

Hal Sutton

venue for the European Open. Winners have included Bernhard Langer and Greg Norman. Between 1974 and 1979 Sunningdale attracted the top women players of the world for the LPGA European Championship, won on two occasions by Nancy Lopez. In 1934 the club inaugurated its annual Sunningdale Foursomes, a unique and popular event open to both amateur and professional players in mixed pairings. In 1956 the British Ladies Amateur was held here, followed by the English Ladies in 1974. In 1986 it was the venue for the Brabazon Trophy,

and in 1987 it staged the Walker Cup for its first major international event.

Sutton, Hal

1958–. Born Shreveport, Louisiana, USA

Hal Sutton came to the US Tour with one of the best records over a short period in post-war amateur golf. Twice in the Walker Cup team, he carried nearly all before him in 1980, winning the North and South, North Eastern and the Western and US Amateurs. Even more significant, he was leading individual in the World Amateur team event with a 276 which was nine strokes ahead of the field.

On the Tour in 1982, Sutton won at the end of the season and was 11th in the money list but he really became a star in 1983. He won the Tournament Players' Championship and the PGA and was leading money winner. Sutton considers he relaxed the following year and dropped to 26th in the money list. He was back again in 1985 and 1986, however, winning four times, including the 1986 Memorial, and he was seventh and sixth on the money list. He played in the 1985

Ryder Cup team and has seven career wins.

Sweetser, Jess

1902–. Born St Louis, Missouri, USA

In 1922, Jess Sweetser won the US Amateur, after defeating Bobby Jones by eight and seven in the semi-finals, the worst result Jones ever had in amateur competition. Sweetser was a finalist the following year and in 1926 became the first American-born player to take the British Amateur, beating A F Simpson six and five at Muirfield. He played in the Walker Cup between 1922 and 1932 and was later twice non-playing captain.

Sydney, Royal, New South Wales, Australia

In what was once virgin country, the Royal Sydney links course is now in the centre of urban development, similar in a way to Royal Lytham in Britain. Yet it retains its seaside characteristics, and is a fine championship test. The Sydney club was formed in 1893; land was later acquired for 18 holes, and its Royal title accorded in 1897.

The course hosted the Australian Open for the first time in 1906 and the event has returned here on many occasions. Its winners include Bruce Crampton and Gary Player, while the Australian Professional event played here has featured Kel Nagle and Peter Thomson among its winners.

Most of the greens are small and well-bunkered, designed by Alister Mackenzie, and over a shorter first half, the fourth and fifth are testing par fours into the wind, calling for long, slightly uphill approach shots. There are three par fives over the second nine, the best being the 13th. The final hole is a dog-leg par four to a well-bunkered green, with trees making a narrow entrance for the approach shot.

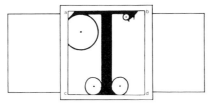

Tait, Freddie

1870–1900. Born Edinburgh, Scotland

Freddie Tait first attracted attention by beating the amateur record for the Old Course, St Andrews, in 1890 with a round of 77. A few years later, he lowered it to 72. Tait was twice third in the Open Championship, in 1896 and 1897, and his finest performances were reserved for matchplay. He won the British Amateur at Royal St George's in 1896, accounting for most of the top players and beating Harold Hilton in the final.

Tait won again two years later and also reached the 1899 final. Having once again beaten Hilton, he lost to John Ball at the 37th. His career was tragically ended at the age of 30 when he was killed in the Boer War.

Taylor, J H

1871–1963. Born Northam, Devon, England

John Henry Taylor (known as 'JH') is always associated with Vardon and Braid. Together, they formed the 'Great Triumvirate' who dominated British professional golf from the mid-1890s to the outbreak of World War I. Taylor won the Open Championship the first time it was played in England, at Sandwich in 1894.

When Taylor won again the following year at St Andrews, a course for which he had a life-long dislike, he had established himself as the leading player of the day. Harry Vardon was beginning to present a new challenge, and in 1896 they tied for the championship at Muirfield. Vardon won the 36-hole play-off.

Taylor won three more Open titles in 1900, 1909 and 1913. In all his five championships, his margins of victory were remarkable: five strokes, four, eight, six and eight. He was also second five times. Among his other wins were the Match Play Championship twice, two French Opens and the German Open. In America, he was second to Vardon in the 1900 US Open.

Taylor was involved in founding the PGA and served as captain and chairman. On his retirement in 1957 as professional at Royal North Devon, the club honoured him by electing him president. He died within a month of his 92nd birthday in the village where he was born.

Thomson, Muriel

1954 -. Born Aberdeen, Scotland

After an amateur career which included the Scottish championship in 1973, two North of Scotland titles and being chosen for the 1978 Curtis Cup, Muriel Thomson turned professional at the launch of the WPGA Tour in 1979. Since then, her worst money list placing has been ninth and she was leading money winner in 1980 and 1983. She has won nine times.

Thomson, CBE, Peter

1929–. Born Melbourne, Victoria, Australia

When Peter Thomson won the Open Championship at Royal Birkdale in 1965, he became the first player of the modern era to win the event five times. Three players before World War I had achieved that distinction — J H Taylor, James Braid and Harry Vardon — and when he won the last Open before the war in 1914, Vardon claimed the all-time record of six titles. Tom Watson claimed five Open titles in 1983.

Peter Thomson

Thomson's record in the Open is outstanding. He was runner-up in 1952 and 1953, then won three in a row from 1954, the only man to do so since the early days of the championship. He was second in 1957 and won his fourth title the next year. Bobby Locke's victory in 1957 robbed him of five titles in succession.

Then the great days seemed to be over, as Player, Nagle, Palmer, Charles and Lema took over, but at Birkdale in 1965, where he had won his first championship, Thomson showed he was no spent force as he triumphed for the fifth time over the rivals who had kept him out of the Open limelight.

Although he was never a dramatic golfer, Thomson's strength was his superb judgement, a feel for distance, a command of links golf, and always swinging with rhythm, perfect balance and well within himself. He first claimed attention in his own country when he was leading amateur in the Australian Open in 1948. He then won the first of nine New Zealand Opens in 1950, and the first of three Australian Opens in 1951. He was a truly international golfer, with more than 50 tournament wins world wide, in Europe, Asia and Japan. In the USA, he played the tour in the 1950s and 1960s, but only part time. His lone victory there was the Texas International Open in 1956, when he beat Gene Littler and Cary Middlecoff in a play-off. With Kel Nagle, he won the World Cup for Australia in 1954 and 1959.

In Britain, Thomson's victories included four PGA Match Play titles, two Dunlop Masters and two Martini Internationals, and he won the Italian, Spanish and German Opens. Retiring from golf, he ran for a seat in the Australian parliament, but after losing narrowly he joined the US Seniors Tour in 1982. His first win came in 1984 in the World Seniors Invitational and he added the PGA title the same year. In 1985, he was in brilliant form with nine tournament wins to finish top Seniors money winner with $386,724. He netted over half a million dollars that year with a bonus award of $125,000. He is also involved in course design, responsible for 40 courses, mainly in Australia and Japan.

Thornhill, Jill

1942–. Born Ely, Cambridgeshire, England

Although finalist in the French amateur championship in 1964 and winner of the Belgian title in 1967, it was in the 1980s that Jill Thornhill emerged as an outstanding player.

In 1983, she won the British championship at Silloth, beating Regine Lautens of Switzerland, four and two. That year she also won the Welsh Open Stroke Play. In 1984 she played in her first Curtis Cup match at Muirfield, when the home team lost by a single point. Two years later she won three matches and halved one as the Great Britain and Ireland team won at Prairie Dunes, Kansas, by 13 to five.

In 1984 Thornhill achieved a long-held ambition when she won the English championship for the first time, an event in which she had competed since 1960 and in which she had been runner-up in 1974. She was British captain in the 1984 Espirito Santo match. She has twice been successful in the Avia Watches Foursomes Championship, at the Berkshire.

Thorpe, Jim

1949–. Born Roxboro, North Carolina, USA

In his third full season on the US Tour, Jim Thorpe led the 1981 US Open with a first round 66 but finished in 11th place. His best Open finish came in 1984 when he was fourth. His best season on the Tour was in 1985 when he finished fourth in the money list with two wins. Although he only has three wins to his credit, two of these were in the 1985 and 1986 Tucson Match Play Championship.

Tillinghast, A W

1874–1942. Born North Philadelphia, Pennsylvania, USA

As a prosperous young amateur, AW Tillinghast visited St Andrews and is thought to have struck up a

Jim Thorpe

friendship with Old Tom Morris. Tillinghast became involved in course design when asked to help out at Shawnee Country Club, and was soon an enthusiast. Some of his most famous work followed at Baltusrol, Winged Foot, Hermitage, San Francisco and Ridgewood. He insisted that his firm should also construct the courses to ensure that his designs were fully carried through.

Tolley, Cyril

1896–1978. Born London, England

A leading figure in British amateur golf between the wars, Cyril Tolley was still good enough to reach the semi-finals of the Amateur Championship in 1950. He won the event in 1920 while at Oxford and took the title again in 1929. A year later at St Andrews, when defending his title, he met Bobby Jones in the fourth round and lost at the 19th. That year Jones completed his Grand Slam.

Tolley won a host of other events and played against the USA seven times in the years 1921–1934. He won the French Open in 1924 and 1928, the only amateur to do so. Later he became an influential figure at the R and A and was captain in 1948.

Torrance, Sam

1953–. Born Largs, Ayrshire, Scotland

Sam Torrance has finished among the top six money winners on the European Tour six times: in 1976 and between 1981 and 1985. He was runner-up to Bernhard Langer in 1984, winning his highest ever prize money of £129,409. He is a long and consistent driver of the ball, but his putting let him down in 1986 when he dropped to 17th place.

Torrance's greatest moment came in the Ryder Cup at The Belfry in 1985 when his putting

Sam Torrance and his moment of glory in the Ryder Cup in 1985 when he won it back after 28 years.

earned him fame. His last-green birdie putt clinched Ryder Cup victory after 28 years. It was his third Ryder Cup appearance and he secured his place in the 1987 match in America.

Torrance has 12 European Tour wins, and overseas won the 1980 Australian PGA. He tied for a US Tour event before the 1983 Ryder Cup but lost the play-off. He won the Italian Open in 1987.

Travers, Jerry

1887–1951. Born New York, USA

One of the first great American amateurs, Jerry Travers was renowned for his putting, but a poor driver, he would often rely on an iron off the tee.

Travers won four US Amateur titles, surpassed only by Bobby Jones who won five. He first won in 1907 and again the following year. Then he did not compete until 1911. He won again in 1912 and 1913. In 1915, he became one of only five amateurs to win the US Open, and never played in another national championship, concen-

trating on his business in Wall Street.

Travis, Walter

1862–1925. Born Maldon, Victoria, Australia

The first overseas player to win the British Amateur, Travis was always regarded as an American. At the time of his Sandwich victory in 1904, Travis had been playing golf for only a few years. His putting throughout was thought phenomenal and attributed to his centre-shaft Schenectady putter. A few years later they were banned by the R and A but not by the USGA.

Although this was his most sensational victory, Travis also won the US Amateur three times in 1900, 1901 and 1903. He took up the game at the age of 35, only four years before his 1900 victory.

In 1905 Travis founded and edited one of the best golf magazines ever, *The American Golfer*, which closed in the 1930s in the Depression. He also worked in golf course design: Garden City and Ekwanok were his best work.

Trevino, Lee

1939–. Born Dallas, Texas, USA

As well as being one of the greatest players of the game, Lee Trevino has also made his mark as one of its greatest personalities. His wise-cracking has become as legendary as his golf has become indelibly inscribed on the game. His superb performances, which have brought him six major championships, earned him the title of SuperMex.

Trevino came to golf by helping at a driving range as a boy. Brought up by his mother and grandfather in a shack in Dallas, he never knew his father. He served four years in the Marines, where he was given time to play golf; he turned professional in 1960. After winning the Texas State title in 1965, he played in the US Open the

Lee Trevino at the British Open in 1980, one of his best seasons. He is a superb golfer and a great personality.

following year, and tied for 54th place at the Olympic club. In 1967 at Baltusrol, he finished sixth behind Jack Nicklaus, collected $6,000 in prize money and was on the US Tour to stay.

A year later, Trevino was celebrating as US Open champion at Oak Hill. Its severe rough did not worry Trevino, who rarely missed a fairway with his individual swing, aiming down the left and curling the ball back into the fairway. Although Bert Yancey led after 36 and 54 holes, Trevino went into the lead over the final nine holes, winning by four strokes as Yancey slipped to 76. Few thought that Trevino, with his awkward swing, would last. He proved them wrong, for his action kept the ball low and it has stood the test of time.

After his 1968 Open victory, Trevino never looked back. In 1970, he topped the money list and was

second the next two years. More major titles came his way in possibly his greatest year, 1971, when he was named US Player of the Year. He beat Nicklaus in a play-off for the US Open at Merion, and in the space of five weeks added the Canadian and British Opens. That first Open in Britain appropriately came at Royal Birkdale, where in 1968 as reigning US Open champion he had made his first appearance in the Alcan Golfer of the Year event. In 1971, he won an exciting duel for the Open title with Mr Lu who had endeared himself to the fans.

In 1972, Trevino retained his title at Muirfield, the first player to win two in succession since Palmer 10 years previously. His chip into the hole from the back of the 17th green destroyed Jacklin, who looked to have the championship won but then three-putted to lose the hole and the title.

Of the two other majors, Trevino was only able to add the US PGA which he won in 1974 and again in 1984. He was then 44 and triumphed over Gary Player and Lanny Wadkins at Shoal Creek by shooting all four rounds in the 60s. The Masters eluded him: it was a course which did not suit him and he never cared for the aura which surrounded the event.

Until winning his second PGA in 1984, Trevino had failed to win a tournament for more than three years. He had suffered back problems, thought to have originated when he was struck by lightning at the 1975 Western Open, and later underwent an operation for a fused disc.

One of Trevino's best seasons was in 1980 when he won three tournaments for second place in the money list with $385,814, and won his fifth Vardon Trophy with a scoring average of 69.73, the lowest since Sam Snead's 69.23 in 1950. The 1984 PGA took his tour wins to 27.

By 1987, his career winnings totalled $3,300,000 — only Nicklaus, Watson and Floyd have won more. Trevino won the Canadian Open three times and the Canadian PGA twice and also won in Australia, Mexico, Morocco and France. In Britain, he won the Benson and Hedges International in 1978, and in 1985 at last gained a Masters title. In the Dunhill British Masters at Woburn, he manoeuvred a three-wood from the right rough at the final hole to within inches of the cup for an eagle three which earned him victory.

Trevino made six Ryder Cup appearances and captained the unsuccessful US team at The Belfry in 1985.

Troon, Royal, Ayrshire, Scotland

Founded in 1878, Royal Troon is one of a number of links courses which run along the Ayrshire coast, with fine views out to sea to the hills of Arran and the rocky Ailsa Craig, which dominates Turnberry.

It was given its Royal title in its centenary year. It has been host to some outstanding championships, the first Open here being in 1923 when a British win was recorded by Arthur Havers. Fifty years later, he was an honoured guest at the age of 75 when he watched the elegant Tom Weiskopf win a rain-soaked Open.

Many changes to the course have been made over the years: length has been added and new greens introduced. Bobby Locke won Troon's second Open in 1950, and the course was lengthened in 1962 when on a hard, dry course Arnold Palmer won his second Open in a row and set a new championship record of 276. This was equalled by Weiskopf on a sodden course, and beaten a few miles away at Turnberry in 1977 by Tom Watson's remarkable 268. Palmer won by six

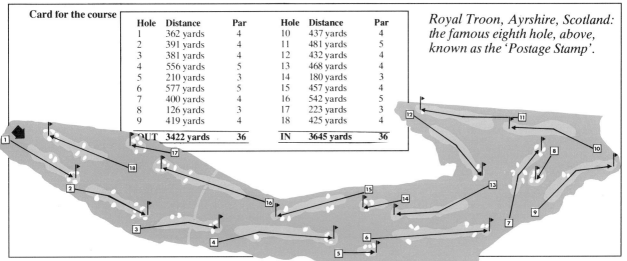

Card for the course

Hole	Distance	Par	Hole	Distance	Par
1	362 yards	4	10	437 yards	4
2	391 yards	4	11	481 yards	5
3	381 yards	4	12	432 yards	4
4	556 yards	5	13	468 yards	4
5	210 yards	3	14	180 yards	3
6	577 yards	5	15	457 yards	4
7	400 yards	4	16	542 yards	5
8	126 yards	3	17	223 yards	3
9	419 yards	4	18	425 yards	4
OUT	3422 yards	36	IN	3645 yards	36

Royal Troon, Ayrshire, Scotland: the famous eighth hole, above, known as the 'Postage Stamp'.

strokes from Kel Nagle, reversing the result of the St Andrews Open two years earlier. When he returned for the Open of 1982, Palmer was honoured by the club who granted him honorary life membership. Watson won his fourth Open here in 1982, and the club is to host the championship again in 1989.

One of Troon's most famous holes is the eighth, the 'Postage Stamp,' at 126 yards the shortest on Open courses. Here in 1973 the legendary Gene Sarazen, like Havers making a nostalgic return at the age of 71, holed in one and danced in delight round the tee with his partners who included former Open champion Max Faulkner. One of the toughest holes is the long par four 11th, with a narrow driving line along the railway. Here in his first Open in 1962 Jack Nicklaus took 10, opening with a round of 80; here Arnold Palmer took a hold on the title, playing it one under par for the four rounds.

The Amateur Championship was first played at Troon in 1938 when Charlie Yates, so long associated with Augusta National, beat Ireland's Cecil Ewing. It has returned on three further occasions, with Michael Bonallack among the winners. The Ladies British Open, first played here in 1904, has been staged four times, and it has been the venue for many Scottish Amateur and Ladies championships, as well as home internationals.

Turnberry, Ayrshire, Scotland: a spectacular links course.

Hole	Distance	Par	Hole	Distance	Par
10	452 yards	4	1	350 yards	4
11	177 yards	3	2	428 yards	4
12	448 yards	4	3	462 yards	4
13	411 yards	4	4	167 yards	3
14	440 yards	4	5	441 yards	4
15	209 yards	3	6	222 yards	3
16	409 yards	4	7	528 yards	5
17	500 yards	5	8	427 yards	4
18	431 yards	4	9	455 yards	4
IN	**3477 yards**	**35**	**OUT**	**3480 yards**	**35**

Card for the course

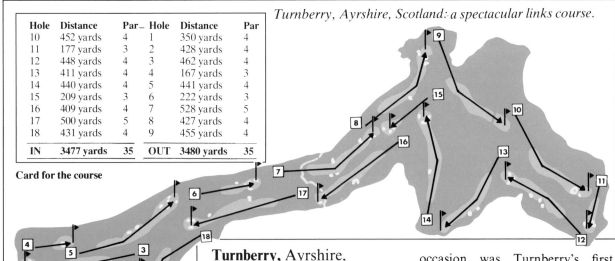

Turnberry, Ayrshire, Scotland

This superb links course is dominated on one side by its outstanding hotel and out to sea by the mighty rock Ailsa Craig. It was the setting for one of the most classic duels in golfing history between two of the greatest players, Jack Nicklaus and Tom Watson. The occasion was Turnberry's first Open Championship in 1977, an event which first saw Mark Hayes lower the championship record with a round of 63, and reached its climax on the final day after Nicklaus and Watson had matched rounds of 68, 70 and 65. Watson went ahead at the 17th and put his approach to the final green two feet from the hole, but Nicklaus played superbly out of the rough on the right to reach the green and hole a monster putt for a birdie three, leaving Watson to hole out for the title with a round of 65 to 66. In heatwave conditions, their brilliant play is underlined by the fact that Hubert Green, who finished third, was 10 strokes behind Nicklaus.

When the Open returned in 1986 in biting winds and rain, Greg Norman triumphed with a total of 280, 12 strokes more than Watson. He had to contend with penal rough as well as the conditions, and still managed a round of 63. The Amateur Championship came here in 1961 to give Michael Bonallack the first of his five wins. It also staged the Walker Cup in 1963, when the home team went down to the Americans after leading the first day.

The Ladies British Open was played here for the first time in 1912. The way in which weather conditions can affect this course was shown in the John Player Classic of 1972 when 11 players were under par on the first day. When a gale blew on the last day Bob Charles finished one over par to take the title, with Gary Player blown to 85.

World War II saw the RAF take over two holiday courses, but afterwards the then owners British Railways brought in Mackenzie Ross to construct the championship 'Ailsa' lay-out, with the 'Arran' following. Its most spectacular hole is the par four ninth, 'Bruce's Castle' by the lighthouse, with the tee jutting out and washed by the sea, and a long carry to a sloping fairway.

Tway, Bob

1959–. Born Oklahoma City, USA

The 1986 season on the US Tour developed into a duel for top honours between former All-American amateur player Bob Tway and

Bob Tway

the Australian who has become his country's top star, Greg Norman. In the end, each could claim a success over the other, but it was Tway who dealt a crushing blow to Norman as they battled for the US PGA title at the Inverness club in Toledo.

Norman had won two tournaments, Tway three on the tour in 1986 and the Australian had won the British Open at Turnberry a month earlier. For three rounds Norman led the PGA; Tway came into the reckoning with 64 on the third day, but still trailed by four strokes. As Norman faltered on the last day, Tway came through the field, and as they played the final hole they were level. Tway's approach to the 18th green fell into a bunker and Norman seemed favourite for his second major title, but Tway holed from the trap for a birdie which Norman was unable to match.

The pair were left to fight for the title of leading money winner. Nor-

man ended his season to play overseas and Tway had the opportunity to overtake him; he failed to do so by the narrow margin of $516. Tway finished Number Two, having won $652,780, and also collected another $500,000 for heading the season's Vantage Cup standings. He was named the tour's player of the year.

Tway, named 1981 college player of the year at Oklahoma State University, joined the tour in 1985 after failing three times at qualifying school, and finished in 45th place with $164,000. His first victory came in 1986 in the Andy Williams Open, in which he tied with Bernhard Langer in an event reduced to 54 holes by rain, and won the play-off. He had two more wins before adding the PGA title. While waiting to win his place on the US Tour, Tway played in tournaments in Europe and Asia, but with little success. He is an excellent striker of the ball and his putting is a strong part of his game.

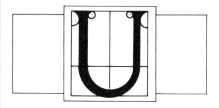

US Amateur Championship

In 1893, Newport Golf Club decided to organize a strokeplay tournament over 36 holes to attract prominent amateurs. Twenty players entered, with Charles Blair Macdonald the favourite. He led by four strokes after an opening 89, but after incurring penalty strokes in the afternoon when his ball came to rest against a wall, Macdonald lost by a stroke. He said the wall had no business on the golf course and that strokeplay was no way to settle a national championship. The next year, the St Andrews club staged a national matchplay championship. Macdonald lost again and claimed this also was not a national championship because the event had not had the approval of every club in the country.

In 1895, Macdonald had no complaints in the first USGA event. He won by what is still the record margin of 12 and 11 against Charles Sands.

Most of the early US Amateur Champions, like Macdonald, had learned their golf in Britain. One foreign-born player to win the Amateur was the Australian, Walter Travis, victor in 1900, 1901 and 1903, who took up golf in his mid-30s and learned the game in the USA. The only other non-American winners after the first years were Englishman Harold Hilton in 1911, the Canadian Ross Somerville in 1932, and his fellow-countryman Gary Cowan in 1966 and 1971.

Travis was the first really good player to win the title and the next was Jerome Travers, champion four times in 1907, 1908, 1912 and 1913. Shortly afterwards, the era of

Bobby Jones began at Merion when he won his first two matches in 1916 at the age of 14. He reached his first final in 1919 and won the title for the first time in 1924.

Afterwards, Jones was almost unstoppable. He was a record five times champion at the time of his retirement in 1930, and no golfer since has monopolized the event the way Jones did.

Before the early 1950s, relatively few Amateur champions joined the paid ranks but the reverse has been the case since then. Only Jay Sigel and Gary Cowan, who remained amateurs, have won more than once in the last 30 years. From its inception the US Amateur Championship was regarded as more important then the Open and years went by before the Open was given precedence by the USGA.

US Masters Tournament

The Masters has acquired its own tradition, although the first Augusta National Invitation was played as recently as 1934. Much of the mystique stems from its founder, the legendary Bobby Jones, one of golf's all-time greats, who created his dream course at Augusta and whose influence and personality still remain. After completing his Grand Slam in 1930 and retiring from competitive golf, Jones favoured the Augusta area for a course of championship quality because of its warm winter climate. With Clifford Roberts, a New York investment banker who often wintered there, Jones found the ideal site, a former horticultural nursery.

Jones chose Alister Mackenzie, designer of Cypress Point, as his architect, and Jones's own ideas became features of the lay-out, reflecting some of his playing preferences — vast, undulating, fast greens, demanding two-shot holes which favour the long, right to left player in the Jones mould.

The course opened early in 1933, with membership drawn from the upper echelons of American business and military society, with a small number of local members. Roberts suggested that Augusta could stage an event different from all the rest, if Jones invited the participants, acted as host and played himself. The first Augusta National Invitation Tournament was held in March 1934 with Jones in the field more than three years after retiring from the game.

The event might have faded away during the 1930s, but for the achievement of Gene Sarazen in 1935. Playing the par five 15th in his final round, he needed three birdies to match Craig Wood's score. After a good drive, he holed his second shot of 230 yards. His albatross or double eagle became the most famous shot in golf history, arousing tremendous public interest in the event, which became officially known in 1938 as 'The Masters'.

The prestige of the Masters grew and after the war in 1946, players welcomed playing in an event with a special appeal. Above all, people were impressed by the beauties of the course with its colourful shrubs, its pre-Civil War clubhouse and the presence of Bobby Jones, generally regarded as the greatest golfer ever.

Between 1949 and 1954, Sam Snead, Jimmy Demaret or Ben Hogan won, all great names. In 1954, an amateur, Billy Joe Patton, came close to winning. He led after two rounds, dropped back with a 75 and went into the final round five strokes behind. He holed in one at the sixth and although he came to grief in water on the two par fives, the 13th and 15th, he finished only a stroke behind the play-off between Snead and Hogan. Snead went on to win by 70 to 71, beating Hogan, the man regarded as almost invincible, who in 1953 had the best year of anyone since Jones, winning the Masters and both British and US Opens.

A new hero was waiting in the wings. Arnold Palmer won his first prize money as a professional at the 1955 Masters. He finished 10th and that was worth $696. In 1957, he went into the final round a stroke off the lead before a 76 left him in seventh place, well behind Doug Ford who holed from a bunker at the last for a round of 66.

This was the beginning of the Palmer years and Augusta itself gave birth to 'Arnie's Army'. His first victory came in 1958 amid controversy. Palmer hit through the green on the short 12th in his final round and his ball was embedded in soft ground. The PGA rule allowed a lift anywhere on the course (except in hazards). The Masters rule appeared to differ and apply only to a ball plugged on the fairway. The official on the spot was unsure and asked for two balls to be played. Palmer took five from the embedded lie and chipped and putted for his par when allowed to move his ball. The rules decision went Palmer's way, giving him a par three and the lead over his playing partner, Ken Venturi.

Palmer went on to eagle the next hole while Venturi began to three-putt.

In 1959 Palmer reached the short 12th with a two-stroke lead in the final round, but his tee shot pitched just short of the putting surface and spun back into Rae's Creek. He took six. Art Wall, who had begun the day six strokes behind the leaders, birdied five of the last six holes to win. Palmer was third, two strokes behind.

In 1960, Palmer led after every round, yet with two holes to play needed to birdie one of the last two holes to tie Ken Venturi, who had finished his round. Palmer birdied both to win.

This feat was at the heart of the Palmer legend ever after — he was the man who could pull out the

Top: Sam Snead and Gene Sarazen, both winners of the US Masters, travel cheerfully together.

Above: Jack Nicklaus acknowledging his triumph at the 1986 US Masters, another highlight in a dazzling career.

shots when he needed them. It was the same story, but in reverse, in 1961. Palmer went into the last round four shots behind Gary Player but, as he stood on the 18th tee, Player was in with 74 and Palmer needed par for 69 and a one-stroke victory. His drive was excellent, but he pushed his approach into a bunker, put his

recovery over the green and took six.

In 1962 Palmer played the first three rounds in 70, 66, 69 to lead Dow Finsterwald by two and Player by four. Even so, he came to the last three holes needing two birdies to tie Player and Finsterwald. He got both.

The next day in the 18-hole play-off Palmer struggled out weakly in 37 but roared home in 31 to become the third man, after Snead and Jimmy Demaret, to win the Masters three times.

In 1963, Nicklaus won his first Masters, greatly helped by a 66 in the second round. Although Palmer won with strokes to spare in 1964, his reign at Augusta was over. Nicklaus won three times in only four years. In 1965, he set the four-round record of 271 and equalled the course record in the third round with a 64. The next men, Palmer and Player, were nine strokes behind.

Nicklaus took his fourth title in 1972, and Player his second in 1974. The next year saw one of the greatest Masters' contests. Nicklaus opened with 68, 67 but then faltered with a 73 as Johnny Miller came back from a poor start with 65, and Tom Weiskopf with 66 took the lead. In the final round, no one else was in it. Nicklaus, playing the 16th, was one behind Weiskopf but two ahead of Miller. A birdie two to Weiskopf's four put Nicklaus in the lead. Miller came into the picture when he birdied the 17th. He and Weiskopf needed birdies on the last to tie Nicklaus. Both played superb second shots but the putts failed, and Nicklaus became the first to win five Masters.

In 1976 Raymond Floyd equalled Nicklaus's 271 aggregate, and Tom Watson won his first title in 1977. Long before this, the Masters had become one of the four major championships. Its image has been helped by the green blazer for the champion with the previous winner helping the new man on with his coat. Other traditions were also introduced successfully. One of these involves former great players playing a nine-holes 'lap of honour.' Once, it was Jock Hutchison and Fred McLeod, followed by Byron Nelson, Sam Snead and Gene Sarazen.

On the Monday of Masters week the club plays host to the amateur contestants, followed by overseas entrants the next day. Then comes the most hallowed of those occasions, the past champions' dinner, started by Ben Hogan in 1952. The defending champion always pays and his guests finish their evening by watching the film of his victory. All champions are given their own private lockers, but can only wear their Masters coats at Augusta itself.

Over the years, Clifford Roberts, who had given it the Masters title, was responsible for most of the ideas which helped to improve it. Jones died in 1971 of a crippling spinal disease. In 1977, in failing health and with preparations for the 1978 tournament well under way, Roberts took a revolver from his clubhouse desk, wandered on to the course and shot himself.

The dramas, especially over the

Larry Mize on his way to winning the US Masters in 1987. This victory saw him pass the $-million mark in Tour winnings.

final nine holes, continued. In 1978, Player came home with 64, with seven birdies in the last 10 holes. In 1979, after the decision to introduce sudden death instead of 18-hole play-offs, Fuzzy Zoeller won on his first appearance, beating Tom Watson and Ed Sneed at the second extra hole. A couple of years later, the 23-year-old Seve Ballesteros became the youngest champion. At one point in his final round he was 10 strokes in the lead, stumbled — but won comfortably enough in the end. Another victory followed in 1983. Starting one behind in the final round, Ballesteros started birdie, eagle, par, birdie and reached the turn in 31 before winning by four strokes. Another European, Bernhard Langer, won in 1985.

The Augusta magic was still there in 1986 with a remarkable finish which produced the oldest Masters winner, Jack Nicklaus, aged 46. His final round of 65 included seven birdies and an eagle. It was his sixth victory, and an impregnable record to the present generation of golfers.

US Open Championship

The beginnings of the US Open were no more grand than the first Open Championship at Prestwick in 1860. On October 4 1895 one amateur and 10 professionals assembled at Newport and played round the nine holes four times.

Horace Rawlins was the first winner with rounds of 91 and 82. A 21-year-old Englishman from the Isle of Wight, he had emigrated to the USA earlier in the year to be assistant professional at Newport. It was only the third competition he had played in and it was worth $150. The early winners were all American-based but British-born.

The year 1900 was an exception which showed the difference in standards between golf in America and Britain. Vardon and Taylor were over on an exhibition tour and entered the Open. The two Englishmen dominated the event, Vardon winning with 313 to Taylor's 315 (72 holes came in from 1898).

In the following years, Willie Anderson established an unbeaten record, winning four times, and the first American-born champion, Johnny McDermott, arrived in 1911. Aged 19, he remains the youngest winner. McDermott had already lost a play-off for the title and won again in 1912.

In golfing legend, however, McDermott's feats were soon eclipsed by another home-bred player, Francis Ouimet, a 20-year-old amateur. Vardon was on tour in the USA again, this time accompanied by Ted Ray, winner of the British Open the previous year. In a desperate finish, Ouimet managed to catch them to complete a three-way tie. No one gave him a chance in the play-off over 18 holes. Even so, he held his own on the first nine and went into a lead he never relinquished on the next hole. He eventually cruised home with a five-stroke lead.

Although golf was already booming in America, Ouimet's astonishing victory added to the momentum and led to greater press coverage of golf. Amateurs won three of the four events from 1913 to 1916 but the 1914 championship, won by a professional, was even more significant. The winner was Walter Hagen, the most flamboyant of the major golfers. He won the title in 1914 and 1919, and was to make more news for his performances in the PGA and the British Open.

After Hagen's second victory, the age of Jones was at hand. He came a close second in 1922, the start of a bewildering sequence. From 1922 to 1930, Jones was only once out of the top two! Others might beat him but they could only do it once. The US Open in this period was very much a matter of Jones against the field. He missed out in 1927. Otherwise, he was

Walter Hagen who won the US Open in 1914 and 1919, an erratic golfer who achieved results although he never practised.

The great Ben Hogan in 1956 when he came second in the US Open. He won it in 1948 and 1953.

champion in 1923, 1926, 1929 and 1930, lost play-offs in 1925 and 1928 and was second in 1924.

With Jones retired and Hagen a spent force, much of the glamour left the US Open. Recovery came towards the end of the 1930s as a new crop of players appeared: notably Ralph Guldahl, Sam Snead, Lawson Little and Byron Nelson. Snead came close to winning the first time he played in the Open but, in spite of trying for some 30 years, he never succeeded. Twice-champion Gene Sarazen bowed out as a serious contender when he lost a play-off in 1940.

Shortly after World War II, Ben Hogan experienced a period of dominance similar to that of Jones. He won his first title in 1948, was almost killed in a car crash in 1949 but with great courage returned to win in 1950 and 1951. He was third in 1952, champion again in 1953, sixth in 1954 and then in 1955 he lost a play-off to the unknown Jack Fleck, which robbed him of a record five titles. He was second again the following year.

Although Hogan came close

once more, in 1960, a new generation was at hand: Arnold Palmer, Jack Nicklaus and Gary Player. Palmer's victory was to go into immediate legend. It was one of his famous last-round charges as he went to the turn in 30 and then held it together on the homeward nine for a 65 to win by a stroke from Nicklaus, who had the best finish by an amateur since 1933 — one which has not since been equalled.

When Nicklaus turned professional, it was appropriate that he made the 1962 Open his first victory, beating Arnold Palmer in a play-off. It was one of three play-offs featuring Palmer, who lost them all and only has one US Open title to his name.

One of the players who stopped him was Billy Casper. With the rest of the field virtually nowhere, Palmer led Casper by seven strokes with nine holes to play and had the Open scoring record in his sights, but amazingly the pair were level after 72 holes. In the play-off, Palmer again went into the lead, but then went down to hand Casper his second Open.

In the meantime, Gary Player had won the 1965 championship, his only victory, and Nicklaus won again in 1967. The following year saw the arrival of the unknown Lee Trevino who was to be a key figure of the 1970s. Remarkably he scored under 70 in every round. He had a repeat victory in 1971, with Nicklaus losing a play-off. Nicklaus made up for this the following year, taking his third title when the championship was staged at Pebble Beach for the first time.

In 1973 the fearsome Oakmont was humbled by Johnny Miller. He followed 76 in the third round with a record 63 which enabled him to overhaul the field. After Hale Irwin took the first of his two titles in 1974, there followed Lou Graham, Jerry Pate, Hubert Green and Andy North. With only one US Tour win, North has the unique

Tony Jacklin in 1970 when he won the US Open less than a year after he had won the British Open. He became the first Briton to hold both titles simultaneously since Harry Vardon in 1899.

record of twice winning the US Open, in 1978 and 1985.

After a long gap, Nicklaus came back emphatically in 1980 to take his fourth championship, setting the Open record of 272 in doing so. Two years later at Pebble Beach, it looked as if the record-breaking fifth title might well come his way. When Nicklaus had completed his round, there was only one man who could catch him — Tom Watson. Playing the par three 17th, Tom Watson's tee shot finished in deep grass, but he popped it out with his sand iron, and the ball ran into the hole for a birdie and victory.

Raymond Floyd's fourth major title in 1986 made him the oldest winner of the US Open about three months before his 44th birthday. He had a 66 in the last round to win by two strokes.

The event began to take off in 1920 when 265 players entered; an entry of 2,000 was first achieved in 1958, 3,000 10 years later, 4,000 in 1971 and more than 5,000 in 1987. The record number of 1920 also marked the year when the status of the championship began to rival that of its British equivalent.

Golfers who had learned to play the game in England and Scotland, notably Willie Macfarlane, Tommy Armour, Bobby Cruickshank, Jim Barnes, Jock Hutchison and Macdonald Smith, continued to feature strongly in the 1920s. In the next decade, the US Open was dominated by the home-born-and-bred golfers and has virtually remained so. Since Jones (1930) and Johnny Goodman (1933) all have been professionals; the greatest of these to fail to win the championship is undoubtedly Sam Snead. Ted Ray was the last foreign-based player to win until Gary Player in 1965 and Tony Jacklin five years later.

The policy of the USGA has always been to move their championship around the country, unlike the R and A, who play all events on links courses in Scotland, north-west and south-east England. Even so, most champion-

When Raymond Floyd won the US Open in 1986, he became its oldest winner. He won by two strokes.

ships have been played in the eastern half of America, but with ventures into the South and several in California. Perhaps the most popular courses with the USGA are Merion, Baltusrol, Winged Foot, Pebble Beach, Inverness, Cherry Hills, Olympic, Medinah, Oakland Hills, Oakmont, Southern Hills and Oak Hills. The decision to take the 1986 championship to Shinnecock Hills, site of the second US Open, was a courageous one, because of the low population in the area.

Courses for the US Open are rigorously prepared. Great attention is given to the greens so that they are hard — holding only well-struck shots — and very fast to putt and chip. Collars of dense rough have been allowed to grow around them, sometimes ruling out a running approach shot. Fairways are narrowed and, if necessary, the semi-rough is fertilized so that the ball settles down into dense grass.

US PGA Championship

Although the Western Open, first played in 1899, is the oldest event on the US Tour, the PGA is not far behind. It was founded as a match-play event in 1916, the same year that the US Professional Golfers' Association came into being.

Foreign-born players were much to the fore in the early years. The first championship was won by Cornishman Jim Barnes, who defeated Jock Hutchison from Scotland. Barnes again won the next time the event was contested, in 1919, with another Scotsman his victim, Fred McLeod. But domination by foreign-born players had not long to run. Hutchison was in the final again in 1920 and came through to beat a recent arrival from England, Douglas Edgar.

The following year saw the first victory by a fully-fledged American — Walter Hagen, who was to give the championship its greatest days and earn the reputation of being the greatest match player of all time. However, Hagen was not too impressed with his achievement. The US and British Opens meant far more to him. In 1922, he did not defend his title. It went to the man soon to be recognized as his main professional rival, Gene Sarazen, who had recently won the US Open. Sarazen was then 20, and still the youngest PGA champion.

By 1923 Hagen had lost his British Open title and was keen to compete for a major title. He entered and cruised through his semi-final with a 12 and 11 victory. Facing him in the final was Sarazen. After the 36 holes, the pair were level. Sarazen's putt stopped on the edge and then toppled in at the next. At the 38th, Sarazen appeared to hook out-of-bounds, but his ball was found in play and thrown back, Hagen always thought, by a friendly hand. Sarazen hit his second shot stone dead while Hagen's approach finished in a bunker.

It was to be several years before Hagen lost another match in the PGA. In 1924, he disposed of Jim Barnes for the second time, and reserved some of his best play for 1925. After winning his first two matches, Hagen then met Leo Diegel, possibly the most talented

Densmore Shute, winner of the US PGA in 1936 and 1937. He also won the British Open in 1933.

shot-maker of his generation. Diegel was two up with two to play and Hagen had to match his birdie at the 34th to survive. On it went to the 40th hole before Hagen came through.

After deciding not to compete the following year Hagen had a last-minute change of heart. Such was the informality then that he was able to turn up the afternoon before the championship began and was allowed to play. His eventual victory gave him four in a row, a record in major championships only paralleled by Young Tom Morris in the British Open.

Hagen had won 20 consecutive matches in the four years against the best that America had to offer. He lost only one match out of 30, the final with Sarazen in 1923. The run continued a little longer. Hagen came through two rounds in

Leo Diegel, whose career peaked in 1928 and 1929 when he twice won the US PGA Championship.

1928 and was then beaten at last, three and two, by Leo Diegel, who went on to take the championship, a victory he repeated the following year. Again he beat Hagen en route.

In the years leading up to World War II, there were some remarkable finals, none more so than 1931, won by Tom Creavy, a 20-year-old unknown who achieved little else in his career. One of the most remarkable matches of all time occurred in 1932. It was between Bobby Cruickshank and Al Watrous, the latter being nine up with 12 to go in their 36-hole match. After Watrous had casually conceded a six-foot putt, Cruikshank began to produce unstoppable golf and birdie followed birdie; the pair were tied and they went into extra holes, the first three being halved. On the fourth, Watrous with two for the match, went a couple of feet past and missed the return. When Watrous three-putted later, it was all over.

One of the Old Guard to win during the 1930s was Sarazen, champion for the third time in 1933, while Tommy Armour reached the 1935 final. By the end of the 1930s, there were new names to conjure with, in particular Sam Snead and Byron Nelson. One or other of them appeared in every final from 1938 to 1945. Snead was the first to do so and lost to Paul Runyan, while Byron Nelson lost a close contest with Henry Picard.

Both made the final in 1940, Nelson winning one up. Snead won for his first major championship in 1942 and Nelson won in 1945, the fifth final he had reached in six years.

The PGA became Hogan's first major championship in 1946 and he won again in 1948. There is little doubt he would have won more but his severe road crash in 1949 meant he could no longer cope with a succession of 36-hole matches. Snead marched on, winning in 1949

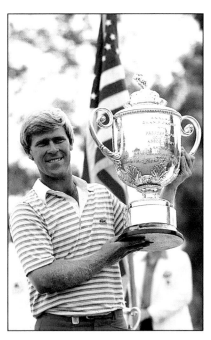

Hal Sutton with the US PGA trophy in 1983, the year he really became a star – and leading money winner.

and 1951 to become one of only three golfers to win the PGA three times as a matchplay event.

Television now began to take a close look at golf and decided it did not like the matchplay variety. Too many of the great names could be knocked out in the early rounds and matches finished far from home, with the cameras covering only the closing holes.

In 1958, it became just another Tour event as strokeplay. Arnold Palmer may have saved it as the major it is today by declaring he wanted to do the Grand Slam and including the PGA as part. Even so, its prestige lags far behind the US and British Opens and the Masters. A man who wins any one of these has his place in golf history; not so with the PGA. For most of its history, there does not seem to have been any great effort to ensure that the championship was played on courses of true stature, and strange names can be found among the venues chosen. That is now changed. Since the early 1970s, the courses have usually hosted a US Open. The few that have not are accepted as formidable tests — Firestone and Shoal Creek are examples.

The PGA has also been helped by dramatic finishes. In 1977, Lanny Wadkins overhauled the old maestro Gene Littler, whose game collapsed almost totally. In 1979 came the play-off between David Graham and Ben Crenshaw, in which Graham holed a couple of unlikely putts before winning through.

Tom Watson who, like Palmer, still seeks to win this championship, went into the last round in 1980 with a seven-shot advantage over John Mahaffey and saw it all drift away. In 1982 there was anticlimax as Raymond Floyd, with the championship record in his pocket, dumped a little pitch into a bunker, but still won with shots to spare. A bunker came into it again in 1986 as Bob Tway played the shot of the year from a bunker to take the title from Greg Norman.

In 1986 Bob Tway played the shot of the year from a bunker to take the US PGA Championship.

Larry Nelson, winner of the US PGA Championship in 1987. Nelson did not take up golf until he was 21.

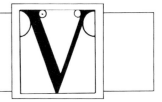

Valentine, MBE, Jessie

1915–. Born Perth, Scotland

One of Scotland's outstanding players, Jessie Valentine (neé Anderson) won the British Championship three times. After her first victory in 1937, there was a lapse of 18 years before she was successful again in 1955. Her third title came in 1958. In between, she was twice runner-up.

In Scottish events, Valentine claimed a string of victories. She won the Scottish championship six times between 1938 and 1956, and won the East of Scotland title four times from 1936 to 1950. She also won the New Zealand title in 1935 and the French in 1936.

Valentine made seven Curtis Cup appearances, playing in winning teams in 1954 and 1956. She was a Scottish international from 1934 to 1938 and turned professional in 1960.

Vardon, Harry

1870–1937. Born Grouville, Jersey, Channel Islands

Usually given precedence over his friendly rivals James Braid and J H Taylor, Harry Vardon is considered one of the greatest golfers ever. His supremacy rests on his record of six Open Championships, the last at Prestwick in 1914. Braid faded after a good first round, but Taylor was as eager as Vardon to become the first man in history to win six Opens.

After two rounds, Vardon led on 150, with Taylor a couple of strokes behind. For the two rounds of the final day they were drawn together. Taylor hit back with 74 to Vardon's 78 to give him a two-

stroke lead into the final afternoon's play. On the first hole, Taylor missed a two foot putt: it would
have given him the four-stroke lead
he needed. Soon after, there came
what Taylor called 'the greatest
tragedy of my golfing life'. Vardon
drove safely between bunkers and
the Pow Burn. Taylor bunkered his
tee shot, got out only a few yards
and into the burn, picked out and
three-putted. It was a seven to Vardon's four. The sixth championship
was Vardon's. As Taylor later
generously wrote: 'Harry Vardon
deserved the high honour. He was
the better player.'

Nearly 20 years before, few had
doubted this. Vardon took his first
title in 1896 and two more in 1898–
1899. He was second the following
three years before winning again in
1903. In ordinary tournament play
during this period he was almost
invincible. Then came tuberculosis.
Vardon recovered, but felt his lack
of confidence on short putts dated

Harry Vardon (left) in 1908, con-
sidered to be one of the greatest
golfers ever. He won six Open
Championships, the last at Prestwick.

from his illness. However, he won
again in 1911, when into his 40s,
and then came that final Open.

In Vardon's day, there was only
one other major championship, the
US Open. In 1900 both Vardon
and Taylor took part in exhibition
matches in America and when they
entered for the US Open that year,
no one else was credited with a
chance. So it turned out, as Vardon
took the title on his first appearance by two strokes from Taylor.

In the 1913 Open, Vardon tied
with countryman Ted Ray and 20-
year-old American amateur Francis Ouimet, who in spite of being
given no chance against two of the
outstanding professionals of the
day, won the play-off with 72 to
Vardon's 77 and Ray's 78. In 1920,
Vardon finished second, a stroke
adrift, as Ray this time took the
title.

Vardon's overlapping grip
remains the standard for most
golfers. His high, upright swing
became the ideal, and many strove
to achieve his high, carrying ball.
On his American tours, his easy,
graceful swing was a revelation to
enthusiasts who flocked to see him.

Ken Venturi

Venturi, Ken

1931–. Born San Francisco,
California, USA

Ken Venturi's golf career was a tale
of disaster and triumph. As an
amateur, he came close to winning
the 1956 Masters. He opened with
rounds of 66 and 69, followed with
75, and led into the final day by
four strokes. In poor weather, he
shot 80, yet everything hinged on
the 17th hole, a par four. Here Venturi took five as Jack Burke had a
birdie three to win.

Venturi turned professional that
year and by the time his next
chance in the Masters came round
in 1960, he had nine Tour wins to
his credit and one season had
finished third in the money list.
After a 70 in the last round, only
Palmer could catch him with a birdie at one of the last two holes.
Palmer birdied them both.

In 1960 Venturi was second in
the money list, 14th in 1961 and he
then fell away to 66th and 94th in
the next two seasons. Then in 1964
came his greatest triumph. He
qualified to play the US Open for
the first time in four years, played

two steady rounds and then picked up five birdies in the first nine holes of the third round to match the Open nine-hole record of 30 and make up six strokes on the leader, Tommy Jacobs. His 66 still left him two strokes behind Jacobs, but a final 70 gave him the title. His victory was a remarkable comeback after it seemed that a complete loss of form had ended his career.

Sadly, his career ended soon after one more victory to bring his total to 14. A disease of the hands caused loss of feeling and he could no longer play. He is now an authoritative TV commentator on golf.

Verplank, Scott

1964–. Born Dallas, Texas, USA

Victory in the 1985 Western Open for Scott Verplank made him the first amateur to win on the US Tour since Gene Littler in 1954. Doug Sanders won the 1956 Canadian Open as an amateur, when the event was not a part of the US Tour.

Roberto de Vicenzo

Verplank's win capped a successful amateur career for he won the 1984 US Amateur and the 1986 NCAA title. He played in the Walker Cup in 1985. In 1986, still as an amateur, Verplank tied for fourth place in the Tournament of Champions and turned professional for the US Open. He tied for 15th.

Vicenzo, Roberto de

1923–. Born Buenos Aires, Argentina

Probably the most prolific tournament winner ever, and Argentina's most famous player, Roberto de Vicenzo is credited with some 240 wins. Many have been on the South American scene; even so, his record includes more than 100 international successes.

De Vicenzo's greatest achievement was to win the 1967 British Open at Hoylake. He led Player by two strokes and Nicklaus by three after three rounds, and held on to win by two strokes from Nicklaus. It was an emotional victory for de Vicenzo, and a popular one with players and fans: he had striven since 1948 to win the Open, had finished third on five occasions and been runner-up in 1950. At the age of 44 he thought his chance had gone. He was second again in 1969.

In 1968 de Vicenzo should have tied for the Masters, but he failed to notice that a birdie three at the 17th had gone down on his card as a four. He signed the card and the score had to stand at 66. Three weeks later he won his ninth and last US Tour event. He has represented Argentina in the World Cup 17 times, and won the individual title when the event was held in his home town of Buenos Aires in 1970.

De Vicenzo's superb swing has lasted into his 60s. He continues to play on the Seniors Tour, and has won three tournaments.

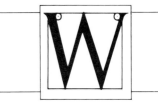

Wadkins, Lanny

1949–. Born Richmond, Virginia, USA

Lanny Wadkins joined the US Tour after an excellent amateur career, having won the 1970 US Amateur, two Southern, the Western and Eastern Amateurs. He played twice in the Walker Cup team.

On Tour, he won in his first season in 1972 and came 10th in the money list. The next year was even better: fifth place and two more wins. Then he went three years without a win, and he dropped out of the top 50 money winners.

In 1977 Wadkins won his first major championship, the US PGA, at Pebble Beach after a play-off with Gene Littler. Later the same

Lanny Wadkins

year he won the World Series. He was third in the money list, winning $244,882, was third again in 1983 and had his most successful season in 1985 when he finished second in the money list.

His approach to the game of attacking the course brought him victory in 1985 in the Bob Hope Classic, the Los Angeles Open and the Walt Disney Classic, and earned him $446,893. He also won the Player of the Year award.

By the end of 1986, Wadkins had 15 US Tour wins and had been successful in Australia, Japan and Canada. He has made four Ryder Cup appearances, and in 1983 at the PGA National, a brilliant pitch to the 18th green for victory over José-María Canizares was decisive in a one-point win for the United States.

Walton Heath, Surrey, England

The two courses, the Old and the New, are among the best of their type in England: testing heathland golf, high on the downs, with heather-lined fairways, cross bunkers and greens, the courses are true yet fast and hard to read. Both courses were laid out by Herbert Fowler, the first, the Old, in 1904. There have been many changes over the years, the latest resulting from the intrusion of the M25 motorway and the building of two new holes at the top of the course. Two of the outstanding holes on the Old are the fifth, a drive downhill and then up to a plateau green, with the possibility of three putts as it is not easy to get near the pin, and the 17th, recently altered, which has bunkers all the way round the front of the green.

The Old course was a popular venue for the PGA Match Play tournament, first held here in 1905, when James Braid won the second of four titles. It has also been the venue for the British Amateur, the

Brabazon Trophy and the British Ladies Championship. In recent years the European Open was played here over a composite lay-out of the two courses; the winners in 1978 and 1980 were Americans Bobby Wadkins and Tom Kite, respectively. The event returned here in 1987.

In 1981, the Ryder Cup was played here. One of the strongest American teams ever fielded beat the Great Britain and European players by 17 matches to eight, with three halved. Jack Nicklaus and Tom Watson won their three matches in a formidable foursomes and fourball partnership, and Larry Nelson, in two appearances in 1979 and 1981, achieved the remarkable record of winning all his nine matches.

James Braid, five times Open champion, has a special place in the history of the club, for he was professional from the start, and continued until his death in 1950.

Waterloo, Royal, Belgium

One of the first professionals of this famous club was Henry Cotton, who took up his post here in 1932. Two years later he not only won

Walton Heath, Surrey, England: the Old and the New courses provide testing heathland golf. James Braid was professional here until 1950.

the Belgian Open here, but went to Sandwich to capture his first British Open.

Royal Waterloo's first course was opened in 1923. It suffered during World War II and was later restored, but in 1960 British architect Fred Hawtree designed a new 18-hole lay-out at Ohain, near Brussels. Much of the course stretches over an undulating plain, but from the 11th to the 16th it climbs and then drops through a beech wood.

Two years after leaving the club in 1936, Cotton won the Belgian Open again here. The club's professionals have also included Flory von Donck, who won the first post-war Belgian title here, and later Donald Swaelens, who tragically died while still in his 30s.

There have been breaks in the continuity of the Belgian Open since 1959: after South African Gavin Levenson claimed the title here in 1979, the championship lapsed, but returned to Royal Waterloo in 1987.

Waterville, County Kerry, Eire

Ireland's famous Ring of Kerry is the setting for several fine courses, and one of more recent origin is Waterville in the south-west. Like the more famous Ballybunion, it is exposed to the winds which sweep in from the Atlantic to present an outstanding challenge.

While some of the earlier holes lack true linksland qualities, the second nine are as tough as can be found among hills and sand dunes, with a finish along the coast. Former Irish emigrant John Mulcahy, who made his fortune in steel in America, came home to Kerry to build his own course. He was closely involved in its planning, and designed one of its most famous holes himself. This is the 17th of 205 yards, named Mulcahy's Peak, with a high tee, an island green and a wilderness between and around. Depending on the conditions, the tee shot can vary from a five-iron to a driver.

For several years, the course hosted the Kerrygold Classic won twice by the club's long-hitting professional Liam Higgins in 1974 and 1977, by American George Burns in 1975 and by Tony Jacklin in 1976. It is the venue for Irish tournaments and a popular annual pro-am.

Watson, Tom

1949–. Born Kansas City, Missouri, USA

Although Tom Watson had established himself on the US Tour with two tournament wins by 1975, it was his achievements in Britain

Waterville, County Kerry, Eire: the 16th hole of a course exposed to fierce Atlantic winds, often the venue for Irish tournaments.

that really put him among the all-time greats. He had won the Byron Nelson Classic before coming to Britain for the first time in 1975 to play in the Open at Carnoustie, and took the title from a field which included Nicklaus, Palmer, Weiskopf and Floyd. He finished in a tie with Jack Newton of Australia, and won the play-off 71 to 72. Eight years later he won his fifth Open at Birkdale to equal Peter Thomson's record in the modern era and leave him one behind the six titles won by Harry Vardon.

In America, Watson had twice squandered chances in the US Open. At Winged Foot in 1974, he led going into the last round by a stroke and slumped to 79. At Medinah in 1975 he led after two rounds of 67, 68 which equalled the championship record. The last two rounds cost him 78 and 77. In 1977, he proved himself in America in the Masters. After the 14th hole of the

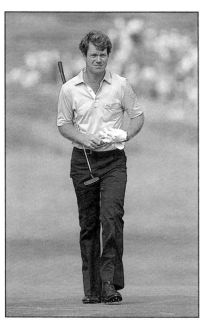

Tom Watson

last round he was tied with Nicklaus, but a long birdie putt at the 17th gave him the lead and he went on to win by two strokes.

Defending his British Open title at Birkdale in 1976, Watson surprisingly missed the two-round cut, but in 1977 when the Open was staged for the first time at Turnberry, he and Nicklaus fought out a stirring duel. They matched each other the first two days with rounds of 68, 70, and were paired together for the final two rounds. In what became virtually a matchplay contest, they produced a classic exhibition, possibly the finest ever to decide a major championship. Again on the third day, they matched each other with rounds of 65; in the final round Nicklaus went ahead by three strokes, but Watson hit back. The 15th and 17th holes proved decisive. First Watson dealt a cruel blow to his rival; short of the green at the par three hole, he holed a monster putt for a birdie, and at the 17th Nicklaus missed a putt of four feet to go behind for the first time. Watson hit a superb approach to two feet at the final hole, but Nicklaus, in deep

rough on the right with his drive, responded with a superb recovery to reach the green and hole a long putt for a birdie. But Watson made no mistake with his two-footer and the title was his by a stroke. For the second time that year he had triumphed over Nicklaus. His 65 to Nicklaus's 66 gave him an Open record aggregate of 268. Third-placed Hubert Green finished 11 strokes behind Watson.

On the US Tour Watson was leading money winner for four consecutive years from 1977; his most successful year was in 1980 when he won six tournaments and became the first player to pass half a million dollars winnings in a season, winning $530,808.

In Britain in 1980, he won the Open again at Muirfield, going into the last round four strokes ahead after a 64 and never challenged. Two years later, he won again at Troon, and in 1985 came his fifth win at Birkdale, resisting strong challenges from Hale Irwin, Andy Bean and Lee Trevino to win by a stroke. He made sure with a stroke worthy of a champion; his two-iron

Tom Watson, winner of the US Open in 1982, leaving the Pebble Beach course with Jack Nicklaus whom he had beaten at the 17th.

approach to the final green covered the flag all the way.

At St Andrews the next year, Watson's hopes of a sixth title were dashed at the notorious 17th Road hole when, again with a two-iron, his ball bounded through the green, just as Ballesteros birdied the final hole for victory.

Watson won his second Masters title in 1981, and after striving without success to win a US Open, his sensational shot at the 17th short hole at Pebble Beach in 1982 gave him the title as he once again foiled Nicklaus. Watson's tee shot finished in thick greenside rough and a par seemed the best he could hope for; instead, his pitch shot rolled into the hole for the birdie he needed to beat Nicklaus.

In 1984, he was again leading money winner, and although suffering a loss of form, he brought his career earnings to more than four million dollars by 1987, second only to Nicklaus. He challenged for the 1987 US Open at the Olympic club, losing by a stroke to Scott Simpson. He has been a Ryder Cup player three times and has also won in Japan.

Weiskopf, Tom

1942–. Born Massillon, Ohio, USA

Tom Weiskopf is one of the best strikers in the history of golf, blessed with a majestic swing. He joined the US Tour in 1965 with the Western Amateur behind him and in 1968 won two tournaments. He was third in the money list and never worse than 19th until 1979, a record of consistency that few could match. In 1968, 1973 and 1975 he was third.

Weiskopf came close to many major championships but won only the 1973 British Open at Troon. Weiskopf led all the way and won by two strokes in a rain-soaked event from Johnny Miller and Neil Coles. His four-round total of 276 equalled what was then the Open

Tom Weiskopf

record set by Palmer in 1962, also at Troon.

This breakthrough might have been the spur for Weiskopf to scale all the heights. He had played brilliantly all season, with steely resolve. But he found it hard to remain motivated, and an uncertain temperament often ruined his chances.

Weiskopf was second in the 1976 US Open and was four times runner-up in the Masters between 1969 and 1975. He won the World Match Play in 1972 and played in the Ryder Cup in 1973 and 1975. He gained his 15th US win in the 1982 Western Open. He also won the Canadian Open, South African PGA and Argentine Open.

Wentworth, Surrey, England

Of England's inland courses, Wentworth is one of the most famous and well-known to millions of television viewers, for it was here that the first live television screening of golf in the UK took place during the Daks Tournament in 1952. It was followed by the Ryder Cup a year later and the Canada (now World) Cup in 1956.

The West course, the famed Burma Road test, has been the venue since 1964 for the event with which Wentworth has become synonymous — the World Match Play Championship. This has

Wentworth, Surrey, England: the clubhouse of one of England's most famous inland courses.

attracted the world's top golfers and has been seen on television by countless millions around the world. The East course opened in 1924, two years before the West, and staged what was to be the forerunner of the Ryder Cup, a match in 1926 between British and American professionals. Home professional George Duncan led his team to a 13 to one victory over Walter Hagen's team. The Curtis Cup match in 1932 was also played over the East.

The legendary Ben Hogan and Sam Snead won the Canada Cup for America over the West; Hogan opened with eagle, birdie, and played his first 10 holes in England in 33 strokes, seven under par. Runners-up were Bobby Locke and Gary Player for South Africa. The former won the Dunlop Professional and Daks Tournament here. Player was five times winner of the

World Match Play title, and Severiano Ballesteros in 1986 claimed his fourth success in the event. Ballesteros and Bernhard Langer met in four matchplay duels, with the Spaniard the winner each time, but in the Whyte and Mackay PGA Championship of 1987 it was Langer who produced possibly the most outstanding golf seen on the West course when he returned all four rounds in the 60s to win the event from Ballesteros with a record total of 270, 18 under par.

Like St Andrews, Wentworth has also a famous 17th, a long par five, and one of two finishing holes rated by Arnold Palmer, twice winner of the World Match Play, as outstanding as any in golf. Now

Wentworth, Surrey, England: the 14th hole. To the famous West and East courses will be added the South, due for completion in 1990.

Wentworth is to get a third course, to be called the South, designed by John Jacobs. Gary Player and Wentworth professional Bernard Gallacher will be consultants. The South will be completed in 1990.

West Norfolk, Royal,
Norfolk, England

A straight out and back links, Royal West Norfolk has changed little since it was founded in 1891 under the patronage of the Prince of Wales. Although it lost two holes to the sea in 1939, these were replaced after the war. A testing course, it has carries over cross bunkers and large bunkers have to be cleared from the first two tees. The links lie between ridge and marsh, with the latter a threat at many holes.

The second nine holes, though much shorter than the outward

half, are often tougher as they are played into a strong wind. One of the most demanding is the par five eighth, which calls for a tee shot diagonally across the marsh and then an approach over a second inlet to a long plateau. The ninth, a fine dog-leg right par four, also calls for a drive over the marsh. The course has an excellent finishing hole to an island green.

Wethered, Joyce
(Lady Heathcoat Amery)

1901–. Born Malden, Surrey, England

Joyce Wethered came to prominence at Sheringham in the 1920 English Ladies' Championship. She had entered for fun and to keep a friend company but swept through to the final. Here she faced Cecil Leitch, the most formidable woman golfer of the day. No one gave Wethered a chance, particularly when Leitch went into lunch four up and then won the first two holes in the afternoon. But Wethered began to play matchless golf and came back to win two and one. The British star of the 1920s had arrived.

Wethered was not enthusiastic about competitive golf. She played in the English event only four more times and won all of them. She was almost as effective in the British Ladies. In 1921, she lost to Cecil Leitch in the final, reversed the decision the following year with a crushing nine and seven victory, and went out in the semi-final in 1923. She won in 1924 and 1925, and then virtually retired from championship golf.

In 1929, the British Ladies' Championship was scheduled for St Andrews, and Wethered entered again and reached the final. It became a contest to decide who was the world's best woman golfer, as her opponent was Glenna Collett, the outstanding American player. Collett went five up after

Joyce Wethered

nine holes but was pulled back to a lead of two at lunch. Afterwards, Wethered took charge to win by three and one. It was her last championship. In the British Ladies', she had played 38 matches and won 36; in the English, she won all 33.

Later Wethered competed in foursomes tournaments, where she carried a succession of male partners to victory. She also toured the USA as a professional in the mid-1930s for a long series of exhibition matches.

Wethered, Roger

1899–1983. Born Maldon, Surrey, England

The last British amateur to come close to winning the Open Championship, Roger Wethered tied with Jock Hutchison in 1921, in spite of the handicap of a penalty stroke for having trodden on his ball. His finish of 72, 71 was superb, but he lost the play-off.

Wethered won the amateur title only once, in 1923, but he was a formidable competitor for years, reaching the 1928 and 1930 finals when he lost to Phil Perkins and

Bobby Jones. He was a superb iron player but less secure with the driver. He played six matches against the USA.

Whitcombe, Reg

1898–1958. Born Burnham, Somerset, England

One of three outstanding golfing brothers, Reg Whitcombe was not considered the best, but only he won the Open. In 1937 at Carnoustie, he led with a round to go but was foiled by a superb last round from Henry Cotton. The following year at Sandwich, Whitcombe was well up the field after two days with a pair of 71s. For the 36 holes of the final day, the gales arrived. Whitcombe mastered it better than most, and his scores of 75 and 78 brought him home by two strokes.

Whitcombe had come to the top at the age of 40. Unlike his brothers, he never made a Ryder Cup appearance. Charles was in every team between 1927 and 1937 and was captain after the war. Ernest played in four Ryder Cups and finished second in the 1924 Open, a stroke behind Walter Hagen.

Whitworth, Kathy

1939–. Born Monahans, Texas, USA

Kathy Whitworth's record makes her the most successful player ever. Her 88 wins on the US PGA Tour put her six ahead of Mickey Wright and four ahead of Sam Snead's men's record. She has never won the women's Open, although she has won five major championships.

Appearing on the LPGA Tour in 1959, Whitworth's first win came three years later. In 1963 she won eight times and was on her way. She was leading money winner in 1965, 1966, 1967, 1968, 1970, 1971, 1972 and 1973; Player of the Year in 1966, 1967, 1968, 1969, 1971, 1972 and 1973; and won the Vare

Trophy in 1965, 1966, 1967, 1969, 1970, 1971 and 1972.

Whitworth was at her peak from 1963 to 1973. She has twice won seven tournaments in a season, eight three times, and nine and 10 once each.

Wilson, Enid

1910–. Born Stonebroom, Derbyshire, England

Enid Wilson won the British Ladies Championship in three successive years, 1931, 1932 and 1933. She had won the English title in 1928 and 1930. She was four times Midlands champion. While British champion, she reached the semi-final of the US Amateur Cham-

Winged Foot, New York, USA: one of America's most famous golf clubs, founded in the early 1920s.

pionship in 1931 and 1933. She made one Curtis Cup appearance in 1932.

Wind, Herbert Warren

1916–. Born Brockton, Massachusetts, USA

One of the best of modern golf writers, Herb Wind has been on the staff of the *New Yorker* since 1947. His first golf book, *The Story of American Golf*, which tells the development of golf in the USA through the great names, is a classic. Two years later, in 1950, he wrote *Thirty Years of Championship* with Gene Sarazen. Then came *The Modern Fundamentals of Golf*, written with Ben Hogan, which contains Hogan's incisive thinking, well ordered by Wind. His *The Greatest Game of All* is the story of Jack Nicklaus.

Wind has also produced two anthologies, one of golf writing, the other of his own.

He has always been interested in golf course design and has often written on the subject. His articles on Dornoch and Ballybunion greatly increased appreciation of these great courses.

Winged Foot, New York, USA

Founded in the early 1920s, Winged Foot takes its name from the emblem of the New York Athletic Club, some of whose members were responsible for setting it up. Its architect was the renowned Albert W Tillinghast, designer of two courses, the West and the East. The longer West is generally acknowledged as a 'man-sized course', and has been the

scene of some outstanding US Open Championships. The first was in 1929 when Bobby Jones needed a play-off to beat Al Espinosa, after being left with a curling putt of 12 feet on the 72nd hole to tie, and reading it perfectly to send it in the hole.

Three more Opens have followed: in 1959 when the winner was Billy Casper, in 1974, won by Hale Irwin, and in 1984 when Fuzzy Zoeller also needed a play-off after Greg Norman had holed a monster putt, again on the 72nd hole. Over the last few holes of the round, Norman had scrambled to save par and came to the final hole knowing he needed a par four to tie. After a long drive, he sent a wild shot into spectators in the grandstand on the right, played from the dropping zone and pitched on to and over the green. The ball stopped on the fringe. From 40 feet, the putt, with a break from left to right of a yard or more, swung in, hit the flagstick and dropped to such a roar from the crowd that Zoeller, waiting to play, waved a white towel as a token of surrender, thinking Norman had

birdied the hole.

The next day, it was Norman's turn to wave the towel as he went down 67-75.

The course, near the village of Mamaroneck, has 12 demanding par fours, 10 of them over 400 yards, with the 17th, a slight dog-leg right, with four big bunkers waiting, requiring an accurate approach to a narrow green, well bunkered. Of its four short holes, the 10th has a green of subtle undulations demanding the most careful reading. The US Open has been here four times, but the par of 280 has only been beaten by Zoeller and Norman, with 276.

Woburn, Buckinghamshire, England

Two fine courses, which wind through the thickly-wooded estate of the Duke of Bedford at Woburn Abbey, were created by the late Charles Lawrie, although sadly he did not live to see all the 36 holes completed. Now the home of the Duke's son, the Marquess of Tavistock, who is president of the golf and country club, the courses,

Woburn, Buckinghamshire, England: two fine courses on the Duke of Bedford's thickly-wooded estate are now the home of the Duke's son, the Marquess of Tavistock.

named the 'Duke's' and the 'Duchess', wind through a forest of pine, birch, beech and chestnut, with a profusion of rhododendrons. The 'Duke's', the more demanding championship lay-out, was opened in 1976. The 'Duchess' followed a few years later, and is notable for its tight fairways.

As well as trees, both courses feature heather, bracken and gorse, bordering springy fairways built on sandy sub-soil. The short third hole on the 'Duke's' course is one of the most spectacular, with the tee level with the treetops on the far side of the green, which is set deep in a hollow, with ferns and bracken all round. Although only 134 yards it is so deceptive that many shots finish in the high bank behind the green or in the bunkers guarding it. The 12th, the longest hole, has bunkers to catch both drives and second shots, and needs accurate play.

The 'Duke's' course hosted its first major event, the Dunlop Masters, in 1979, and has since attracted the Brabazon Trophy, the Ladies British Open and a women's professional event, the Ford Classic. In 1985 it staged the first Dunhill British Masters when Lee Trevino provided a spectacular finish to take the title. As the layout had been changed to make the normal first hole the 18th for this event, Trevino came to this final par five needing at least a birdie to win. He pushed his drive into semi-rough before playing a superb three-wood which faded into the green 255 yards away, rolling to six inches from the hole for an eagle three.

Wood, Craig

1901–1968. Born Lake Placid, New York, USA

When Craig Wood played at Augusta in the 1935 Masters, Sarazen had to birdie three of the last four holes to tie and produced a spectacular two on the par five 15th hole, tied his opponent and won the play-off. The year before Wood had been beaten by a birdie par finish by Horton Smith. In 1933 at the British Open at St Andrews Wood hit two phenomenal shots, one put him into the Swilcan Burn in front of the first green for an eventual six and then one of the all-time fluke drives on the fifth which travelled 430 yards into a bunker. He tied with Shute and lost the play-off.

Even by the time of Sarazen's unique shot Wood had lost yet another major championship unexpectedly, when his massive hitting was countered in the final of the 1934 US PGA by Paul Runyan's superior short game skills.

For the following few years, major championships eluded Wood. Then in the 1939 US Open, he tied with Densmore Shute and Byron Nelson, and his 68 in the

Woodhall Spa, Lincolnshire, England: a fine inland course, now a regular venue for amateur championship events.

play-off ended in another tie with Nelson. Out they went again. Nelson pitched dead on the third hole, and then holed his one-iron for an eagle on the next, and Wood was unlucky again.

Wood eventually broke through in the majors in the 1941 Masters. He began with 66 and played coolly for the next two rounds. In the final round he faltered to 38 on the first nine, and was caught by Nelson. This time, Wood played better than Nelson on the back nine and had his first championship.

On to Colonial for the US Open. Wood had a sore back and was fitted with a brace. Early on, he found himself in a ditch. The brace was hurting and a storm had blown up. But he went on and finished his first round with 73. At halfway, he tied for the lead and was two ahead after 54 holes. A 70 in the final round gave him victory.

Wood's first Tour win had come in 1925 and the US Open was

almost the last of his 17 US victories. After striving unsuccessfully for so long for a major championship, he won two in the same number of months.

Woodhall Spa, Lincolnshire, England

Built on sandy soil, and with heather, silver birch and pine trees, this fine inland course is one of the best of its kind in England, although not as well known as some. Opened in 1905, Harry Vardon and H S Colt played some part in its early lay-out, but it was completely redesigned by its owner, Colonel S V Hotchkin after World War I, and is now a regular venue for amateur championship events.

Although the greens are not difficult and there are no tricky slopes, the bunkers are among the toughest to be found, and one of its most demanding holes is the par four 11th, slightly downhill, with two deep bunkers across the fairway short of the green.

Michael Bonallack won the fourth of his five English Amateur titles here in 1967. It has also been

the venue for the English Ladies: its winners include that grand old lady Molly Gourlay, who still kept an active interest in the game 60 years after taking the title in 1926. In the Brabazon Trophy of 1954, Philip Scrutton made up seven strokes in wind and rain over his opponents to claim an outstanding victory. The Home Internationals were played here in 1981; Scotland won all their matches.

Woosnam, Ian

1958–. Born Oswestry, Shropshire, Wales

Welshman Ian Woosnam, of stocky appearance and determined character, possesses all the attributes of two former outstanding countrymen of his, Dai Rees and Brian Huggett, and could surpass the achievements of those former stalwarts of the European Tour. In the last few years, Woosnam has matured into a world-class player, with his performances early in 1987 sending him soaring to the top of the Tour's Epson Order of Merit.

Ian Woosnam, who won the 1987 Lancome Trophy and £50,000, bringing his winnings to £244,166.

His climb to tournament success started in 1982, when he broke through for his first major victory in the Swiss Open, and went on to win the Masters tournament in front of his home fans at St Pierre in Wales. He won the Scandinavian Open in 1984, the Zambian Open in 1985, and in 1986 the Kenya Open and Lawrence Batley TPC. He capped his year by challenging for the Open Championship at Turnberry, finishing third to Greg Norman.

A trio of tournament wins in the early months of 1987 set him on the path to the greatest year of his career. After finishing fifth in the Moroccan Open, he won the Jersey Open, was second in the Suze Open and won the Madrid Open in successive weeks. He finished runner-up in the Dunhill British Masters, tied for second in the Belgian Open, was third in the Carrolls Irish Open, and at Glen-

eagles destroyed the opposition in the Bell's Scottish Open. He led from the start with rounds of 65, 65, 66, and a final 68 gave him victory by seven strokes.

An eighth place in the Open at Muirfield raised his prize money to £175,000, passing his previous season's total by £50,000.

Like Rees and Huggett, Woosnam makes up for lack of height — he is 5 feet 4½ inches tall — with a good punch with hands and arms.

He gained his place for the third time in the 1987 Ryder Cup team, having been a member of the winning team at The Belfry in 1985.

Wright, Mickey

1935–. Born San Diego, California, USA

Although Kathy Whitworth later overhauled her in total victories, Mickey Wright won 79 of her career total of 82 in the nine years 1959–1968, averaging nearly eight wins a year.

As an amateur, Wright played only one full year when she won the World and All-American titles, being a finalist in the US Ladies and fourth in the US Open. On the LPGA Tour, she began winning in 1956 and in 1958 won five, including two majors, the LPGA and the Open. From that year until her last in 1966, Wright won a record 13 major championships, including the LPGA and Open four times each. She is the only player to win both titles the same year twice.

Between 1956 and 1969, Wright was always in the top 10 money winners. She led the money tables for four consecutive years 1961–1964. In 1963 she set a new record: 13 wins. As late as 1979, she tied for a tournament but lost the play-off to Nancy Lopez. Almost alone of prominent LPGA Tour players, Wright is acknowledged to have had a faultless swing and the crisp hand action that enabled her to play the long irons so well.

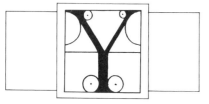

Yancey, Bert

1938–. Born Chipley, Florida, USA

A superb swinger of the club, Bert Yancey won seven Tour events in the years 1964–1975. He is now recognized as a leading theorist on the golf swing. His name is beginning to fade, mainly because he did not win a major championship. He came close several times, notably in 1968 when he began the US Open with rounds of 67 and 68 and went on to be five strokes in the lead with a round and a half to go. Then came Trevino.

The Masters was his main aim, and Yancey even built models of the greens to study them. He was

Bert Yancey

third on two occasions, but his career was brought to a halt by medical problems.

Yomiuri, Tokyo, Japan

Japan's leading architect Seichi Inoue, was the designer in 1964 of the Yomiuri Country Club course. He created an excellent lay-out, which the Japan Golf Association chose for the World Cup two years later. The event was won by the United States with their outstanding team of Jack Nicklaus and Arnold Palmer, though individual honours went to the Canadian George Knudson after a play-off with Japan's Hideyo Sugimoto.

The event brought Inoue's layout international recognition; it set a severe test in its hilly terrain, with deep valleys having to be carried, requiring accurate shots, as well as some blind shots from the tees. It is a regular tournament venue on the Japan circuit. The final two rounds of the Japan Series are played here, and its winners include two of the country's most famous players, Isao Aoki and Tsuneyuki Nakajima. The two opening rounds are played over the sister course at Osaka. It has also staged the Nissan Cup.

Hole	Distance	Par	Hole	Distance	Par
1	396 yards	4	10	425 yards	4
2	180 yards	3	11	507 yards	5
3	403 yards	4	12	432 yards	4
4	508 yards	5	13	450 yards	4
5	384 yards	4	14	364 yards	4
6	541 yards	5	15	194 yards	3
7	389 yards	4	16	410 yards	4
8	197 yards	3	17	510 yards	5
9	448 yards	4	18	224 yards	3
OUT	**3446 yards**	**36**	**IN**	**3516 yards**	**36**

Card for the course

Yomiuri, Tokyo, Japan: a first-class course designed in 1964 by Seichi Inoue, Japan's leading architect.

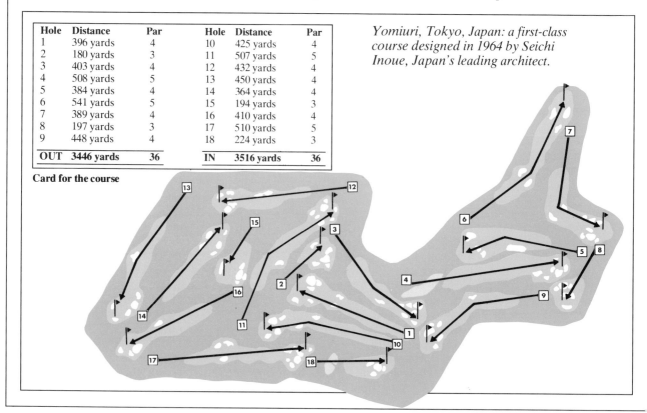

Bottle Strong nerve at the crisis of a match or tournament.

Boundary The perimeter of a course. To go beyond these limits is to be out-of-bounds and suffer the stroke and distance penalty.

Bowmaker A form of competition where usually three players are allowed to take their best individual score to count for their team.

Box A system of scoring for matchplay with three players. When one player wins a hole over the other two he goes into an imaginary box. If he then wins a hole he scores a point; if he halves a hole, he stays in the box; if he loses, he leaves the box. It can also be called 'chairman of the board'.

Brassie A wooden club with a brass soleplate intended to protect the wood in contact with the ground. Because it had slightly more loft than a driver its modern equivalent is often said to be the No. 2 wood. Many drivers today have as much loft as the old brassie.

Break The amount of turn on a putt from left to right or right to left.

Buggy A powered vehicle for carrying golfers and their equipment around a golf course.

Building a stance A player is not allowed to improve his stance by scraping footholds, for example, or holding down boughs of trees. Neither may he lay anything down to stand or lie on.

Bunker A depression, either deep or shallow on the course, usually part filled with sand and either natural or man-made. Earth and grass bunkers can also be found.

Bye There are two distinct meanings. The first is used in knock-out competitions where the number of players needs to be arranged in order to arrive at a later figure of 64, 32 or 16. Some players are then given a bye and move on to the next round without playing a match. The second meaning occurs in matchplay when the game is over before the end of the round. The players may decide to play a bye over the holes which remain.

Cackhanded Grip of a right-handed player who places his left hand below his right but also sometimes used of a left-hander with an orthodox grip.

Caddie A person employed on a fee basis to carry golf clubs and perform other services. The word comes from the Scots 'cady', a person who carries and does other odd jobs. It probably came from France with Mary Queen of Scots in the form 'cadet', a page.

Callaway system A form of handicapping decided by deducting the worst three holes on a player's card for the first 16 holes of a round. If a player had three sixes, but nothing worse during these holes, his handicap would be 18.

Cambuca A game played in England from the 14th century in which a leather ball stuffed with feathers and a curved club or stick were used. A stained glass window in Gloucester Cathedral dating from the mid-14th century shows a figure who is probably playing cambuca. He is often called 'The golfer'.

Carry The distance from where the ball is played to where it lands. Often used when there is an obstacle to be carried, such as a water hazard, a fairway bunker or a ravine.

Cart A wheeled device on which a bag of clubs is placed and then pulled behind the player.

Casual water Temporary water on the course which is not part of the design and is therefore not a water hazard.

The player is allowed to pick and drop without penalty. If water is brought to the surface when the player takes his stance he can also claim relief from casual water. Snow and ice may be treated either as casual water or as loose impediments.

Centre-shaft A putter where the shaft is not fixed to the clubhead at the heel, but in the centre or some way towards it. Such putters were banned by the R and A from 1909 to 1952.

Championship tees Some courses have teeing areas farther back than the medal tees for championship and tournament use only.

Character builder A putt of a length the player knows he ought to hole but which is by no means a foregone conclusion. Holing them does not perhaps build a player's character; missing a few in a round may well destroy him. The expression is also sometimes used for a testing shot through the green, a delicate pitch just over a bunker or a carry over water.

Chip A low running shot played from close to the green towards the flag.

Choke A player is said to choke or be a choker if his nerve seems to give way when he is in a winning position.

Choke down To grip lower on the club when either less length or more control are needed.

Chole A game played in Belgium and France about 100 years before the first mention of golf in Scotland (1457) and at the same time as cambuca in England. Chole involved playing cross-country with a club and ball, but the object was to hit a landmark not to hole the ball.

Cleek A Scots term for an iron with a rather long, narrow face. Most were the rough equivalent of a modern number two or three iron while others were used for lofting the ball, driving and putting.

Closed face To address the ball or strike it with the toe of the club turned inwards.

Closed stance Used when a right-handed player has his left foot nearer to the target line than the right.

Club A group of people forming an organization for the purpose of playing golf. The oldest known clubs are the Honourable Company of Edinburgh Golfers (1744) and the Royal and Ancient Golf Club of St Andrews (1754). The Royal Burgess Golfing Society of Edinburgh claims to have been founded in 1735 and was certainly in existence in 1773. Similarly Royal Blackheath claims to have been founded in 1608, without written evidence, but a silver club was presented for competition to the Blackheath golfers in 1766.

Club Implements with which the game is played. The limit is 14. The average golfer chooses to carry three woods, 10 irons and a putter. In earlier days, golfers carried as few as five, but during the 1920s and 1930s some began to carry far more than are now permitted.

Club, too much This is said when a player overshoots a green because he has used a number five iron, for example, when a six would have given him the correct distance.

Clubhead That part of the club which is fixed to a shaft and is used to strike the ball.

Cocking the wrists The bend or break in the wrists as the club is swung back from the ball.

Come off the shot This is said of a player whose body lifts up before his clubhead contacts the ball or whose shoulders turn away too early. There can be several results which include a topped shot, a quick hook or a slice, depending on the timing.

Concede In matchplay, a player may give a putt to his opponent if it is close to the hole, or a hole when he thinks he has no chance of a win or half. He may award a match if very far behind.

Course The area of ground, usually with clear boundaries, over which the game is played.

Croquet putting Standing with legs apart, chest on to the ball and swinging the putter, usually centre-shafted, back between the legs. This method was made famous by Sam Snead and banned towards the end of the 1960s.

Cross bunker Once much used by golf course architects, these were broad bunkers in the fairway set to catch tee shots, long second shots and approaches to greens. As thinking about course design developed, it came to be felt they were an unfair penalty for short hitters. The majority are now found at the front of greens to catch weak pitch shots.

Cup Often used instead of the hole.

Cut A ball hit with side spin, causing the ball to move from left to right through the air, either deliberately or by accident.

Cut, to make the To score low enough, usually over the first 36 holes in a 72-hole competition, to qualify to play the remaining two rounds.

Cut up A shot where the clubhead is drawn sharply across the ball from out to in, causing it to rise quickly and stop quickly, after moving right, on landing. Usually played from short range with a pitching club though such shots can be played from longer range with woods and long irons, perhaps to hold the ball against a wind or slope of the green.

Dead A ball is dead when it is so close to the hole that it seems impossible to miss the putt.

Dimples The indentations on a golf ball which help to make it fly well, and improve its grip on the clubface.

Direction posts Posts set up to guide the player for blind shots, most often used in the case of tee shots.

Divot A piece of turf removed by the clubhead in the playing of a shot.

Dog-leg A hole where the fairway bends sharply left or right at driving distance. There is often a hazard, such as a bunker, bushes or rough at the angle of the dog-leg to discourage players from attempting to drive across it.

Dormy A player in matchplay is dormy when he has moved as many holes up as there remain to be played. He cannot be beaten unless the match goes to extra holes.

Double bogey A score of two over par for a hole.

Double dog-leg A hole, usually a par five, where the fairway bends sharply twice.

Double eagle A score of three under par on a par five. American version of an albatross.

Downhill lie When the player has to strike his ball from a downslope.

Draw A gentle movement of the ball from right to left in the case of a right-handed player.

Drive A full shot played from the tee, usually but not necessarily with a driver.

Drive for show and putt for dough An American expression which means that although long driving may be the most appreciated by golf spectators, good putting wins the money.

Driver A wooden club with little loft used for getting maximum distance.

Drive the green To reach the green from a tee shot, usually at a short par four. The expression can be used for a par three of maximum length.

Driving mashie A club of similar loft to a No. one iron formerly used for accuracy from the tee.

Driving range Places where golfers may go to hit practice shots with all clubs, usually under cover and in bays.

Drop A player drops a ball when he has hit out-of-bounds or lost his original ball. He may also drop his ball back into play when given relief by the rules or under penalty if he thinks the ball unplayable.

Duck hook A hook which bends sharply and flies low.

Duff To strike a very bad shot, usually by contacting the ground well before the ball.

Eagle A score of two under par on a hole.

Eclectic A total for a round of golf arrived at by taking the player's best score on each hole, usually for several or more cards in a long-running competition. Golfers sometimes also talk of their 'lifetime eclectic'. This means the total of their best scores on each hole of a particular course.

Equipment Anything designed to help the golfer play. Waterproofs, trolley and umbrella are included. Under the rules, however, it does not include the ball in play.

Equity If the rules of golf or local rules do not seem to cover a point of golfing law, a decision has to be made in accordance with equity. This matter of what is fair has caused many arguments and appeals being made to committees at both club and national level.

Etiquette The conduct expected of players towards opponents, other golfers on the course and the course itself.

Explosion A sand shot played with the aim of propelling both ball and sand out of a bunker.

Extension A term used of the stretching of the arms through and after impact and usually considered essential in a good swing.

Extra holes Holes played after a match has finished level to decide a winner.

Face The part of the clubhead intended to strike the ball. Also the part of the bunker that confronts the player as he makes his shot. The term is not used unless the face is steep or rises some distance from the floor of the bunker.

Fade A shot which flies straight for much of its flight and then, in the case of a right-handed player, drifts from left to right.

Fairway The closely mown part of a golf hole between tee and green. Its boundaries will usually be semi-rough or rough and the apron of the green.

Fat A shot usually hit with an iron, so that the clubhead takes turf a little before the ball with the result that it does not reach its target.

Feathery A kind of ball which began to go out of use in 1848 and was quickly replaced by the gutta percha ball. A top-hatful of boiled feathers were forced into a sewn-hide casing. The result was a hard, serviceable ball in dry weather, though it was seldom perfectly round. In the wet, the ball was easily cut, or burst as it soaked up moisture, and lasted only a short time.

Feel Used of the sensitivity of the hands which enables a player to play shots, for example, where touch not power are needed.

Firm left side Henry Cotton taught that a golfer should hit against a firm left side. The achievements in particular of Byron Nelson greatly lessened belief in this theory.

Flagstick A thin marker for the hole, usually 6 feet long, with a piece of coloured cloth at the top. It is also called the pin, the flag or the stick.

Flat swing A backswing where the club is swung back nearer the horizontal than vertical so that the club passes over the top of the upper arm or the lower. In spite of the example of Ben Hogan, this came to be considered a fault with the successes of Jack Nicklaus. The pendulum is now swinging the other way.

Flight The path taken by a golf ball through the air.

Fluff A stroke where the clubhead meets the ground considerably before the ball so that it moves hardly at all. It is most common on short shots such as a chip.

Flyer A shot, usually into the green, where the ball flies further than the player intended. It is usually caused by grass, especially if wet, coming between clubface and ball with reduction of backspin.

Follow through The movement of the body, especially the arms, after the ball has been struck.

Fore! The traditional warning cry given when a player sees his ball flying towards another person.

Forecaddie Caddies used by a club committee or competition organizers to observe where players' balls have come to rest, usually after blind shots.

Forward tees Set ahead of the medal tees, these are mainly used either to make the course slightly easier for general play or to reduce wear on the competition teeing area.

Fourball Usually a match in which two count their better ball score against the better ball of the other two players.

Foursome A match for four players, with each pair using one ball and hitting alternate shots on each hole. Before play begins the team of two decides who is to hit the first tee shot.

The other will then play from the second tee, and so on.

Free drop A drop without penalty, such as away from ground under repair or casual water.

Freeze A condition in which a player, as a result of nerves, is unable to play his shot. It happens most often in putting and in other parts of the short game, but many players also remain immobile over a drive.

Friendly bounce A bounce which favours the player in which a ball luckily skips over a bunker, for example, or kicks from a bank towards the target.

Friendly game or match So called in contests within a club, or club against club, when nothing very much is at stake.

Front door The edge of a hole nearest to the line of a putt.

Front nine The first nine of an 18-hole golf course.

Frost holes Temporary greens used when it is thought that normal greens would be damaged if used when they are frozen or thawing.

Gamesmanship A word coined by Stephen Potter to mean the art of winning games — not only golf — by talk or conduct aimed at putting off the opponent.

Gate money The first time money was charged to watch golf was in 1892 for a match between two well-known British professionals. More than 30 years passed before spectators at the Open Championship paid to watch.

Gimme A putt short enough to be conceded.

Give To give a putt is the same as to concede one.

Go down the shaft To grip lower to improve control of the club, or sometimes to reduce the distance obtained from a particular club.

Golf widow A wife whose husband is very often away from home pl golf.

Good bounce A bou which favours taking it ne

Also used of a drive that lands on a down slope or hard area, causing the ball to run further.

Gooseneck A twist or curve in the neck of a putter.

Grain Grass on a green where the blades are not vertical but lie horizontal in some direction. This is sometimes natural but usually caused by cutting. A putt with the grain travels further than one against it.

Grand slam A term used in 1930 of Bobby Jones's success in winning the Open and Amateur Championships of both the USA and Britain in the same year. Today's equivalent would be the winning of the four majors in one year. In 1953, Hogan made the nearest approach, winning the Masters, the US and the British Opens, but he did not compete in the US PGA.

Great Triumvirate A phrase used to describe Harry Vardon, J H Taylor and James Braid, three great players during the 20 years immediately preceding World War I.

Green fee A playing charge paid by visitors to a golf club.

Greensome A variation of foursomes play where both players in a team of two hit from the tee and then select the best shot. Alternate shot play then continues.

Grip The way a golf club is held by a player. It is also the part of the club so held.

Groove Used of a swing which seems to repeat identically.

Gross A player's score before his handicap is deducted.

Ground the club To place the sole of the club behind the ball prior to swinging. The club may not be grounded in a water hazard or bunker.

Ground under repair Any part of the course so marked as unfit for play. Also material piled for eventual removal.

Guide post A post erected to indicate the line a blind shot should be played.

Gutta percha A substance like rubber from the latex of Malaysian trees, used from 1848 for making golf balls.

Guttie A ball made from gutta percha which lost popularity quite rapidly with the introduction of the wound ball early this century.

Hacker A poor golfer who is apparently more successful at removing turf than at striking the ball.

Half A drawn hole or match.

Half shot A shot where approximately a half swing and half power are used to keep a ball low into the wind, using a club with less loft than usual.

Ham and egging A term used in pro-ams to indicate how a handicap player can help his professional partner by making use of his strokes.

Hand action The use of the hands in the golf swing. Some theorists, especially Henry Cotton, have stressed the importance of strong, lively hands to good golf. Jack Nicklaus feels that leg action is more important.

Handicap A system of allotting a player strokes so that, as in handicap horse racing, all should finish level at the end of an event.

Hanging lie A lie in which the player has his front foot lower than the rear because of a downslope.

Haskell A name once used for the rubber core, wound ball after its inventor, Coburn Haskell. This kind of ball replaced the guttie from the turn of the century in the USA and from 1902 in the UK.

Hazard Any bunker, and stream, ditch, lake or pond defined as such by a club's committee.

Head A shortened form of clubhead.

Head cover A cover to protect woods and, occasionally, putters.

Head up A fault in which the head is lifted too quickly, perhaps before the ball has been struck, in order to follow its flight. The cause can also be a bad swing that forces the head up.

Heavy To strike the turf a little before the ball, reducing the distance the ball travels.

Heel The part of the clubhead nearest the golfer as he prepares to play. Also where the shaft enters.

Hickory The wood which, from about

the middle of the 19th century, replaced other woods for the making of club shafts. In its turn steel replaced it from the late 1920s.

Hitting across The movement of the clubhead from out to in at impact, and one cause of a slice.

Hitting early Using hand action too early in the downswing.

Hitting late Unleashing hand action late in the downswing, often so that the hands are ahead of the clubhead at impact.

Hole This must be four and a quarter inches in diameter and sunk to a depth of four inches. The liner must be set one inch or more below the surface. The word is also applied to the entire area between tee and green.

Holed Any shot, usually a putt, that enters the hole.

Holed out A completed hole.

Hole high Used of a shot which covers the distance to the hole but not on the exact line.

Hole in one To strike a tee shot directly into the hole.

Home course The course a player is more active on than anywhere else.

Home green The last hole which brings golfers home to the clubhouse.

Home of golf A title given to St Andrews in Fife.

Honour The privilege of playing first from a tee.

Hood To set the hands ahead of the clubface and therefore to reduce the loft of the club.

Hook A poor shot which curves from right to left in an exaggerated way, usually unintentionally.

Hosel The part of iron clubhead into which the shaft is fitted.

Hustler A golfer who plays off too high a handicap in order to win bets.

Identify A player must always be able to identify his ball. The brand name and a number are not sufficient and a personal mark should be added.

Impact The time the clubface is in contact with the ball or the moment it meets it.

In contention A golfer is said to be in contention in a strokeplay event when he is one of the group that has a chance of winning. The term is not usually used until after the second round or later.

In play A ball is in play from the moment it is struck on the teeing ground until it is holed out.

Inside to out A swing where the club is swung back inside the line of flight to the target and is travelling outwards at the point of impact. If the clubface is square, a draw or hook results.

Interlocking grip A grip where the hands are bonded together by wrapping forefinger and little finger round each other.

Irons Clubs which have metal heads, usually of steel, and varying amounts of loft.

Jail A player can be described as in jail if he has played his ball to a place where there seems to be no escape, such as into a clump of bushes or deep woods.

Jerk A sudden movement in the swing which destroys all rhythm.

Jigger A club with a narrow face, usually the loft of a No. five or six iron and a fairly short shaft, most often used for run-up shots.

Jitters Nervousness, especially in putting, that prevents the player making a smooth stroke.

Kempshall An early type of wound ball made with rubber tape instead of rubber thread. It rivalled the Haskell ball.

Knock-out competition A competition, usually matchplay, where the loser, or losing team in a round, does not live to fight another day.

Knuckles The merits of the one-, two- and three-knuckle grip have often been argued. When the player looks down at his left-hand grip while in the address position, he will usually see one of these numbers. The one-knuckle position is often called weak and the three-knuckle strong, though in fact only a strong player can use the one-knuckle grip and weaker players tend to use a grip with three knuckles visible.

Kolbe, kolf, kolven, kolve An earlier form of golf in Holland has been traced back as far as 1296, but it was often played over short distances with a stake rather than a hole as the target on ice. Golf developed on Scottish linksland, but the name golf came from the Continent where it meant 'club', while 'put' meant 'hole'.

Ladies tees The par of golf courses and individual holes is rated differently for women than men. Ladies' tees are normally set ahead of those for men but may occasionally be set farther back, perhaps to make a par four into a five.

Lag Used especially of a downhill putt or any occasion when the player is more concerned to get his putt close to the hole rather than to hole it. Also used of shots through the green.

Laminated Used of wooden clubs where the heads are made of thin layers of wood, glued together, rather than solid persimmon. Such clubs are usually less likely to crack or to be badly affected by damp.

Lateral water hazard This lies parallel to the line of play rather than across it and is lateral when the committee decides it is impracticable to drop a ball behind the hazard and keep the spot at which the ball last crossed the margin between the player and the hole.

Left-hand below right Few players — Sewsunker Sewgolum of South Africa was the outstanding example — have managed to play right-handed but with the left hand below the right on the grip for all shots. Many more have found it an effective grip for putting, partly because it lets them pull the putter into the ball more easily.

Let through When one game on a course waves another through, usually because of slower play or a lost ball.

Lie The position of the ball in relation to the ground beneath. A good lie usually means that most of the ball is visible. A lie becomes progressively worse as the ball settles down in the grass or sand. The term is also used of the way a clubhead sits on the turf. This depends on the angle formed by the clubhead with the shaft and whether or not the player stands near or far from the ball or if he holds his

hands high or low. Players often have the lie of their iron clubs checked if they think one or more is either too upright or flat.

Lift and drop The action of a player when, under penalty or not, he picks up his ball and drops it in a place and manner laid down in the rules of golf.

Like as well A term used when each side has played the same number of strokes. The distance from the hole may be vastly different.

Line The direction a putt should take for the hole, taking any borrow into account. For longer shots it is the direction in which the ball should be hit, taking hazards into account, the length a player can hit and also the position for the shot which will follow.

Links This word probably derives from the Old English 'hlinc', meaning ridge, although others see the term as meaning land which forms a link between the sea and land fit for agriculture further inland. Typically linksland is low-lying, with sand dunes and bristly varieties of salt resistant grasses. Because almost all early British golf was played on such land, the term came to mean 'golf course', even if the holes ran through parkland or water meadow. Today the word is used correctly; other kinds of land on which courses are laid out are called 'downland', 'heath' and so on.

Lip The edge of the hole. A putt can be said to have 'stopped on the lip', 'lipped out' or 'lipped the hole'.

Lob A short, high shot played with a lofted club which will run little because of its angle of descent more than backspin.

Local knowledge The knowledge a player gains through experience of golf on his home course of how to play particular shots.

Local rules Rules made by a club committee to deal with special conditions on the course.

Loft The angle a clubface is set back from the vertical. Among the irons, the loft increases from the No. one to the sand wedge.

Lofting iron (or lofter) An iron of about the loft of a modern No. six which generally replaced the baffy.

Long game Use of the woods and long irons.

Long right arm Used to describe the player who drives his right hand and arm long and low through the ball.

Loop In even the best golf swings the club does not go back and down again on exactly the same area. When the difference between the two is exaggerated, it is called a loop.

Loose impediments These are natural objects not fixed, growing or adhering to the ball and, except in hazards, may be removed as long as the ball does not move when this is done. Sand and loose soil can be deemed loose impediments on greens but not elsewhere and snow and ice anywhere. See 'obstructions' for other kinds of unnatural impediments.

Lost ball A ball is lost if it cannot be found within five minutes of the player or his caddie searching for it. A player may also declare a ball lost without searching for it and a ball becomes lost if a provisional ball is played beyond the point where the original ball disappeared.

Marker Usually a coin or small plastic disc used to mark the position of a ball on the green. Also a person, often a fellow-competitor, who records scores, hole by hole.

Marker post A post erected to indicate the line of play, usually for a blind spot.

Mashie An iron club which first appeared in the 1880s whose modern equivalent is the No. five iron. At the time, a 'masher' was a fashionable young man and it is likely, but not certain, that the name of the club came from this source because it, too, quickly became fashionable.

Mashie niblick An iron halfway between the mashie and the niblick and equivalent to the modern No. seven iron.

Match Usually used of a man-against-man game where holes are won, lost or halved, as opposed to strokeplay.

Matched set A set of clubs made by the same manufacturer and of the same model designed so that each club feels similar in balance and swing as each of the others.

Matches The rules of golf lay down the following types of matches:
Single: One golfer against another.
Threesome: One golfer playing the better ball of two others.
Foursome: Two golfers against two but with each side using only one ball.
Threeball: Three golfers involved with two matches at the same time.
Best ball: One golfer plays against the better or best ball of two or three others.
Fourball: Two play against two with each side counting the better of their two scores. A variant is adding the two scores together and matching the total against that of the other side.

Matchplay The form of golf based on holes won, lost and halved rather than total strokes taken.

Medal Originally these were competitions, usually strokeplay but occasionally matchplay, where a medal was the prize, held for a year or perhaps for ever.

Medal play Strokeplay competitions, with the lowest score winning.

Medal tees The competitions tees at a golf club at the distance the hole was designed to be played from.

Members' tees Tees set a few or more yards ahead of the medal tees for friendly play by members.

Middle the ball To strike the ball exactly in the centre of the clubface.

Mis-hit Any shot not struck precisely in the middle of the clubface.

Missable Used of a putt which a player ought to hole but could easily be missed.

Mixed foursome Normal foursomes play except a woman is paired with a man.

Moved ball A ball is considered to have moved only if it does not return to its original position. Any movement away from that incurs a penalty stroke.

Muff To play a badly mis-hit shot, usually one that moves only a small part of the expected distance.

Mulligan A second chance given to a golfer who has hit a poor first drive. This is against the rules of golf. It is allowed only in the friendliest of games

and even then usually only on the first tee.

Municipal course A course owned by a public body rather than a private club and usually open to all.

Nap A term which refers to the horizontal growth of grass on a putting green, especially in South Africa. A ball putted against the nap will go less far than one hit with the same strength with the slope of the grass. Putting across the nap can be more puzzling.

Nassau Betting where sums of money are involved on the result for the first nine, the second nine and the 18 as a whole.

Natural golf course A golf course where use has been made of the natural features of the terrain and little or nothing has been done in the way of blasting, bull-dozing and so on. In this sense, St Andrews is a natural course.

Neck Part of the clubhead where the shaft is inserted.

Net score A player's score for a round after his handicap has been subtracted from his gross score.

Never up, never in A putt which does not reach the hole, and cannot possibly hole out.

Niblick Once the most lofted iron and the rough equal of a No. nine iron.

Nine A golf course is almost always thought of as being split into two lots of nine holes, as nearly equal in playing qualities as possible.

Nineteenth When the first hole is played again after a match has finished all-square after 18 holes, it is referred to as 'the 19th'. Also referred to as the bar in the clubhouse after a match, the 19th hole.

Not enough club An expression used to mean that a player has misjudged the distance to the green and used, say, a six-iron instead of a five.

Obstructions Unless declared an integral part of the course, anything artificial built or left on a course. If moveable, the player may do so; if not he is allowed to lift and drop.

Old Man Par A term used by Bobby Jones and simply meaning the par of a course. After some unexpected defeats early in his career in matches, he decided to play against par rather than his opponent.

Open An event which in principle anyone can enter but in practice there are usually restrictions. Such competitions at club level are open to non-members, while national open championships seek an international entry.

Open stance To stand to the ball with the front foot drawn back from the target line.

Open to shut Used of a wristy swing in which the clubface is allowed to open on the backswing and become square or closed at impact. As a method by good players it has long been out of fashion.

Open up the hole To play a tee shot so that there are no obstacles between ball and hole for the second shot.

Out The first nine holes. The use derives from many early links courses where the players went 'out' for nine holes and the second nine took them 'in' to the clubhouse.

Out-of-bounds Usually a ball beyond the boundaries of a course. However, there are exceptions. On some seaside courses, the beach is not ruled out-of-bounds and areas of courses such as a practice ground within the boundaries are declared out-of-bounds. In practice, a ball is out-of-bounds if it is anywhere prohibited for play.

Outside agency Anything which affects the flight or run of a player's ball which is not part of a match or, in strokeplay, not the player, his equipment or caddie. Examples are a referee, spectators, animals and vehicles.

Out to in A swing path where the clubhead comes from outside the line of flight and moves inside at impact. If, at this time, the clubface is square or open, a slice results; if shut, the ball will be pulled.

Over par To score more than par for a hole or to be in that position for a round either at any point during it or the end.

Pacing the course Before a tournament begins, competitors often measure distances by pacing so that they will know which club to play from certain points during the competition. Nowadays, they are usually assisted by course charts and in effect are merely adding more detail to these. The job is often done for them by their caddies.

Par The standard score for a hole, in most countries based on its length. Holes up to 250 yards are par threes; up to 475 yards par fours and over 478 yards the remainder par fives.

Pell mell Also called pall mall and paille-maille, the names derive from the Latin *pila*, a ball and *malleus*, a mallet or hammer and the game is regarded as a likely fore-runner of both golf and croquet. It was not a cross-country game and both mallet and ball were made of wood. It came over from France to Scotland in the 16th century and Mary, Queen of Scots played both this game and golf. She was criticized when she did so soon after her husbands' murder. The Stuarts later brought both games to England.

Penalty stroke A stroke or strokes added to a score because of a breach of the rules of golf.

Persimmon A wood found at its best in Kentucky but also in Louisiana, Florida and other Southern States in America which almost totally replaced others in the making of wooden clubheads. In its turn, persimmon was replaced by beech and maple laminates but has since made a strong comeback. Today, persimmon is demanded for a top-quality driver.

Piccolo grip Many early golfers allowed the club to move in the right hand and also let go with the last two fingers of the left hand, so they looked rather like piccolo players when at the top of the swing. Hardly any good player does this today.

Pin *See* flagstick.

Pin high A shot to the green which finishes level with the flagstick but not necessarily close to it.

Pitch A fairly high shot played to a green from approximately 150 yards down to shots of just a few yards. The eight, nine wedge and sand iron are usually regarded as the pitching clubs.

Pitch and run A shot of lower trajectory than the pitch usually intended to land short of a green and run on to the flag. Not often played when greens are well watered.

Pitch mark The mark or indentation caused by a ball as it lands on a green.

Pivot The turning movement of the body during the backswing.

Placing Because of winter conditons or the poor state of a golf course, local temporary rules are sometimes introduced to allow a player to move his ball a short distance to a better lie, either by hand or by pushing it with the clubhead.

Plane The angle of the swing are in relation to the ground, ranging between flat and upright.

Playing short To hit the ball so that it does not reach some hazard.

Play-off When there is a tie in a competition, the players involved may go on to play further holes. In major championships, play-offs used to be over 36 holes or 18 but the demands of TV for a quick result mean that most play-offs today are 'sudden death', with the exception of the US Open. Whoever first wins a hole wins the event.

Play through To be allowed through by a game in front, normally as a result of a lost ball or slow play.

Plugged ball A ball resting in the depression it made on landing, usually in a bunker.

Plumb bob A method of holding a putter up at the end of the grip and letting it hang vertical with arm extended looking along the line of putt. The angle made by the shaft with the surface of the green may reveal the direction of any slope.

Plus handicap A golfer with a handicap better than scratch.

Pot bunker A small, round bunker, usually quite deep.

Practice ground An area set aside for practice shots.

Practice swing A swing made either to loosen up or to rehearse the feel of the shot to be played.

Preferred lies *See* placing.

Press To try to hit the ball harder for extra distance. Also, a bet when a side in a match falls behind.

Pro-am A competition in which amateurs form a team with professionals.

Professional A golfer who accepts prize money or fees for playing golf, as an instructor by word of mouth, in print or other media, or for otherwise serving as a professional golfer.

Professional side of the hole The higher side of a hole set into a side-slope. So called because a putt which misses tends not to run far from the hole.

PGA Professional Golfers' Association.

Provisional ball A ball played in the expectation that the previous one is lost or out-of-bounds.

Public golf course A course which is usually owned by a local authority, on which anyone may play.

Pull A shot which flies to the left, without noticeable curve on it, usually caused by the swing path being left of target.

Punch shot A shot played mainly with the forearms, with the hands in front of the clubhead and the wrists held firm.

Push A shot which flies right of target and straight, caused by the swing path being to the right of the target.

Putt Any stroke made with the intention of running the ball along the ground.

Putter A club designed to run the ball along the ground and with little loft.

Putting green A green intended for practice.

Quadruple bogey A score on a hole of four over par, for example a seven on a par three.

Rabbit A very poor golfer who will probably never improve.

Rap Used of a putting stroke where the player restricts both backswing and follow-through.

Recovery A shot which removes the ball from a poor position resulting from the previous shot.

Referee A person appointed to accompany players and make rulings on matters of fact and the rules of golf.

Release The free action of the hands and arms through impact.

Reverse overlap grip The most popular of the putting grips in which the index finger of the top hand is extended down over the fingers of the bottom hand. This position helps prevent the top wrist breaking before the ball is struck.

Rim out A putt which catches the rim of the hole but does not drop.

Roll the shoulders To turn the shoulders too much on a horizontal plane.

Roll the wrists The normal hingeing action of the wrists in the golf swing.

Rough Grass which has been allowed to grow in order to penalize off-line shots,

Round Eighteen holes of golf.

Round Robin A form of competition where each of the competitors plays each other. The fields are limited.

Rubber core Invented by Coburn Haskell, this ball with a rubber centre covered by many yards of wound thread and cased in gutta percha replaced the solid guttie from the turn of the century.

Rub of the green Used when an agency outside the game affects the run or flight of a player's ball. The result may be either lucky or unlucky.

Rules of amateur status These rules tell amateurs what they may or may not do if they wish to remain amateurs and not be adjudged to be making money from golf.

Rules of golf The first set of rules which have survived were issued by the Honourable Company of Edinburgh Golfers in 1744 but the Royal and Ancient Golf Club has a set dating to 1754. With the expansion of golf towards the end of the last century, R and A rules became accepted in most of the golfing world but the United States Golf Association legislates in America. The two bodies meet to discuss changes and today's rules are virtually unified world-wide.

Run The distance a ball travels after it has landed on the ground.

Sand iron A usually heavy club with a flange designed so that the clubhead rides through soft sand rather than digs down. The rear of the flange, not the leading edge of the club, is lower.

Sand trap American term for bunker although trap is increasingly used in Britain.

Sand wedge *See* sand iron.

Scorecards These probably came into use for the first time in the 1865 Open Championship. They are printed cards on which scores for individual holes and eventual totals are recorded.

Scotch foursomes A term used in the USA for foursomes. Scotch because the game is presumed to have been invented in Scotland.

Scratch A golfer with a zero handicap.

Seeding Spacing the best players through a draw so that, in theory, they do not meet until a late stage of the competition.

Semi-rough The grass between the fairway and the uncut rough. Considerable attention is often paid to its length and density in important events.

Shank To hit a ball, using an iron at the place where the head joins the shaft. The ball flies away from the player nearly at right angles.

Shoot the lights out To score brilliantly low.

Short When the ball fails to reach the target.

Short game Putting, chipping, bunker play and short pitching.

Short set Less than the full complement of golf clubs.

Shutting the face The loft of the club is reduced because the hands are ahead of the clubhead at impact. Achieved by setting up to the ball with the hands ahead or having the ball back in the stance, with the same result. The result will be to keep the ball low, perhaps into the wind or under the branch of a tree.

Shut to open A deliberate effort is made on the backswing not to allow wrist action to open the clubface so that at the top the clubface, rather than the toe of the club, may be aiming down the target line. The clubface then opens on the downswing.

Side saddle A stance adopted by some players, notably Sam Snead, when putting between the legs in croquet style was banned. The player stands chest on to the hole and strokes the ball from near the right edge of the right foot.

Sidespin Left-to-right or right-to-left rotation of the ball, resulting in a shot that bends right or left.

Silloth terms A form of handicapping invented at Silloth Golf Club in Cumbria for pairs golf which tends to penalize a partnership with a low handicap golfer.

Single A match between two players.

Sitting down Used of a ball lying well down in the grass.

Sitting up Used of a ball in a good lie.

Sky Usually a wooden club shot where the ball is struck by the top edge of the club and soars upwards.

Slice A ball that curves to the right for the duration of its flight.

Snap hook A hook which bends very quickly.

Socket A ball hit on the joint between shaft and clubhead and which shoots off almost at right angles to the player.

Sole That part of the club which rests on the ground when the player addresses the ball.

Spade mashie An old club with a deep face, used for shots from sand and deep rough.

Split hands putting A putting grip where the hands are kept apart with the stroke made mostly by the bottom hand.

Spoon An old club, equivalent to the modern No. three wood.

Square When the clubface is at right angles to the target line.

Square stance To stand with both feet parallel to the target line.

Stableford A scoring system in which one point is awarded for a bogey, two for a par, three for a birdie, four for an eagle and five for a double eagle. Handicap strokes are included. If a player equals his handicap, he will score just under 36.

Stance The placing of the feet before playing a shot.

Standard scratch score The score a scratch player should do on a particular course.

Steel shafts The first steel shafts were made before the turn of the century but were banned. The USGA allowed their use in putters from 1924 and they were legalized by the R and A in 1929, some years after the USGA approved them. They rapidly replaced hickory because they were both lighter and had little torsion.

Strict par Basically the score that a very good professional should have for a round. For instance, the par of a course with four par fives might be 72 but the professional should reach all of the par fives in two strokes, thus making the strict par 68.

Stroke A forward movement of the club made with the intention of striking the ball.

Stroke hole A hole where a stroke is received.

Stroke index For the purpose of giving and receiving strokes, all club cards are rated from one to 18 because it is reckoned a good player can be expected to play the most difficult holes more effectively than the poor player. In practice, however, strokes are equally divided between the first and second nines of the 18 holes so the system depends on deciding which is the most difficult hole on the course and the second most difficult is then reckoned to be in the other nine. So the numbering continues, alternating.

Strokeplay A form of competition in which the winner is the player with the lowest total score for the number of holes played. It seems to date back to the 18th century.

Strong A shot which travels too far.

Stymie A situation in which a ball about to be putted had another ball on its route to the hole. Players had to attempt to loft their balls over the obstruction. The rule was changed early in the 1950s.

Sudden death Often played in tournament golf after a tie. When two players are involved, the first to score lower for a hole than the other wins the event. If a greater number of players is involved, all who do not equal the best score on a

hole have to drop out.

Sweet spot Usually in the centre of the clubface but sometimes inclining slightly towards the heel. A ball struck here will travel further than when hit anywhere else.

Swing All the movements a golfer makes in moving the club away from the ball, back to it and then continuing until all momentum is spent.

Swing weight The static measurement of the weight and balance of a club. A matched set of clubs should all be the same swing weight.

Syndicate In fourball play a syndicate bet is won by the player with the lowest score on a hole.

Take away The first few inches of the backswing.

Target golf Golf where shots to the green can be flown directly at the flag, the target, with the knowledge that the ball will grip and stop quickly as a result of the density of the grass or softness of the green or perhaps both, combined with backspin.

Tee The prepared area from which the first shot to a hole is played.

Tee peg A device on which to set a ball for the first shot at a hole.

Tee up To place the ball on a tee peg or, on the practice ground particularly, putting the ball on a good lie.

Tempo The timing and rhythm of the golf swing where the take away is smooth and the backswing and beginning of the downswing are unhurried.

Texas scramble A form of golf where players go out in teams of two, three or even four. Each team member hits a tee shot and the best is selected. Each then hits from that position and so on until the ball is holed out. Low scores result.

Texas wedge A shot played with a putter from well short of the green.

Thin A shot hit with the bottom edge of a club, or quite close to it.

Threeball A match where each of the players is playing a separate single against the others.

Threesome A match in which one player plays against the two others, either their better ball or, less often, the two playing as a foursomes partnership.

Through the green All of a hole except hazards, the teeing ground and the green.

Tie When players return the same score in a strokeplay event.

Tiger A very good golfer.

Tight A tight golf course allows little room for inaccurate driving. The fairways will be narrow and hazards may threaten to either side. A tight lie usually refers to a fairway shot where the ball is lying less than ideally.

Timing When maximum clubhead speed is reached just before or at the moment of impact rather than too early or too late.

Toe That part of the clubhead at the opposite end to the heel.

Topspin The spin which results when the ball is struck above centre. Many shots wrongly described as having topspin (as opposed to being simply topped) actually have less backspin than usual.

Torsion The twist, rather than bend, in a clubshaft. Hickory shafts caused problems when they had excessive torsion; steel shafts have little.

Touch player A golfer who relies on ability to vary the kinds of shot he can play rather than depend on a rigid mechanical method, repeating the same basic swing for every club. The touch player tends to excel in the short game.

Trajectory The flight of a golf ball and the characteristics of its parabola.

Trap A bunker.

Triple bogey A score of three over par on a hole.

Trolley A device with wheels for carrying a golf bag.

Twitch A quick, nervous, jabbing movement at the ball caused by a player's nerves. It is seen mostly in putting, but also sometimes in chipping.

Under par A player is under par when, either during a round or at the end of it, his total score is less than the par for the holes played.

Up and down Taking only two more shots to hole out when a player has missed a green.

Upright stance To stand comparatively erect in the address position.

Upright swing The club is swung up rather than round, almost to the vertical.

Utility shots The playing of strokes far different from the normal golf swing such as from unusual stances in bunkers or on slopes, from under bushes.

Vardon grip Harry Vardon was one of the first golfers to use a grip in which the little finger of the bottom hand was curled around the fore-finger of the top hand.

Vs When a golfer looks down at his grip on the club, he sees two Vs, formed by the thumb and forefinger of each hand. A majority of good golfers have these Vs pointing towards the rear shoulder.

Waggle Some players move the club backwards and forwards before playing a stroke. This can either be a

nervous habit, or to rehearse the feel of the stroke or to help keep the muscles from becoming tense.

Walk-over When an opponent fails to appear at an arranged time, a golfer receives a walk-over and proceeds to the next round of a matchplay competition.

Water hazard These include sea, lakes, rivers, streams, ditches, or anything ruled to be a water hazard, regardless of whether it contains water.

Wedge A pitching club with more loft than a nine-iron, varying between different models of club. The sole is usually broad but, unlike the sand iron, the leading edge is lower than the trailing edge.

Weight transfer Movement of the weight backwards and forwards during the golf swing.

Whipping On a wooden club, thread wound round the point where the shaft fits into the head in order to strengthen the joint and support the wooden neck.

Whippy Used of a club shaft which flexes more than the norm.

Width Used of a swing with a wide arc.

Winter greens Prepared surfaces, sometimes of fairly poor quality, for putting on when it is desirable not to play on the normal greens. Usually brought into play when the ground is very wet or frosted.

Winter rules These usually permit a player to clean his ball through the green and move it a short distance to a more favourable lie.

Winter tees Tees provided to rest the normal tees while there is little or no growth of grass.

Wry-necked Used of putters with a pronounced curve in the neck designed to improve the playing qualities of the club.

Yardage charts Printed or personally prepared charts of golf holes which show the distances from one point on a hole to another.

Yips Caused by nerves when putting, this distressing condition can make a player unable to swing his putter back and his eventual stroke becomes a convulsive jerk or jab.

Jacklin inspires Ryder Cup triumph

Sixty years after the first Ryder Cup match in Massachusetts, former Open Champion Tony Jacklin led his European team to a historic victory in 1987 at Muirfield Village in Ohio for the first success on American soil.

In his third appearance as European captain, Jacklin inspired his team to another magnificent performance after their victory two years earlier at The Belfry. A final result of 15 points to 13 gave Jacklin and his men special satisfaction in defeating the United States team captained by Jack Nicklaus over the course that he had created.

With Europe leading $10\frac{1}{2}$-$5\frac{1}{2}$ on the final day, the Americans staged a determined fight-back in the singles, with the issue in the balance almost to the end. The suspense for the European team was ended by Eamonn Darcy, who holed a crucial and testing five-foot putt on the final green to win against Ben Crenshaw and Seve Ballesteros. He followed this with a tremendous 2 and 1 victory over Curtis Strange to win the Cup for Europe.

Lyle, MBE, AWB (Sandy)

1958-. Born Shrewsbury, Shropshire, England

Almost as soon as he could walk, Sandy Lyle was hitting his first golf balls with a cut-down club under the watchful eyes of his father Alex, the professional at Hawkstone Park in Shropshire. It was the natural talent of the boy combined with the expert coaching of his father that saw Lyle develop and mature into one of the world's top players and realize the ambition that had always been his goal as he achieved his greatest triumph in 1985 when he captured the Open Championship at Royal St George's, Sandwich.

Lyle became the first home winner of the title since Tony Jacklin in 1969. Going into the final round three strokes in arrears to Bernhard Langer and David Graham, Lyle conjured two crucial birdies at the 14th and 15th holes to move into the lead as his challengers faltered. Even a bogey at the last, when he fluffed a chip from a grassy lie just off the green, did not matter in the end as he secured victory by a stroke from American Payne Stewart. Yet Lyle had turned possible disaster into success at the long 14th, where a pulled drive finished in the rough and he could only pitch out over the Suez Canal. With 220 yards to the flagstick, he drilled a 2-iron to 20 feet and holed the putt for a brilliant birdie, and holed from 13 feet for a birdie at the next.

Although Shropshire born, Lyle took his father's Scottish nationality

Sandy Lyle holds the Open Championship trophy after his victory at Royal St George's in 1985.

on turning professional in 1977 after a fine amateur career, gaining international honours at boy, youth and senior level, and winning the British Youths and English Stroke Play Championships and earning Walker Cup selection. He won the PGA European Tour Qualifying School and a few months later captured the 1978 Nigerian Open, posting a round of 61 on the way. In 1979 he celebrated a hat-trick of victories in the Jersey, Scandinavian and European Opens to finish the year as European Number One, retaining the Vardon Trophy title the next year.

With at least one tournament win a year, he was never lower than fifth in the rankings until again claiming the Number One position in 1985 with prize money of £199,020. As well as the Open, Lyle also won the Benson and Hedges International, and was honoured with the award of the MBE for his services to golf. Lyle made his first impact in America in 1984 when he won the Kapalua International in Hawaii and followed by winning the Casio Open in Japan. Although failing to win in Europe in 1986, he gained his first US Tour success in the Greater Greensboro Open, and in 1987 followed with a superb victory in Florida in the Tournament Players Championship, a title that earned him a ten-year exemption for the US Tour and brought him the biggest prize money of his career of $180.00.

Lyle ended a lean two-year spell in Europe when he won the 1987 German Masters. After a record-equalling final round of 66, Lyle, in a play-off with Bernhard Langer, took the title at the second extra hole where the German was out of bounds.

With five Ryder Cup appearances, Lyle played his part in magnificent European victories at The Belfry in 1985 and again in the historic triumph at Muirfield Village in 1987. He reached the final of the Suntory World Match Play for the fourth time in 1987, but once again finished runner-up, this time to his Ryder Cup colleague Ian Woosnam.

The publishers regret the omission in the alphabetic sequence of Sandy Lyle's biography, due to production problems.